About this Book

In this pioneering work Siraj Sait and Hilary Lim address Islamic property and land rights, drawing on a range of socio-historical, classical and contemporary resources. They address the significance of Islamic theories of property and Islamic land tenure regimes on the 'webs of tenure' prevalent in Muslim societies. They consider the possibility of using Islamic legal and human rights systems for the development of inclusive, pro-poor approaches to land rights. They also focus on Muslim women's rights to property and inheritance systems. Engaging with institutions such as the Islamic endowment (*waqf*) and principles of Islamic microfinance, they test the workability of 'authentic' Islamic proposals. Located in human rights as well as Islamic debates, this study offers a well researched and constructive appraisal of property and land rights in the Muslim world.

About the Authors

Siraj Sait is a graduate of the University of Madras (India), London and the Harvard Law School and is Senior Lecturer in the School of Law at the University of East London. His expertise lies in the areas of human rights and development, immigration and asylum laws, and Islam and the Middle East. He has held several key appointments in India including Supreme Court appointed Commissioner on Forced Labour, Legal Advisor to the Government of Tamil Nadu and State Prosecutor on Civil Rights. He has been a consultant for the UNHCR, UNICEF and UN-HABITAT. He has been closely associated with several NGOs, as a consultant for Minority Rights Group and as a trustee of the Commonwealth Human Rights Initiative. He is currently Legal Officer, Land and Tenure Section, Shelter Branch, UN-HABITAT.

Hilary Lim is a Principal Lecturer in Law at the University of East London, where she teaches land law, equity and trusts and child law. Her research interests are concerned with children's rights, land law and gender. Most recently she participated in a DfID-funded project to explore the role of land titling in poverty alleviation in peri-urban settlements under different land tenure regimes.

Land, Law and Islam

Property and Human Rights in the Muslim World

Siraj Sait and Hilary Lim

UN-HABITAT

Zed Books
LONDON & NEW YORK

Land, Law and Islam: Property and Human Rights in the Muslim World
was first published in 2006
by Zed Books Ltd, 7 Cynthia Street, London N1 9JF, UK and
Room 400, 175 Fifth Avenue, New York, NY 10010, USA.

www.zedbooks.co.uk

Cover designed by Andrew Corbett
Set in 10/12.6 pt Bembo by Long House, Cumbria, UK

A catalogue record for this book
is available from the British Library

US Cataloging-in-Publication Data
is available from the Library of Congress

Paperback ISBN-10: 1 84277 813 7
Paperback ISBN-13: 978 1 84277 813 5
Hardback ISBN-10: 1 84277 810 2
Hardback ISBN-13: 978 1 84277 810 4

Contents

Abbreviations

AFDISN	Awqaf Fund for the Disabled and Individuals with Special Needs
BIS	Bank of International Settlements
CAMEL	capital adequacy, asset quality, management, earnings and liquidity
CEDAW	Convention on the Elimination of All Forms of Discrimination against Women
CERD	Convention on the Elimination of all Forms of Racial Discrimination
CGAP	Consultative Group to Assist the Poor
CMW	International Convention on the Protection of the Rights of All Migrant Workers
CRC	Convention on the Rights of the Child
CSR	Convention relating to the Status of Refugees
D8	Group of 8 developing countries
DfID	Department for International Development
ESCWA	Economic and Social Commission for Western Asia
FIG	Fédèration Internationale des Geomètres (International Surveyors' Federation)
ICCPR	International Convention on Civil and Political Rights
ICERD	International Convention on the Elimination of All Forms of Racial Discrimination
ICESCR	International Covenant on Economic, Social and Cultural Rights
IDP	internally displaced person
IFSB	Islamic Financial Services Board
ILO	International Labour Organization
IMF	International Monetary Fund
ISNA	Islamic Society of North America
KAPF	Kuwait Awqaf Public Foundation

MFI	microfinance institution
MNA	Middle East and North Africa Programme
NAFSA	National Awqaf Foundation of South Africa
NAIT	North American Islamic Trust
OECD	Organization for Economic Cooperation and Development
OHCHR	Office of the High Commissioner on Human Rights
OIC	Organization of Islamic Conference
OICC	Organization of Islamic Capitals and Cities
UDHR	Universal Declaration of Human Rights
UIDHR	Universal Islamic Declaration on Human Rights
UN	United Nations
UNCHS	United Nations Commission on Human Settlements
UNDP	United Nations Development Programme
UN-HABITAT	United Nations Human Settlements Programme
UNHCR	United Nations High Commissioner for Refugees
UNRWA	United Nations Relief and Works Agency (for Palestinian Refugees in the Near East)
WLUML	Women Living Under Muslim Laws

Acknowledgements

This research would not have been possible but for the vision, initiative and efforts of Dr Clarissa Augustinus, the Chief of the Land and Tenure Section, Shelter Branch, UN-HABITAT. Not only did Clarissa commission this study, but she also stayed involved at every stage of the research and writing with generous inputs and meticulous feedback.* Ideas and inspiration for this research flowed from various quarters, with special mention owed to Professor Rob Home and Dr Lynn Welchman. Numerous UN-HABITAT staff including Farouk Tebbal, Roman Rollnick, Tom Osanjo, Lucia Kiwala, Mohamed El Sioufi, Ulrik Westman and Florian Bruyas provided support and guidance. This research and publication was made possible through funding to the UN-HABITAT's Global Campaign for Secure Tenure from the Governments of Belgium, Italy, the Netherlands, Sweden and Norway.**

Fiona Fairweather, Head of the Law School, University of East London, provided leadership, institutional support and encouragement throughout the project. Further, Fiona went out of her way to create all the time and space needed for this research. The authors also benefited a great deal from the wise counsel and support of the Law School's research leader, Dr Kofi Kufuor, as well as other staff and researchers at the Law School. We are also grateful to the post graduate researchers, Suzanne Abdallah and Neezla Kureembokus who assisted in the research, as well as Keegan Le Sage for all her technical skills. Gratitude is also owed to Patricia Berwick and Sharon Senner who provided administrative support and all the warmth, Mr W. L. Lim at UEL and Liliana Contreras at the UN who taught us a great deal about budgets. The librarians at the University of

* The Global Land Tool Network (GLTN) also provided valuable support.

** The authors are grateful to Mohammed Elewa, Government of Egypt, and Manaf Hamza who ably presented this work in a range of fora, and Al-Azhar in Cairo for reviewing the draft.

East London and in different parts of the United Kingdom and the world generated the materials that matched often insatiable and unreasonable research demands. But it is Anna Hardman and Susannah Trefgarne at Zed Books whose enthusiastic backing and guidance for this project finally turned it into a book.

Lastly, we would both like to thank our families – our exceptional partners Lim Soo Chneah and Asma Sait, our inspiring dads Bernard Robinson and Saleh Mohamed Sait and our activist kids Adil, 9 and Nilofer, 6 – without whose patience and understanding this work would never have been completed. A special mention should be made of Aladin, who was born during the preparation of this book.

This book is dedicated to the memories of two amazing women – our mums, Pat Robinson and Najma Bai – who would truly appreciate such a cross-cultural endeavour.

Foreword

As part of its global mandate, UN-HABITAT is actively involved in promoting access to land and protecting security of tenure. While land, property and housing rights are generally cross-cultural and asserted within every socio-economic and political system, it is recognized that practice regarding their regulation and protection may take different forms. As part of its study of different systems and approaches, UN-HABITAT commissioned this study of land strategies in the Muslim world, which accounts for about 20 per cent of the global population.

UN-HABITAT has a rich and fruitful experience of working in countries with significant Muslim populations. In the course of its work in countries ranging from Afghanistan to Indonesia and from Iraq to Somalia, UN-HABITAT has been increasingly aware of the importance of Islamic land tenure systems and land rights. This pioneering study will fill a gap in our understanding of the distinctive land, housing and property issues and practices in that part of the world. I am pleased that, far from being seen as a theoretical exercise, this study has been recognized by several governments and the premier Islamic institution, the Al Azhar.

This initiative is part of UN-HABITAT's 'best practices' approach to develop affordable, pro-poor and flexible tenure types and land tools, particularly for women. We hope that through a cross-fertilization of Islamic and universal approaches, we can help develop approaches which are both authentic and durable, in keeping with international standards. This work will feed into UN-HABITAT's global campaigns for Secure Tenure and Urban Governance, which support the attainment of the Millennium Development Goals and the commitments contained in the 2005 World Summit Outcome. UN-HABITAT's goal is to promote a vision of an urban future based on inclusion, and social and economic development – on human opportunity and on hope for all.

Foreword

I am pleased that the Global Land Tool Network (GLTN) has recognized Islamic tools as a priority development area. Through GLTN's work, UN-HABITAT strives to make available pro-poor, innovative and scalable Islamic tools to governments, civil society and all stakeholders for their advocacy work and for implementation of relevant laws and policies. I trust that this pioneering study by Siraj Sait and Hilary Lim will further contribute to ongoing efforts to recognize the positive contributions that Islamic strategies can make in appropriate contexts.

Anna K. Tibaijuka

United Nations Under-Secretary-General and
Executive Director of UN-HABITAT

1

Researching Islam, Land and Property

> The concept of dual ownership [human being–God] is one of the special features of the Islamic doctrine of economics. Islam protects and endorses the personal right to own what one may freely gain, through legitimate means.... It is a sacred right. Yet, human ownership is tempered by the understanding that everything, in the last analysis, belongs to God.... What appears to be ownership is in fact a matter of trusteeship, whereby we have temporary authority to handle and benefit from property. (Abdul-Rauf 1984: 19)

Land, property and housing rights are generally cross-cultural and asserted within every socio-economic and political system, but the practice regarding their regulation and protection may take many forms. However, there has been little research on the complex and distinctive forms of land tenure and land rights found in Muslim societies, despite the fact that over 20 per cent of the world's population is Muslim. Although there has been extensive literature generally on Islam and human rights, there has been very little focus on Islam and property rights. This book seeks to address this gap in the literature. Too often global reviews of land tenure and strategies fail to take into account Islamic principles and practices because they are assumed to be either non-existent or irrelevant. By way of illustration, Hernando de Soto's (2000) influential and best-selling work *The Mystery of Capital*, which predicates economic development and poverty alleviation upon the formalization and legal protection of land titles, does not explore Islamic conceptions of land, property and housing rights. His proposals for converting 'dead capital', by which he means informally owned property, into formally recognized property rights, through surveying, mapping, registration, monitoring, maintenance and facilitative mechanisms, have led to plaudits (Clinton 2001; USAID 2002), as well as critiques (Home and Lim 2004; Payne 2002) but are considered automatically applicable in the Muslim world. Though Egypt is on de Soto's study list, he merely explores its symptomatic problems, particularly the bureaucratic delays in asserting property rights. The issues faced by Muslim countries, however, are far more complex than problems with red tape and apathy.

Islam is considered by Muslims to be a complete way of life, and property conceptions go far beyond theorization to impact on the lived experiences of Muslims. They also inform, to varying degrees, state policies and land rights discourse. Better understanding of, and engagement with, Islamic dimensions of land may potentially support land rights initiatives in Muslim societies, which have implications for programmes relating to land administration, land registration, urban planning and environmental sustainability. No generalization can be made about the extent to which Islamic dimensions may be relevant or appropriate to a particular context – that is for land professionals, policy makers, civil society and ultimately the people to determine. The fear of Islamizing the land discourse is exaggerated because Islam, as this research demonstrates, is never a stand-alone and there is a dynamic interplay between universalist, human rights, customary, informal and Islamic conceptualizations and applications. Rather, the lack of engagement with the internal Islamic dialogue risks creating land systems that are bereft of authenticity and legitimacy and thereby of effectiveness and durability. Even where well-intentioned donor-driven efforts to establish modern land systems succeed, the obduracy of informal norms, practices and processes leads to unattended dualisms that undermine the prospect of integrated and unifying land policies.

This chapter provides an introduction to the context, methodology and scheme of this research, to distinctive conceptions of land tenure and rights in Islamic theory, as well as to key economic principles promoting private ownership and their present and potential role in promoting access to land. Furthermore, it outlines the application of Islamic perspectives on land registration, urban planning and environmental sustainability.

Scope of the Research

This research was initiated by the Land and Tenure Section (Shelter Branch, Global Division) at UN-HABITAT, which carries out systematic research into distinctive land, housing and property issues and approaches in various regions of the world. During its work in a range of countries from Afghanistan to Indonesia, UN-HABITAT has been increasingly aware of the importance of Islamic land tenure conceptions and land rights. It therefore commissioned us to carry out a year-long, in-depth study of the Islamic and other dimensions of land and property rights in the Muslim world. The eight research papers which emerged from the study provided the chapters of this book.

The general findings of the research point to distinctive Islamic conceptions of land and property rights that vary in practice throughout the Muslim world. Though Islamic law and human rights are often important factors in the Islamic conceptualization of land and property rights, and their application, they intersect with state, customary and international norms in various ways. In doing so, they potentially offer opportunities for the development of 'authentic' Islamic land tools which can support the campaign for the realization of fuller land rights for various sections of Muslim societies, including women. However, in order to facilitate that role, the various stakeholders must constructively review the normative and methodological Islamic frameworks and their relationship with other systems of formal and informal land tenure.

This chapter will show that Islamic property and land concepts are part of a mature and developing alternative land framework operating alongside international regimes. The roles of Islam, history, politics, culture, kinship and custom – operating in different dimensions within Muslim societies – are intertwined in distinctive property conceptions and structures. In the Islamic system, private property rights are promoted but the ultimate ownership of God over land is assumed and requires all rights to be exercised within the Islamic legal and ethical framework with a redistributive ethos. It is argued that engagement with Islamic dimensions of land may potentially support land rights initiatives in Muslim societies and has implications for programmes relating to land administration, land registration, urban planning and environmental sustainability.

Chapter 2 considers Islamic law in relation to land rights and tenure systems in Muslim societies. A striking feature of Islamic societies is the high degree of reliance on legal cultures, arising in part because of the sophistication and breathtaking scope of the Shari'a. Though it is a site of struggle between conservatives and liberals, Islamic law is not medieval and static, but a 'living' field. An appreciation of the distinctive features and sources of Islamic law, its methodologies and diversity in application and its dispute resolution mechanisms may contribute towards strategies aimed at enhancing security of tenure.

Chapter 3 explores how the multifaceted, generally distinctive and certainly varied nature of land tenure concepts, categorizations and arrangements within the Islamic world leads to the 'web of tenure' in contemporary Muslim societies. An appreciation of the historical context of land tenure in Muslim societies and the range of land tenure forms contributes towards the development of authentic and innovative strategies for enhancing access to land and land rights.

Chapter 4 sets out to examine the relationship between international human rights and Islamic conceptions of human rights in theory and practice. It argues that, with respect to land rights, the difference between these two sets of rights appears minimal and a sensitive and careful recognition of Islamic religious and political sensitivities can help deliver international human rights more effectively in Muslim societies, without offending Islamic principles.

Chapter 5 explores the nature and scope of women's rights to property and land under Islamic law (Shari'a) through a socio-historical background to women's property rights, an appraisal of modern legal reforms and the avenues for enhancing their security of tenure. It argues that, despite assumptions to the contrary, there are potentially empowering strategies for women through Islamic law that can enhance women's access to land and enforcement of their other property rights.

Chapter 6 considers how Muslim societies generally derive from religious sources their inheritance rules for the division of an individual's property upon death, some of which are controversial. Yet, it argues that the application of these formal inheritance rules pertaining to designated shares must be understood in a broader socio-cultural and economic context and within wider systems of inheritance practice.

Chapter 7 outlines the *waqf* as a key Islamic institution, which has incorporated within its legal sphere vast areas of land within the Muslim world, connected firmly with the religious precept of charity. Modern reforms in several Muslim countries have abolished or nationalized religious endowments, or subjected them to strict regulation, but the *waqf* remains influential and there are clear signs of its reinvigoration. The chapter evaluates the role of the *waqf* in strategies to improve security of tenure based on its legal foundations, history and socio-economic impacts.

Finally, Chapter 8 considers the increasing demand from within Islamic communities that financial services be compliant with the Shari'a. This chapter explores the Islamic context which stimulates such alternative credit systems, the key distinguishing features of Islamic banking models, the development of Islamic microfinance practices, and the practical challenges to these innovations. It considers how Islamic finance, banking principles and credit, particularly housing microfinance, can contribute to security of tenure and help to transform the lives of the poor.

This is a preliminary study which seeks to contribute to the debate about appropriate strategies to realize innovative and pro-poor land tools in their particular context. With that in mind, it has been written for a general audience without any assumption of knowledge regarding Islam, law or property rights, offering basic information as well as an opportunity to revisit first principles.

Methodology

A project that seeks to explore key themes and developments within the Muslim world raises fundamental questions regarding the scope and methodology – even feasibility – of such an endeavour. Resident in over 57 Muslim-majority countries (member states of the Organization of Islamic Conference, OIC), or as significant minorities in the West and from China to Russia, there are an estimated 1.2 billion Muslims amongst the world's population. Though Muslims see themselves as a universal community (*Umma*), they are, in fact, divided into several nationalities and, contrary to popular assumptions, only 20 per cent of Muslims reside in the Arab world. They include many different ethnic groups and speak dozens of languages, including Arabic, Turkish, Urdu, and Persian. The lived experiences of Muslims – reflecting various socio-economic conditions, political affiliations and religious practices – cannot be essentialized or simplified. The Muslim holy book, the *Qur'an*, celebrates this diversity:

> O mankind! Truly We have created you out of a male and a female, and We have made you into nations and tribes, that you may know one another (*Qur'an* 49: 13). And among His signs is the creation of the heavens and the earth, and the difference of your languages and colours. Verily in that are signs for men of sound knowledge. (*Qur'an* 30: 22)

Callaway notes, in the context of Africa, that 'in each major region of each country, the impact of Islam is different. No study can reasonably blanket the region with one set of generalizations about how Islam interacts with society and shapes it' (Callaway 1994: 1). Given the enormous range of Muslim identities intertwined with indigenous and Western practices, a project such as ours, which uses thematic approaches, can only provide selective case studies, often in a comparative mode. It cannot generalize or universalize these experiences as a homogeneous Muslim position. Rather, the research underscores the considerable variations in the doctrine and practice of land tenure arrangements driven by local socio-economic, customary, cultural and political factors, as well as by secular influences. The prefix 'Islamic' has been preferred to 'Muslim' for conceptual formulations or attempts at authenticity because land issues are mostly theorized from the *Qur'anic* and other Islamic legal principles. It is equally true, though, that Islam is a contested zone and is ultimately a matter of human interpretation of divine intent. There are differences between the Muslim Sunni and Shi'a sects, as well as within the *maddahib* (schools of jurisprudence) within the sects. However, this project avoids referring to states, societies or individuals who invoke Islam as 'Islamic' (except sometimes by way of emphasizing distinctive puritanical approaches), preferring 'Muslim' because they are practitioners of Islam rather than embodiments of it.

At the same time there is much that unites Muslims. The term 'Islam' comes from the Arabic word-root *s-l-m,* which has a general reference to peace and submission. Specifically, Islam means submission to the will of God, and a Muslim is one who makes that submission. Muslims are identified as those who share *shahada* (common faith) in the oneness of God (Allah or the God, in Arabic), acceptance of the Prophet Muhammad (peace be upon him, hereafter referred to as 'the Prophet') as being the final Prophet in a long line of Judeo-

Christian messengers including Adam, Abraham, Moses and Jesus (peace be upon them). This first pillar of Islamic faith is accompanied by four others: *salat* (prayer) which is performed five times a day, *zakat* (charity, literally purification), fasting during the Islamic month of Ramadhan and the Hajj (pilgrimage to Makkah), although the last is only an obligation for those who are physically and financially able to perform it. As Esposito (1980: ix) points out: 'A distinctive feature of the Islamic tradition is the belief that Islam is a total, comprehensive way of life'; it is 'integral to all areas of Muslim life – politics economics, law, education and the family'. It is not surprising, therefore, that Islam has much to say about various aspects of land, property and housing rights and regulates property relationships within the family, communities and between individuals and the state.

This book is co-authored by a Muslim and a non-Muslim, a male and a female, a Southerner and a Northerner coming from different fields of expertise and experiences. Together, the team has sought to be academically neutral, pursuing internal and external critiques and debates. Through a dialogic method of research, they have adopted a general approach that Islam, like other religions and cultures, must be constructively analysed to discern its potential benefits as seen by Muslims as well as other communities. This research uses international, cross-cultural human rights and development standards as the framework for engaging with Islamic principles. A range of materials was used, including Muslim and non-Muslim sources, though largely restricted to English-language resources and translations. However, the researchers have been sensitive to arguments over orientalism (Said 1978; Tibawi 1964; Macfie 2000) – texts that generate essentializing statements about 'the Orient', amounting to an exercise of power. Postcolonial approaches to and critiques of Western imperialism were incorporated along with caution over occidentalist trends in literature, as reactive to orientalism (Buruma and Margalit 2004). As Smith argues, scholars and foreign affairs experts agree that Islam's teachings are humane but many Westerners have considered 'radical Islam one of the gravest threats facing the free world' (Smith 2000). At the root of this constructive endeavour is a predisposition to see land, property and housing rights as basic and universal aspirations though there may be different pathways to realizing them, including Islamic approaches.

Land and Property Rights in Muslim Societies

The extent to which land rights are protected within Muslim countries is difficult to detail or even generalize because of the sheer diversity of Muslim countries as well as the lack of systematic and reliable data. The annual *Index of Economic Freedoms* published by the Heritage Foundation and the *Wall Street*

Journal points to why a comprehensive review of land rights is difficult to achieve (Feulner *et al.* 2005). The *Index*, with its free market orientation, recognizes 'property rights' as one of the ten broad categories or factors guaranteeing economic freedoms. Other factors include trade policy, fiscal burden of government, government intervention in the economy, monetary policy, capital flows and foreign investment, banking and finance, wages and prices, regulation and informal market activity (Feulner *et al.* 2005). The *Index* is primarily concerned with the extent to which private property is recognized by the state and protected from expropriation. To assess this it reviews law and practice, the rule of law and the independence of the judiciary, freedom from corruption and the ability of individuals and businesses to enforce contracts. The *Index*, thus, takes a particular view of property rights and is not concerned about issues of broader access to land or security of tenure nor is it able to recognize informal or collective forms of land ownership (Feulner *et al.* 2005).

The *Index* of 2005 covers 161 countries, including a large number of Muslim ones. Egypt, Qatar, Oman, Saudi Arabia, Tunisia, Turkey and the United Arab Emirates are assessed at 'Level 3' property protection. This classification indicates 'a moderate court system, inefficient and subject to delays; corruption may be present; judiciary may be influenced by other branches of government; expropriation possible but rare'. Pakistan, Indonesia, Kuwait, Lebanon, Malaysia, Morocco and Yemen are found to have 'low property ownership; weakly protected; court system inefficient; corruption present; judiciary influenced by other branches of government; expropriation possible' (Level 4). Iran and Libya are ranked at the bottom of the table at Level 5 with 'very low private property outlawed or not protected; almost all property belongs to the state; country in such chaos (for example, because of ongoing war) that property protection is non-existent; judiciary so corrupt that property is not effectively protected; expropriation frequent'. No Muslim country figures in the top list (Levels 1 and 2) where protection of property is very high or high and an independent uncorrupt judiciary enforces those rights (Feulner *et al.* 2005). This top list is composed in the main of Western countries.

These tables, problematic as they may be in their standpoint, methodology and sources, fuel general assumptions about the precarious state of land, property and housing rights in the Muslim world. These are by no means conclusive. Public opinion polls carried out in Algeria, Jordan, Lebanon, Morocco and Palestine in late 2003 by the United Nations Development Programme (UNDP) found that the right to own property ranked high on the list of freedoms presently enjoyed in the five countries (UNDP 2005). Yet there are concerns about property rights in the Muslim world that in turn raise a number of questions. Is there something inherently Muslim or Islamic that frustrates property rights in these countries? Do competing Islamic property rights regimes impede universal land, property and housing rights standards? If Islamic principles do exist as a coherent, sophisticated body of rules and arrangements, what are their implications and relevance to contemporary land rights debates? Islam may well be considered irrelevant or problematic in some contexts, but often it cannot be ignored. As a holistic, authentic and workable system it could invigorate the search for universal property rights in several contexts in the Muslim world.

Theorizing Islam, Land and Property

We have said that the Islamic property rights framework conceives of land as a sacred trust but promotes individual ownership with a redistributive ethos. However, at the outset it should be emphasized that Islam is by no means the only factor in Muslim societies and often coexists with customary, secular and other influences. The impact of Islamic land theories is best understood through an analysis of particular national and local histories, dominant economic principles and the interplay of customary and cultural practices in each context. The present structures may reflect choices at the societal level or through a top-down, state-dominated approach. The land rights paradigm in Islamic theory is circumscribed not only by external human rights and development strategies promoting a just and equitable society, but equally by internal dynamics. These religious and moral dimensions of land may be internalized and incorporated into property transactions of many societies in multiple ways. Our research explores how Islam potentially impacts on all stages of the property cycle, from acquisition to management and transmission. In this chapter some of the factors impacting on contemporary land discourse are identified, including religion, history – particularly Ottoman history – family, kinship and culture. Disentangling these factors will help to clarify the potential and limits of an Islamic dimension to land rights.

In investigating the various factors impacting on the development and practice of Islamic land theories, the role of the Muslim state in ordering and implementing Islamic and internationally guaranteed land rights is considered. Under Islamic theory, the state's role in land management is seen as supervising land ultimately beonging to God. Thus, the state is mandated to administer land, efficiently and fairly, in accordance with God's laws and ethical and moral principles. While it may be argued that there is no specifically Arab or Muslim mode of governance, the Islamic framework does contain the important and influential concepts of *shura* (consultation) and *adl* (justice). The experience of Ottoman land administration is utilized to demonstrate that effective land management systems, land registration, titling and cadastre have been enduring features of the Muslim world. Potentially, within the Islamic framework states have the scope and the means to promote security of tenure and access to land.

That same framework is capable of responding also to modern urban planning and environmental challenges, although the nature of these current demands could not have been envisaged in the classical Islamic period. In several aspects Islamic land principles and practices run parallel or are similar to contemporary international standards; in other ways they offer an alternative paradigm. However, Islamic land concepts and models in all their diversity potentially support the quest for security of tenure and offer a sophisticated and alternative land framework *vis-à-vis* international regimes.

Rights to land are part of a broader set of property rights that includes real (landed) property interests and personal property, the latter in turn distinguished as tangible and intangible property (stocks, intellectual property). Land rights include not only the right to use land but also benefits from property, such as usufruct or rent. Generally, they imply the right to exclude others. Lawyers, philosophers, sociologists, anthropologists and economists have differing perspectives on the nature and scope of property rights, but they are conventionally understood to be a bundle of rights that includes the acquisition, ownership, control, use, management, transfer and sale of property (Alchian 1977). Despite the widespread assumption that property rights originated in Western philosophical and socio-political thought, they are evident also in Islamic theory ('Abd Al-Kader 1959). Property governs relations not merely of persons to things but, equally, relations between persons with respect to things (Vandevelde 1981; Munzer 1990). As such, human relationships are a part of social relations, as distinct from matters relating to *ibadat* (worship). Property, however, is a part also of a larger scheme, as Harris notes (1996: 3), 'governing the use of most things and the allocation of some items of social wealth', the latter being 'all those things and services for which there is a greater potential total demand than there is a supply'. While property rights are mediated within society to maximize wealth, they are often subject to transaction costs (in distributing resources) and the vagaries of individual power and leverage. Property rights are allocated in different ways, through the private use of markets, informal communities or governmental actions.

The nature and scope of property rights have long been at the centre of philosophical debates over natural law (God-guided or morality-driven principles) and legal positivism where legitimacy is derived from the authority of the law maker rather than morality (Becker 1980). Islamic law relating to land is inspired by the concepts of sanctity of land, divine ownership and righteousness of use. While Muslims may show the same drive as non-Muslims towards acquiring land, it is generally understood that land is a sacred trust rather than just a property, commodity or wealth (*mal*) ('Abd Al-Kader 1959). While Muslim societies are absorbing secular practices, religion and politics in the Islamic context are not viewed in any sense as separate from one another. Therefore, Islamic arguments on property rights, like those on other human rights, are ordered in more absolute terms within a vertical relationship governing 'how man discharges his duties towards God' in dealing with fellow human beings (Weeramantry 1988: 116–17). This is similar to other religious approaches that consider property as God's bounty and hold human beings accountable for its use.

There are scores of references to land in the *Qur'an* (Hamza 2002) that provide for and respect property rights (*Qur'an* 2: 205, 2: 220, 4: 2, 4: 5-6, 4: 10, 4: 29, 16: 71, 38: 24, 59: 8). Private property rights are well established but constructed as a sacred trust based on *tawhid* (doctrine of unity), *khalifa* (stewardship) and *amana* (trust). Property and land vest in God, but are temporally enjoyed by men and women through responsibility or trust (*Qur'an* 2: 30, 36: 54; see Moors 1995). According to a literal religious philosophical tradition, man is allowed to use resources such as land but can never own it. Abdul-Rauf quotes extensively from the *Qur'an* and *Sunna* (tradition of the Prophet) to conclude that there is a concept of dual ownership (human–God) under Islamic principles (1984: 19). The existence of rights to own (*raqaba* or full ownership), enjoy or alienate land is not in the main contested but these rights are conditional on their legitimacy as derived from Islamic principles.

Some argue that Islamic conceptions of property rights, which promote private ownership with limits arising out of ethical and redistributive considerations, are amenable to socialist dogma (Mannan 1970). Others such as Behdad (1989: 185) view Islamic property rights as largely oriented towards a capitalist economy. Since the 1973 oil boom in the Middle East, there is more talk of Islam and capitalism in contrast to the weakening influence of Arab socialism (Cummings 1980: 25). At the same time, the 1979 Iranian Islamic revolution and resurgence of Islamic economics from Sudan to Pakistan have intensified the debate over the true potential of 'stand-alone' Islamic economics. There is a growing literature on Islamic economic principles and practice (Chapra 1970; Khan 1994), although at this stage in contemporary life the cohabitation of Islam with principles according with a capitalist economy seems more in evidence (Pryor 1985).

What are the implications of a distinctive tradition in Islamic property rights as a 'third way'? Are Islamic economic principles merely rhetoric or part of a more fundamental quest for authenticity, as indicated in the recent OIC call for greater adherence to Islamic economic principles? For many Muslims, the question is not merely one of economic development but rather 'whether [Muslims] want the right things in the light of the Shari'a … [and that] the development involving production, distribution and exchange process has to be distinctive to Muslim societies' (Mannan 1984: 62). Rosser and Rosser (1999) find that Islam as a 'new traditional economy' may not exist as a fully developed system yet, but 'it exists as a perspective in the form of an ideal model which has become an ideological movement of significance around the world in many societies'. Kuran (1977: 37) argues that 'the significance of the steps to give economics an Islamic character lies only partially in their economic content. Much of their importance lies in their symbolism, in the present and future distribution of political power and their cultural meanings'. Whether or not Islamic economics are a pragmatic strategy or a utopian ideal, their guiding principles, particularly regarding property rights, can be used to promote access to land.

Despite similarities with Western liberal conceptions of property rights, Islamic rights to legitimate use of property have 'much wider significance than [those] enjoyed in the narrowly material accounting of capitalism' (Tripp 1997: 15). Writing on the 'Islamic approach to development', Ishaque (1983) notes the 'radical difference between the vision of a good and successful life in the worldview of Islam and that of the capitalist or the socialist world'. He contends that in 'the former it consists of fulfilling one's covenant with Allah and of living out the worldly life in terms of divine guidance as preparation for a more beautiful life awaiting mankind' (quoted in Esposito 1983: 268). One of the basic aims of Islam is to create an egalitarian society where every person may obtain his/her basic rights and enjoyment from life, and the Islamic approach includes several economic regulations – some moral and others material. Thus, Islamic property conceptions and arrangements have potentially important implications for individual ownership, access to land and secure tenure. It is an argument which will be returned to in succeeding chapters, particularly with respect to the potential for Islamic credit and microfinance, but also in discussions about the distinctive Islamic charitable endowment or *waqf*.

Islamic Concepts of Land Tenure and Access to Land

In theory capitalist private property rights are largely unfettered, while property rights in Islam are circumscribed. Rights in land depend upon Islamic principles emphasizing that land is a sacred trust for human beings and should be put to continuous productive use. However, excessive exploitation and hoarding of land are prohibited. Islamic property rights are conditional on the requirement that property not be used wastefully or exploitatively, or in a way that will deprive others of their justly acquired property (*Qur'an* 2: 188; see Rodinson 1973; Mannan 1970). As Guner (2005: 4) notes, 'Islam is against those who accumulate property for the purpose of greed or oppression as well as those who gain through unlawful business practices.' These Islamic principles contribute to a distinct framework shaping categories of land tenure and usufruct rights that are capable of giving rise to flexible and creative arrangements for access to land.

Property rights in Islamic law may be divided conveniently into three categories – public, state and private (Normani and Rahnema 1995). Public property includes forests, pastures, rivers and mines and everything found in the sea. However, like *mewat* (dead land) which can be converted into private land by reclamation, fish caught from the sea and trees felled for timber convert from public to private. With regard to public land, the state exercises supervision to ensure that no exploitation of it occurs contrary to public benefit. Hussain (1999) points out that one of the features of the Islamic property regime is that public and state land can be converted to private ownership by private use and the state's determination of public interest, just as unused land can in some cases revert back to the state. Thus, land ownership in Islam is linked to land use. Behdad (1989) points out that while private property rights are well established, an individual who uses the land will have priority of access to a patch of land over another who has failed to use it. Unworked land cannot be owned, and according to theorists cannot be rented (Behdad 1989); indeed, whether any land can be rented at all was itself a matter of Islamic debate, although leases are now widely accepted (Johansen 1988). This debate arose out of the *hadith* (saying of the Prophet): 'He who has land should cultivate it. If he will not or cannot, he should give it free to a Muslim brother and not rent it to him.'

That unproductive land should not create wealth is similar to the well-known Islamic prohibition on *riba* (interest), which stipulates that money by itself should not create money. There are those such as Bethell (1994) who find the injunction against hoarding and the emphasis upon use of land as fundamental to secure tenure to be both unwelcome and obstructive. However, the ethical and moral dimensions of Islamic property doctrine, as found in the Islamic legal principles prohibiting unreasonable profiteering, exploitation through 'usury' or *riba* and hoarding, are part of a broader structure assuring important rights, including respect for property rights of all persons regardless of religious faith (*Qur'an* 3: 75). Minority rights have been posited as a problem in some commentaries regarding the application of Islamic law, but non-Muslims enjoy the same property rights as Muslims, although, as will be explained in more detail later in this chapter, the tax structure varies (Doi 1997: 426). The *Qur'an* also has rules ranging from the guardianship of the property of orphans and warnings against its misuse (2: 2, 2: 5 and 4: 10) to the inheritance rights of women (4: 7, 4: 24, 4: 32).

The flexibility of the Islamic framework is enhanced further by distinctive Islamic land tenure arrangements such as *milk* (private full ownership), *miri* (state), *waqf* (endowment) and *metruke* (common land). However, there are other classifications such as *mehlul*, which is unused state land liable to be confiscated and *mewat* land (Lambton 1953). Also recognized, in practice, are *musha* (communal land) and other forms of collective ownership that are based on custom. In the case of state land – *miri* or *emir* land – the state owns the land, as a representative of God, but creates a range of access and usufruct rights for individuals through cultivation or payment of taxes. State land can also be converted by the state into *matruk mahmiyya* (property for general public use such as roads) or into *matruk murfaqa* (property for use by a particular community such as marketplaces and cemeteries). Land in a *waqf* is explicitly designated as owned by God, putting the brakes on private or state ownership over it. It is a form of land tenure with a significant role in promoting access to land for a wide range of beneficiaries and a later chapter is devoted to the *waqf* and Islamic philanthropy. However, it is worth noting even at this stage that the *waqf* and theories relating to the Islamic doctrine of *shuf'a* (rights of pre-emption) were viewed within the colonial perspective as examples of the backwardness of Shari'a law in terms of limiting individual ownership, as opposed to key elements in a creative and flexible arrangement (Messick 2003).

Security of Tenure

Security of tenure is an aspiration, if not a legal expectation, the world over – including Muslim societies. It implies that the right of access to and use of land/property is underwritten by a known set of rules, and that this right is capable of enforcement. Tenure can be realized in a variety of ways, depending on constitutional and legal systems, social norms, cultural values and, to some extent, individual preference. Islamic law provides such a framework, with the recognition and protection of private property rights, remedies for individuals deprived of their property rights and prescribed punishment for theft. As with other branches of Islamic law and practice, every property transaction can be characterized through the Islamic value system as *wajib* (obligatory), *mandub* (recommended), *mubah* (permissible), *haram* (prohibited) or *makruh* (repugnant) (Hallaq 1997: 40). Protection of property rights is well established in Islamic law ('Abd Al-Kader 1959). The Prophet emphasized the importance of property rights in his farewell pilgrimage by declaring to the assembled masses: 'Nothing shall be legitimate to a Muslim which belongs to a fellow Muslim unless it was given freely and willingly.' Kadivar (2003) argues that property and housing fall within the private domain in Islam, and are therefore respected and protected from intrusion, whether by another ordinary man or woman or by government.

Certainly, the *maqasid al-sharia* (hierarchy of legal aims) of the noted Islamic jurist Al-Ghazali (1058–1111 AD) 'included, at its top, the principles of protecting life, private property, mind, religion and offspring' (Hallaq 1997: 112). Muslim scholars are unanimous that these are the five essential values of Islamic law which 'must be protected as a matter of priority … [and] the focus is on the individual' (Esposito 1999: 147). Further, the Shari'a provides remedies for individuals wrongly deprived of property by official action (Mayer 1999a: 45; Behdad 1989). Another well-known Muslim writer, Ibn Khaldun (1332–95 AD), writes:

> To exercise political leadership, the ruler, together with his helpers, must enforce restraining laws among the people, in order to prevent mutual hostility and attacks upon property. Attacks on people's property remove the incentive to acquire and gain property. People then become of the opinion that the purpose and ultimate destiny of (acquiring property) is to have it taken away from them. Those who infringe upon property (rights) commit an injustice. (Al-Araki 1983: 148)

Such is the importance attached to property rights, that theft under Islamic law falls within the crimes which are punishable by a pre-established severe punishment (*Hadd*) found in the *Qur'an* 5: 41.

Islamic Land and Land Reform

Islamic theoretical insistence that ownership of everything belongs to God alone (*Qur'an* 2: 108; 3: 190) signifies that ownership is subject to equitable and redistributive principles. The divine ownership is coupled with repeated *Qur'anic* references to the effect that all of humanity benefits from nature's resources. The Muslim state, as the repository and means of implementation of God's laws and objectives, came to acquire and exercise 'ownership' over large swathes of land out of which a range of land tenure arrangements were created. Further, the interactions between Islamic and customary approaches to land add their own dimensions to this diverse body of land rights, most obviously with respect to communal conceptions of property. However, the Islamic framework does not merely shape diversity in landholdings, but also has redistributive elements.

The central role given to the Muslim state, in which ownership of land is vested on behalf of God, lends itself to the deployment of arguments based on Islamic principles in order to legitimate land reform programmes. Bonne (1960) notes that the concept of *miri* was much broader than Western conceptions of state or crown land since the *raqaba* (nominal ownership) vested in the state but 'possession and extensive rights of usufruct are vested in the private owner'. He further elaborates:

> The idea of supreme ownership on the part of the state and consequently the dual concept of ownership under Islam emerges also from the fact that, contrary to Roman law where a distinction is made between ownership and usufruct, a twofold right of disposal is admitted, that is, one in respect of the land itself and one in respect of its yield. Consequently, a house and the site on which it is built may belong to different owners. (Bonne 1960: 116)

The state therefore assumes land 'ownership' on behalf of God but for the benefit of the community. Caliph Umar, a companion of the Prophet, 'guided by old ideas of divine ownership left large parts of the conquered territories to God, that is, the Moslem community. The interest, that is, yield from the land should belong to man, the capital to God' (Bonne 1960: 118). As noted earlier, Islam obligates Muslims to pay *zakat* (a charitable levy), as one of the five 'pillars' of faith (*Qur'an* 9: 60). Islamic property rights therefore incorporate a redistributive element, which is evident also in institutions such as the *waqf*. Al-Maamiry (1987: 59) notes that in Islam 'what is owed to the poor is a duty on the state as well as the wealthy. It is not a grant or gift; it is an obligatory right as long as this poor person is unable to earn or if the means of earning are not easy for him'. This emerges from a number of *Qur'anic* verses, for example 2: 77:

> It is righteousness to spend your wealth out of love for God, for your kin, for orphans, for the poor, for the travellers, for those who ask and for the release of slaves. Be steadfast in prayer and establish regular charity.

A further instance of the redistributive elements in the Islamic framework arises with respect to the inheritance rules. These establish a broad category of mandatory beneficiaries – albeit, as will be explained in Chapter 5, with opportunities for 'estate planning' by the benefactor. The fixed *Qur'anic* inheritance rules, by guaranteeing access to property for a large number of individuals, foster the break-up of large estates and land monopolies. Furthermore, these rules provide possibilities of co-ownership (Warriner 1948: 64). The view of some commentators that Islamic law creates wasteful land subdivisions will be discussed in later chapters; it does, however, create opportunities for land readjustment and co-ownership of holdings. In addition, there has been considerable interplay between Islamic property conceptions and customary practices where communal or tribal land are a feature of Muslim countries (Warriner 1948: 18; Bonne 1960: 117). An example is *musha* (Arabic for shared) lands, mostly relating to rural agricultural land where the custom is of 'reallocating land in unequal shares (at regular intervals) to which a customary right of ownership attaches' (Warriner 1948: 19). Similarly, *muzara'a* (share-cropping), a contract under which one party works the land owned by the other party in consideration of a share of the crops, has been discussed in Islamic jurisprudence. *Musha*, however, has been on the decline following colonial disapproval and the emergence of liberalized individual property rights regimes.

Islamic conceptions of property therefore offer a range of land rights and a choice among land tenure arrangements. As Kuran (2003: 5) argues:

> During the first few centuries following the rise of Islam, Islamic law had produced a rich set of principles, regulations and procedures to govern contractual relationships. There were rules to support the joint ownership of property. There were also rules to support the pooling of resources for commercial missions.

Muslim governments have often sought to derive legitimacy for their land reform or redistribution measures from Islamic first principles of redistribution, or violation of such principles, as in the case of the nationalization of Islamic endowments. This adaptation points to the political or pragmatic use of Islamic argumentation. For example, the question of whether a land ceiling or redistribution of land was Islamic was hotly contested by the government and the landed class in Pakistan.

Factors Influencing Islamic Land Doctrines

Despite the general principles relating to property rights, the *Qur'an* did not elaborate on land tenure – on its regulation and administration, or on the mechanics for its protection – leaving it to succeeding generations to develop the field. Property rights were widely asserted during the Prophet's lifetime (570–632) given that he and many of his companions were traders and businessmen. The right to property is promoted by a key document, the Prophet's Farewell Sermon (*Khutbatul Wada',* 632 AD), which states 'regard the life and property of every Muslim as a sacred trust. Return the goods entrusted to you to their rightful owners' (see Haykal 1976: 486–7). From the time of the Prophet onwards, property rights were not only asserted but also subjected to litigation (Hamza 2002: 29–30). In the next period of Islamic legal history, the four 'rightly guided Caliphs' Abu Bakr, Umar, Uthman and Ali (632–61) consolidated those principles and developed land surveys, prohibited land as war booty and created equitable land tax structures. Though no generalization can be made about the later rule of the Ummayads (661–750), Abbasids (750–1258), Ayyubids (1171–1250), Mamluks (1250–1517) and Safavids (1501–1722), or the Shi'a Fatimids (969–1171), private land rights were always understood to be promoted by Islam irrespective of some centralization of land processes (see, generally, Humphreys 1995).

It is the records and laws from the Ottoman (Uthmani) period 1281–1918 that establish the highly developed land tenure regimes and land administration system and vibrant land markets, as will be discussed further in the chapter on Islamic land tenure and land reform (see Inalclk 1969; Islamoglu-Inan 1987). Modern land regulation laws in most parts of the Sunni Muslim world are derived, at least in part, from categories of land in classical Islamic law and Ottoman land law, culminating in the Ottoman Land Code 1858 (see Jorgens 2000), which were further fashioned and distorted by the colonial encounters. As will be explored in some detail in later chapters, historical narratives have an impact on the development of contemporary land tenure regimes in Muslim countries. Such narratives offer an explanation as to why classical/traditional concepts persist in the contemporary tenure web. These histories also provide insights into the potential for innovative but authentic tools for enhancing access to land. Equally, the Islamic history of an institution such as the *waqf* clarifies not only its continuing relevance, but also its potential contribution to current debates on land reform. Particular episodes, including colonialism and distinctive local histories, have also been a factor in the evolution of contemporary land regimes in different Muslim countries.

Property rights across the 57 Muslim majority countries, however, cannot be generalized about or too easily attributed to religious influence or history alone. They are as much an outcome of contemporary economic conditions and choices. Some Muslim countries have been quicker to adapt to the calls for economic liberalization or the challenges of globalization than others, a reaction which in turn has often been determined by a variety of factors, including a country's specific socio-political, religious and historical context. The economic performance of parts of the Muslim world, for example the Arab world, has been analysed by various authors (Rivlin 2001). Writing in 1948, Warriner forewarned that there was a need for new forms of tenure in the Middle East to combat poverty due to the high density of the population, unequal land distribution and low productivity (1948: 120). Such warnings are not confined to the Muslim world, but it is perhaps the case, as argued in research on the moral economies in Islam, that the close links between Muslim countries, coupled with the varying economic development between countries, have led to obvious and continuing tensions (Institute of International Studies 1998).

The convergence of customary and Islamic law has also been a particular feature in the development of laws and practices with respect to land in Muslim countries. Land is a fundamental asset: shelter, food production and other activities are all dependent on it (DfID 2002). But it is often more than that. For indigenous peoples, for example, land is fundamental to lifestyle since it is imbued with sacred or ancestral values, and often cannot be traded or compromised. In Muslim societies, too, land has multiple cultural meanings and implications. Writing in the context of the Palestinian Arab community, Husseini and Baidoun (2001) point out that historically land was seen as the most valuable asset of the Arabs as well as fundamental to their personal esteem and honour. It is a status symbol as well as part of familial, tribal, national and religious identities. In many societies, Muslims take their name from the land they come from. The term *milk* or *mulk* in relation to land signifies more than an individual's property; it is their permanent temporal abode. Barakat (1993: 55), however, points out that the significance of formal land ownership differs from the peasant to the nomad (Bedouin), even though both use land:

> Peasants derive their identity from the land and village life. Their relationship to the land is inseparable from their intimate and interdependent kinship relationships. What differentiates Bedouin from peasants is the latter's relationship to land rather than kinship ties. The Bedouin view attachment to land as a source of humiliation. They look down on peasants and see them as slaves of land and of those who have control over it. The peasants, by contrast, seek land and consider it to be the source of their dignity.

Even within communities, there are other important factors such as family and kinship that play an important role in determining the operation and effect of property rights. For instance, Muslim women's access to property, as will be argued in a later chapter, is best understood through the dynamics of custom, family, kinship and the construction of property itself. Conservative interpretations of Islamic law and customary/traditional structures/practices often combine to diminish or altogether extinguish women's rights to property (Doumani 2003; Moors 1999). Vulnerable categories of people such as squatters, slum dwellers, minorities, migrants and children often have great difficulty in accessing land rights. Therefore, it is necessary to determine the true import of Islamic norms in order to distinguish them from other deprecating customary or patriarchal norms where applicable.

Land Administration and Good Governance

The link between good governance and an efficient land policy is well established. It has been the driver of international initiatives from the United Nations Development Programme (UNDP), World Bank, International Monetary Fund (IMF) and UN-HABITAT. With effective governance, it is argued that business, government and citizens, acting as partners, will build a stronger economy, a better society and an effective polity. The UN Millennium Development Goals stress the importance of governance as part of an enabling environment conducive to development, drawing from the familiar language of civil and political human rights. Good governance implies the existence of participatory, transparent and accountable socio-political and economic processes and interaction/dialogue between state and non-state actors. However, the *Arab Human Development Report 2004* concludes that the situation of freedom and good governance in the Arab world ranges from deficient to seriously deficient. Despite sporadic improvements in the human rights situation in some Arab countries, the overall human rights picture in the Arab world appears grave and deteriorating (UNDP 2004).

The problems of land administration faced in Muslim countries are undoubtedly related to the democratic deficit but they also arise out of misuse of limited resources as well as inefficient structures. In many societies, whether Muslim or non-Muslim, land is seen as a currency of political patronage and corruption. Where land administration is complex or dysfunctional, rent-seeking behaviour flourishes at the expense of the poor (DfID 2002). The outcomes of the World Bank's Middle East and North Africa Programme (MNA) 2002 governance workshop in Beirut are instructive. They challenge the 'message' in the *Arab Human Development Report 2002* that the region is exceptional or that governance problems are qualitatively different from other regions. Moreover, they emphasize that there is no 'Arab' or 'Muslim' model of governance. Islam is neither a critical factor in determining the quality of governance nor inherently incompatible with good governance (World Bank 2002; see also Grant and Tessler 2002).

It should be acknowledged, however, that much of the literature regarding Islam revolves around the Islamic state as a utopian past or idealized future. The concept of the Islamic state, and its limits in the postmodern world, has been explored by several commentators (Ayubi 1995; Zubaida 1993). Whatever their orientation, Muslim governments routinely deploy Islamic justifications for their political legitimacy and survival (Esposito 1987: 239). Specifically, there is no doubt about the influential quality of *adl* and *shura*, the concepts of justice and consultation, which are embedded in Islamic consciousness and administrative practice (Rosen 2000). This quality is evident not only in modern liberal thought but equally in the works of Muslim revivalists like Hassan al-Banna, Abul Ala Mawdudi and Sayid Qutb.

Accountability, particularly against misuse of power and corruption, in both the temporal and religious sense, are repeatedly stressed in Islamic literature. As such, these concepts and ideals are deeply entrenched in Muslim consciousness and need to be employed more in land administration issues. In contrast to those who find Islam and democracy incompatible (Kedourie 1994), there is abundant scholarship arguing the opposite, although it is clear that Western and Islamic models vary (Abed 1995; Al-Suwaidi 1995). Brumberg (2002) argues that over the past two decades the Middle East has witnessed a 'transition' away from authoritarianism but seems to be moving back towards it. Zakaria (1997) argues that the mere existence of the opportunity to vote is not enough and that liberal democracies with built-in protections for citizens must be promoted. The record of Muslim states has generally been problematic in terms of open or good governance, but, as Ahmad (2004) argues, often the state in the Muslim world has enjoyed a monopoly position and consequently untrammelled powers to control potential critics in the media or through the polls.

A wide literature exists on the traditional and modern Muslim civil society (al-Ghannouchi 2000; Sajoo 2002). Traditional Muslim civil society, through institutions such as the *waqf* (Hoexter 2002), contrasts in structure and scope with Western-inspired models, though there are now a range of Islamic and secular spaces created by civil society in various parts of the Muslim world. Apart from state restrictions on their operation in several Muslim states, there are theoretical dilemmas for non-governmental organizations regarding the extent to which they can adopt universal standards and methodologies and their relationship to Islam, which often affects their standing with the government and society (Al-Sayyid 1997). However, civil society in most parts of the Muslim world appears to be expanding and gaining a stronger voice commensurate with the inability of many Muslim states to cater sufficiently to the needs of their peoples and adapt themselves to 'the demands of an ever-growing globalizing world economy' (Sahliyeh 2000). This diminishing power of the state – driven by the media and Internet revolution – has spurred civil society, which manifests itself in assorted ways, one of which is through religious and philanthropic organizations.

Islamic activism itself is often directed at efforts to 'produce a viably authentic political and social synthesis which is both modern and true to their indigenous (Islamic) history and values ... and the desire to articulate a more authentic identity' (Esposito 1987: 152). Bowman and Green (1997: 253) note, in the context of urbanization, that

> Islam can function as an important source of political mobilization when abysmal conditions in many of the region's cities lead to popular political dissatisfaction.... It is here that Islamic groups can mobilize urban dwellers on the basis of a government's inability to respond effectively to many of the ills that are by-products of massive urban growth. Such Islamic groups generally portray themselves as viable alternatives to prevailing political orders that do little for their constituents other than to oppress them. Thus, the relationship between massive urbanization and political protests may have as an intervening variable religio-political mobilization.

As Bowman and Green (1997) argue, Islamic groups have taken on a significant role as relief providers: they give the example of aid following natural disasters such as an earthquake which destroyed a part of Cairo, where the Egyptian government itself failed to respond effectively. The extent to which religious and philanthropic organizations can respond more generally to the lack of adequate secure housing and infrastructure for the residents of many cities across the Muslim world is a matter that warrants further attention and will be discussed further in Chapter 7 which focuses on *waqfs* and Islamic philanthropy.

Ottoman Land Administration

Ottoman land history offers an expansive case study of the application of Islamic land principles in a specific context, lessons from which can also contribute to modern debates. The Ottomans by the mid-sixteenth century ruled much of the Middle East, North Africa and Eastern Europe, and, through much of their 600-year dominance, developed an extensive land administration system based on Islamic and local principles. While the time and circumstances of each conquest varied, progressively Byzantine, Mamluk, Turkish and Hungarian practices, together with other land traditions, were incorporated. In theory, conquered land became the tithe land or *'ushr* (based on an obligatory charge on farm produce), whereas land left in the possession of its former holders was subject to *kharaj*, the levy of land tax. *Kharaj* tax, levied on non-Muslims at a higher rate than *ushr*, is usually synonymous with *jizya* (Arabic for 'compensate', in the context of non-Muslims being exempt from other obligations). Relationships governing landholders and the state, or between peasants and landlords or the state, or to do with the cultivation of *mewat* lands, were all inspired by Islamic principles. These continue to inform contemporary land classifications in many of the successor states, despite colonial and postcolonial modifications. Even today the Ottoman land records are being used in land transactions in a number of countries.

Ottoman land administration was driven largely by interests of revenue and taxation, though these had implications for the social and land structures (Cosgel 2004). Land administration was generally carried out through an elaborate network of laws and guidelines. A land grant (*iqta*) was given to soldiers in lieu of a regular wage at a time when the state had limited revenue, and did not create juridical or hereditary rights. At the time of Sultan Suleyman (the 'Magnificent' or the 'Lawgiver'), the empire's territories consisted of 36 administrative provinces. Districts of varying sizes were controlled by a *dirlik* appointed by the sultan and granted his own budget. The *dirlik* managed tax collection and land distribution and could be removed if found to be unsuitable (Biyik and Yomralio 1994). Despite the centralized nature of the Ottoman land and revenue bureaucracy, the vastness of its lands required more local management.

With weakening state power, in the seventeenth century *iltizams* (tax farms) were created where *multazims* (wealthy notables) were in charge of collecting land revenues for the state, initially for a year. The essence of the system was thus the leasing of the right to collect taxes on state land (Baer 1962). The *multazims* were allowed to keep part of the tax for a little more than their overheads but in practice exploitation did occur. Over time, *iltizams* were routinely renewed and even extended for the lifetime of the holders, who came to treat them as their own private property. In 1813, however, Muhammad Ali (or Mehmet Ali), the Ottoman Viceroy for Egypt, brought back centralized land assessment and control as a way of improving state revenues: he cut out the intermediaries and established a direct relationship with the working peasants, who were an important part of his economic agenda (see Pennell 2005). In the second part of the nineteenth century, the landowning class grew in economic and political power as a result of the breakdown of the state's monopolies, Ottoman law (introduced in the 1840s) regarding land ownership, the state's fiscal crisis (necessitating the sale of state lands to private individuals) and the establishment in 1866 of the Consultative Assembly (Moaddel 2002).

The Ottoman land administration experiences, derived theoretically in part from Islamic principles but equally conditioned by other socio-political considerations, establish several facts. First, *milk* freely existed for the landed classes, while for peasants there were limited but definite opportunities to access land – for example, through the reclamation of *mewat* land. Second, there was a concentration of state land (*miri*), although there were interests and rights created for intermediaries and peasants. Third, the cadastre (register of lands) and tax collection indicate that Islamic principles do not inhibit effective land administration systems. Fourth, land settlement patterns were determined by the availability of water and the nature of the irrigation system. Fifth, the role of the state with regard to land was not static but diverse and evolving. The Ottoman experience, a product of its times, went through several phases of centralization and decentralization. Finally, Ottoman land administration has contributed to contemporary land registration systems, as discussed below.

Islam and Land Cadastre, Registration and Titling

One of the significant challenges for land administration is the development of appropriate cadastral systems which can provide necessary information and clarify legal rights. The Cadastre 2014 initiative builds on earlier conceptualizations by seeking a modern integrated system giving a complete description of all legal conditions effective for a piece of land, including all public rights and restrictions. However, as van der Molen (2003) argues, there are 'significant differences' exhibited by the cadastral arrangements in 30 to 50 countries, which either possess, or will possess in the near future, appropriate land administration systems; but another 140–160 countries will not be anywhere near sufficiently prepared. The joint 1999 United Nations–FIG (International Surveyors Federation) Bathurst Declaration on Land Administration for Sustainable Development recognizes the multidimensional, evolving nature and plurality of cadastral work (Williamson and Grant 2002). It is noteworthy that among the members of the working group of FIG Commission 7 (Cadastre and Land Management) were representatives from Algeria, Egypt, Jordan, Malaysia and Turkey. Far from it being a Western concept, cadastre has been found since the time of the Prophet Mohammed, when at his suggestion collective lands around the city of Makkah were marked out with stones (El Ayachi *et al.* 2003). Likewise, the 'fencing' of *mewat* (dead land) properties to establish rights has been a common practice. For Muslim states in later historical periods, land records were considered necessary for resolving land disputes between (usually) private parties as well as to meet the state's desire for land information for purposes of revenue (Larsson 1991).

The Ottoman rulers realized the importance of land information and management, with periodic surveys and reviews of expected tax revenues (Cosgel 2004). During the Ottoman period, a land registration system flourished: particularly in the period 1534–1634, extensive land information records *(Kuyud-u Hakani)* contained all available land-related information. These records included names of villages and farms, landholders' names, annual income of lands, land classifications, boundaries of public-use areas, the natural resources on the land, population and paid tax. In fact, a land registration guide called *Kanunname-i Kitabet-i Vilayet* is available in the Ottoman archives. In addition there were further books, providing more detail with respect to landholdings in a particular province, such as boundary descriptions on the basis of which landholders were given certificates, land tenure and crops (Biyik and Yomralio 1994).

Despite its ambitious scope, the registration was not completed for the entire Ottoman territories but the advantage of Ottoman cadastral experience has meant that Egypt, for example, has had comprehensive land statistics available since 1907, with the techniques of assembling them becoming gradually more accurate (Baer 1962: 71). In Palestine, the Israeli state used the legal basis of Ottoman land law as the framework to aid its nationalization of Palestinian land (Kedar 2001). The power of the Ottoman legacy is illustrated by the fact that the Israeli land title registration office is still referred to as the 'Tabu' office and title registration certificates as 'Tabu' papers, a term which is Ottoman in origin. Many Muslim countries that were colonized experienced the Torrens system or similar titling programmes. The FIG country reports on Muslim countries such as Jordan, Algeria and Morocco show considerable cadastral preparation activity, often with international support. Several other Muslim countries such as Yemen, as well as countries with Muslim minorities such as the Philippines, have received extensive support for land-titling projects, with mixed success. In Muslim countries attitudes towards cadastre or tiling vary, but there is nothing in Islam that frustrates these attempts; indeed, the contrary is the case.

Islamic Urban Planning

Rapid urbanization with its attendant problems is a serious challenge in Middle Eastern and other Muslim cities. Referring to the complications arising from rising population, poverty and politics in urban centres, Bonine asks, 'Are Cities in the Middle East Sustainable?' (1997: 339). Echoing Santos's experience with informal settlements (*favelas*) operating outside formal structures in Brazil (Santos 1995), Hanna addresses the context of Egypt's migration-fed housing problem:

> When a government, anywhere in the world, does not set up a plan to satisfy the basic needs of its people [the people] have to seek ways and means to satisfy their basic needs. They do things according to their means.... There is no clear plan to control or guide this flow, nor is there a plan to solve the housing problem for these country people. (1985: 206)

Many of these urban management problems are similar to those faced by non-Islamic cities but they also have socio-religious dimensions as Islamic concepts of planning have permeated the wider planning debate. Since 1980 the Organization of Islamic Capitals and Cities (OICC), which is a global non-governmental and non-profit organization, has been affiliated to the OIC. It has 141 cities as active members in 54 OIC countries spread across the four continents of Asia, Africa, Europe and South America. Its activities are focused on the achievement of its goals within the framework of sustainable development of human settlements. It publishes a biannual magazine, *Islamic Capitals and Cities*, and through its seminars has produced several books relating to housing, the environment and urban planning.

Contemporary urban planning faces challenges, both in scale and nature, and limitations of resources perhaps not encountered by pre-modern societies, and modern secularized principles of planning efficiency seem to make Islamic concepts of doubtful relevance. However, there is much in Islamic civilization and history on which town planners and architects can draw. Muslim societies have been largely urban: the city of Al-Medina, where the first Muslim community was formed and which was first developed through the planning activities of the Prophet's generation, is often cited as the Islamic urban model. Much Western scholarship on Islamic urban space and socio-religious identity has been concerned with the mosque and the market as focal points, in analogy with the Hellenic city prototype (von Grunebaum 1955: 145). However, the *waqf* played a significant role in the characterization of public space (Ehlers 1992, Bonine 1987). Lapidus underscores the complexities of Islamic urbanization, noting how kinship, community ties (based on the unifying concept of the *umma* or community) and religious consciousness determined the historical evolution of Islamic cities (1973: 33–6). These studies are relevant, for example, in explaining the importance of privacy through courtyards or male communal spaces through *hammams* (public baths). As Al-Asad (1997: 63) points out, planners seeking to alleviate contemporary problems in modern cities should 'approach the city as an entity that fosters the preservation of memories and the creation of a sense of place [and] with sensitivity to psychological, historical and overall cultural issues'.

Given Islamic architectural splendour, it is easy to romanticize the Islamic city of tree-lined broad roads, fountains, exotic bazaars and clear public and private spaces. It has been argued that present-day architects and town planners are implicated in this idealization of an Arab-Islamic model, with the consequence that regional and local differences which are themselves shaped by Islamic history are sidelined (Fuccaro 2001). Bonine (1979: 223–4), writing in the context of Iranian cities, cautions against the single 'Islamic city model' as there are many variations. Abu-Lughod (1987) lists a number of variables that have an impact on Islamic urban space, including territoriality, gender segregation and neighbourhood. However, she debunks the generalizations regarding Islamic cities from patchy case studies as an 'orientalist' misreading. She asks 'Why would one expect Islamic cities to be similar and in what ways?' (1987: 160).

Characteristics of traditional Islamic cities, themselves diverse owing to varied socio-cultural factors, have been modified over time particularly during the modern period. Abu-Dayyeh (2006) argues that where traditional neighbourhoods have survived the onslaught of modernization, the *waqf* and the processes of land succession have stimulated some development, although it is slow and uneven. Therefore, the renewed interest in Islamic planning systems may or may not provide a wholesome alternative paradigm – but does warrant further attention. Traditional Islamic principles relating to land could not have foreseen the challenges of urbanization, land conflicts or newer forms of land use, as well as the difficulties in access to land and security of tenure. These are at a jurisprudential level matters for *ijtihad* (personal reasoning), but at a policy level, a state following Islamic principles has considerable leeway also in orienting its land policy towards the benefit of the community through *maslaha* or public interest. In particular, the rights of landless poor, slum dwellers and/or squatters could be addressed through this policy mechanism and the potential of both *ijtihad* and *maslaha* are addressed in the following chapter, which is concerned in part to discover how the processes of Islamic reasoning and interpretation can enable the emergence of innovative land management tools. This search is also relevant in approaches to contemporary environmental problems.

Islam, Environment and Water

Land management and use have to be integrated within a sound and responsible environmental policy. The *Qur'anic* view holds that everything on the earth was created for humankind. It was *ni'amah* (God's bounty) to humankind, but has to be exercised with care as a trusteeship. Land is a part of that holistic, moral and ethical dimension of *imaan* (religious faith), living in a way that is pleasing to Allah, striving in everything to maintain the harmony of both inner and outer environments (Khalid 2002). Engelmann (2001) points out that over 6,000 verses in the *Qur'an* urge believers to respect the environment and seek intergenerational equity in the use of the natural resources of the earth, which are a gift from God. There are environmental safeguards during peacetime and war. The Prophet not only encouraged the sustainable use of fertile lands; he also told his followers of the benefits of making unused land productive: planting a tree, sowing a seed and irrigating dry land were all regarded as charitable deeds and would lead to ownership of that land. Extrapolating laws from such *Qur'anic* teachings is the challenge in addressing environmental issues in the modern context. These issues range from deforestation and soil erosion to drought and flood, from the application of technology to the preservation of community and culture, from the greenhouse effect to acid rain, from nuclear power to genetic engineering, from population and poverty to North–South equity and from stewardship to sustainable development (Rahim 2001). However, beyond the theory, Khalid (2002) points out that there a large number of institutions and mechanisms to foster environmental protection, including the reclamation of *mewat* land or the establishment of conservation zones in the form of a *waqf* or a *hima*, which is an area designated as a special reserve by the state. The state can also establish *al-haramain*, inviolable sanctuaries where the use of land is severely restricted, or where trees and animals are protected.

Environmental challenges arising out of water shortages and disputes are particularly critical in the Middle East and other parts of the Muslim world (Swain 1998). The *Qur'an* mentions water (*ma*) some 63 times. Water is extensively discussed in the documented sayings and actions of the Prophet (Faruqi *et al.* 2001). Not only did water play a prominent role in Islamic architectural designs and in its settlements, it has a significant role in rituals, particularly *wudu* (obligatory ablution) which precedes the *salah* (five times daily prayer). The Makkan *zam zam* (aquifer) has a *Qur'anic* status. Water is constructed as a gift from God and belongs to the community with the right to drink (*shafa*) and other uses. However, the question of individual ownership over water, in contrast to usufruct or access rights, is still a matter of Islamic debate. In classical Islamic theory all land is held in trust for the benefit of the community, but water rights over individual lands were bought and sold during the Ottoman period (Lambton 1953). Warriner notes that 'water rights are regarded as the personal property of individuals and not annexed to the land which they should naturally pertain' (1948: 73). Thus, land could be sold without water rights and vice versa, leading to confusion and speculative practices (Forni 2005). In most Muslim countries, water is a commodity but the discourse over its use often recalls the religious dimensions of the environmental issue (Caponerea 1973). The Arab Human Development Report 2002 points out that Muslim countries must confront environmental problems as a priority (UNDP 2004: 45–50, Talal 2004).

Conclusions

This chapter's outline of Islamic conceptions of land tenure and land rights demonstrates that there an Islamic dimension to contemporary land debates which is worthy of exploration. Property rights are not only well established under Islamic law, but are indisputably one of the five foundational principles of the Islamic society. As such, land rights must be respected and protected as a matter of priority. Though, in religious terms, all property vests in God, it has never been seriously disputed that human beings as owners assert the usual range of property rights in the land, subject to compliance with the egalitarian provisions of the Shari'a. Moreover, particular Islamic approaches are evident in the fields of land administration, land registration, urban planning, water policies and environmental protection. Understanding the nature and scope of property rights in Islamic society could further secure tenure as the land rights framework emerges from divine edict and the sayings and examples of the Prophet.

There is repeated Islamic emphasis on obligations regarding philanthropy, fairness and poverty alleviation, which are influential in land rights argumentation. The concept of property rights in Islamic economics has implications far beyond the material domain as it lays stress on responsibility, poverty alleviation and redistribution. In the Islamic welfare state, the *Baytul-Maal* (public treasury) has a specific mandate for support of the landless. In addition to taxes, state funds are also comprised of *zakat* and other donations. The state is expected to fund access to land for the landless poor. The formulation that land is a sacred trust implies that land ownership and enjoyment must be just and responsible. As a result, Islamic doctrines engage with entitlement to land rights for a broad range of beneficiaries, including women, children, landless and minorities. Land ownership in Islam is predicated on productive use of land, as evidenced from the principle of ownership of *mewat* through reclamation. Despite the clear foundational Islamic principles relating to land and the evolution of sophisticated land tenure arrangements in many parts of the Muslim world, their application in Muslim societies does manifest itself in different ways. However, there is the basis upon which Islamic access to land through Islamic arguments can be promoted, with a holistic, authentic, moral, ethical and legal land rights code.

Under Islamic theory, the state in land management is seen as supervising land ultimately belonging to God. Thus, the state is mandated to administer land, efficiently and fairly, in accordance with God's laws and ethical and moral principles. The Ottoman land administration narrative is complex and its legacy often disputed, but it demonstrates clearly that systems such as titling, registration and cadastre have a well-embedded history in the Muslim world. In practical terms, there exist no ideal Islamic states, and Muslim states selectively adopt Islamic principles according to their particular interpretation. Further, it has been argued that there is no distinctive Arab or Muslim model of governance, but the concepts of *shura* and *adl* are nevertheless influential. Potentially, an Islamic framework gives states wide leeway in promoting security of tenure and access to land within a transparent and accountable framework. For instance, an opportunity could arise through the redistribution of *mewat* lands or through optimizing *waqf* lands.

Though traditional Islamic practice may not have foreseen the extent or nature of present-day problems, and purely Islamic solutions may be a utopian model, there are aspects of Islamic principles, mechanisms and processes that can provide legitimate and durable solutions through incorporating or at least considering authentic Islamic contributions. This introduction to Islamic land rights has highlighted some key areas for a deeper exploration of the relationship between the theorization of Islamic property rights over land and the impact of those rights in Muslim societies which are the focus of later chapters: Islamic land tenure systems, Islamic human rights relating to land, Muslim women's access to property, Islamic inheritance, the *waqf* and Islamic microfinance. By systematically addressing the distinctive features of the Islamic land framework it is intended to contribute to the quest for international land rights. However, before focusing upon these specific issues, it is important to investigate further Islamic legal cultures relating to land and property, including the sources and methods of reasoning and interpretation. It will be argued in the next chapter that probing Islamic legal doctrines and methodology can enable the development of inclusive land tools, raising important possibilities, for instance, through *maslaha* or public interest within the domain of land administration and *ijtihad* or personal reasoning across a range of areas, including women's property rights.

2

Islamic Law, Land and Methodologies

> Islamic Law is the epitome of the Islamic spirit, the most typical manifestation of the Islamic way of life, the kernel of Islam itself. For the majority of Muslims, the law has always been and still is of much greater practical importance than the dogma. Even today the law remains a decisive element in the struggle which is being fought in Islam between traditionalism and modernism under the impact of Western ideas. It is impossible to understand the present legal development in the Islamic countries of the Middle East without a correct appreciation of the past history of legal theory, of positive law, and of legal practice in Islam. (Khadduri and Liebesny 1955: 28)

Islamic law is a central feature of the lived experiences and consciousness of Muslims across the world, whether or not their states 'officially' implement the law. Contrary to general assumptions, Islamic law is not a 'religious' law but rather a man-made code whose primary source is the holy scripture *Qur'an*, subject to human interpretation of divine intent. In order to be legitimized within an Islamic jurisprudential praxis, interpretation must comply with certain authenticated methodology. How one goes about interpreting Islamic legal principles in compliance with certain protocols is therefore vital to the success of the venture. Rather than assuming that the Shari'a is a monolithic, static or immutable corpus of medieval laws, one may see it as an evolving, responsive and assimilating sphere of competing ideologies and interests. The primary sources of the Shari'a may be divine (the *Qur'an*) but it is *bashari* (human) endeavour or interpretation as well as state preferences that determine how contemporary society actualizes it. As such, Islamic legal conceptions inform and influence the lives of a majority of Muslims, including their attitudes towards land and property rights. Islamic law is an important factor influencing land rights and tenure systems in Muslim societies.

Recognition of the potency of Islamic legal thought processes can pave the way for active and constructive engagement with the internal discourses. Western perspectives of Islamic law tend to be limited, partial or hostile, creating a gulf of cross-cultural misunderstanding that allows myths about Islamic law to develop and leaves the field clear for extremist and obscurantist constructs of Islamic law. An appreciation of the distinctive features and sources of Islamic law, its diversity in application in relation to property and land rights and its dispute resolution mechanisms can contribute towards strategies aimed at development goals and security of tenure. While there are dominant conservative legal opinions alongside egalitarian foundational principles, there exist significant opportunities for interpretation strategies within Islamic law that can promote access to land and security of tenure. This chapter aims to open up these opportunities.

The role of law in land policy will be considered, both in a general sense and with respect particularly to Muslim societies, as well as the significance of Islamic law in Muslim consciousness. The sources of Islamic law relating to land and property rights will be outlined and the pluralism inherent in the articulation of Islamic legal theories and their practice will be explored. Finally, there will be an examination of the role of various legal institutions in implementing Islamic law. It will be demonstrated that delving into the 'authentic' forms of argumentation has its advantages, not least in that it offers an additional means of securing rights in, and access to, land. As argued in the previous chapter, Islamic laws relating to property and land rights have to be assessed within the broader Islamic legal systems, since there is considerable overlap and cross-application of different Islamic legal doctrines. Decoding the sources, structure and normative frameworks of Islamic law enables those working within Muslim societies to explore innovative, proactive and inclusive land tools potentially available within Islamic law. This is particularly relevant for strategies aimed at developing access to land and security of tenure.

Role of Law in Land Policy

Law generally constitutes a significant medium in the development, articulation and implementation of land policies. It defines property rights, informs land tenure systems and regulates land administration (Fernandes and Varley 1998). Law is often such a dominant channel in debates over land policy that reforms or interventions appear primarily directed at changing, reorienting or restructuring law itself. Land law not only provides the legal foundation for land administration but is a key vehicle to systems such as land titling and registration, and in facilitating access to land and security of tenure (Payne 2002).

There appears to be a general consensus among international, national and local actors that land laws potentially provide the framework for ordering equitable, fair and clearer relationships with respect to land amongst individuals, societies and states. Yet law as an instrument of power is malleable and can also be manipulated to disempower particular groups or types of individuals. As is often claimed, 'some people use the law, some people have law used against them'. Therefore questions of the legitimacy, fairness, efficiency and durability of law continue to permeate the debate over the role of law in land policies. Rather than a constant predictable model, law can be used for a variety of objectives from social engineering and empowerment to disenfranchisement and oppression, and is capable of multiple, even unintended effects.

The relationship between law and property is contentious and complex. As Bentham wrote: 'Property and Law are born together and die together. Before laws were made there was no property; take away the laws and property ceases' (1931: 113). Philosophical and jurisprudential debates over the nature and scope of property law have often been central to understanding the nature of law itself, as well as the connotations of property rights in society. Law is not used only by lawyers, however, but also by commentators and consumers from the wide spectrum of society for whom law has different meanings and implications. Some feminists, for example, argue that patriarchal assumptions have shaped the content of property laws (Scott-Hunt and Lim 2001), while those from the Critical Legal Studies movement emphasize the influence of ideology in shaping the content of the law (Kennedy 1994). Proponents of the Law and Economics school argue that areas such as property law 'bear the stamp of economic reasoning' (Posner 1992: 23). Land law at a formal level operates through legislation, rules, policies, judicial reasoning and implementation strategies, but it often incorporates informal or 'extra-legal' norms and practices.

Property rights amount to a socio-economic institution or field of relationships that is much broader than property law, the latter being only one discursive location for property rights. Land rights are considered to be a subset of property rights since the latter often subsume property rights over land. Not all land rights are justiciable and often the cost of transactions, together with the political will to act, can determine their effectiveness. Therefore, rather than the monopoly of the state through statute-based regulations, declared policy and court mechanisms, property rights may be enforced informally through customary norms, institutions or through market forces. Law is thus sometimes the creator of land rights and at other times – by merely recognizing them or preventing abuse – the facilitator of the pursuit of land rights by individuals. However, any discussion about the role of law in land policy will have to contend with its limitations – as evidenced in current global concerns about the rule of law – and resist the temptation of viewing law as a utopian solution and unifying force for land policy.

Throughout the world there are variations in how property rights are established: the types of property rights recognized; the regulation of different types of use and users; and the enforcement mechanisms. This is because systems of law throughout the world exhibit plurality, even as between the two dominant systems: the common law (as in British and US laws) and civil law (as in the French). Though there is increasing interchange of legal experiences globally, each legal tradition or system emerges, among other things, from its own particular historical evolution. The mere existence or creation of laws and mechanisms are not enough; such laws must have legitimacy and be accessible and acceptable to the people to whom they apply (Freeman 1998: 365). Laws include not only state-created norms but a spectrum of tribal, customary and religious laws. The ideas of law in Islamic legal contexts are distinctive in their normative outlines, structure and methodology, but a treatise of Islamic law relating to land and property rights is not offered here, for reasons explained further below. Instead a framework is set out within which these rights can be explored. It is difficult from a non-Islamic perspective to decide among the claims of rival and incompatible accounts of justice competing for moral, social and political allegiance (MacIntyre 1988). However, as Collier (1996) writes:

> In the coming new world order of nationalist struggles and ethnic confrontations, socio-legal scholars may not be able to remain silent, for if we fail to explore connections between Western and Islamic legal systems, we only contribute to media stereotypes of Islamic law as regressive and feudal and of Islamic political activists as religious fanatics.

Relevance of Islamic Law in the Muslim World

Muslim countries do not present a simple dichotomy of Islamic or non-Islamic laws. Islamic legal principles generally coexist and overlap with social constructions of race, gender, family, kinship and the *umma* through customary norms as well as state secular laws. On one hand, there is no such thing as 'the' Islamic law – it manifests itself in a variety of ways owing to choices between competing norms and methodologies – though there are certain agreed Islamic principles. On the other hand, Islamic laws function alongside a host of other legal cultures through a multiplicity of relationships. Islamic laws sometimes absorb or negotiate, and at other times conflict with, foreign elements. However, whatever the extent and form of Islamic law 'officially' sanctioned in Muslim societies, in the consciousness of much of the Muslim world land tenure regimes and concepts are generally constructed or realized, to a noticeable degree, through reference to the Shari'a. Therefore, discussions regarding rights to acquire, utilize and alienate property in Muslim societies are informed by the general belief that property vests in God and that the use of the property must be in accordance with Islamic law (Rodinson 1973). The characteristic Islamic conceptions of ownership and use, as discussed in the previous chapter, are accompanied by the frequent reminder that land use must comply with the norms of the Shari'a.

Property and land rights are evident in the Muslim world (Ziadeh 1993), but writing on Islamic law dimensions of the subject is a difficult enterprise. There is no unified field of legal doctrines relating to property and land rights or systematic development of Islamic norms corresponding to access to land and security of tenure, though there are raw materials. Therefore there is no dedicated discipline of 'Islamic land law' but rather a set of overlapping themes or domains which practitioners will recognize as such. This must also be said of housing rights, another area where Islamic principles should have given rise to a full-bodied field of law but where there is limited literature. How Islamic law relating to property and land operates in reality and practice, as Islamic or secular law, is also an under-researched area. There is sufficient material on how, for example, family courts or criminal courts function, yet the knowledge of formal Islamic dispute resolution mechanisms with relation to land is limited.

Land rights in Islam do not exist in isolation, therefore, but are best understood with reference to other parts of Islamic law. Islamic land rights and tenure regimes are themselves derived from a range of overlapping Islamic fields such as family, public, finance, taxation and commercial laws. Religiously justified specific rights or secularized rights relating to land and property in the Muslim world are often contingent on being authenticated through Shari'a validation. Schacht, the leading orientalist scholar, explained it thus: 'Islamic law is the epitome of Islamic thought, the most typical manifestation of the Islamic way of life, the core and kernel of Islam itself' (1964: 1). Property rights in general are to be exercised in accordance with foundational concepts in Islamic dogma and the Shari'a: human rights are subject to compatibility with the Shari'a; inheritance shares are fixed by the Shari'a; land tenure systems are influenced by the Shari'a; women's access to property has to be understood within the Shari'a; Islamic microfinance products have to be Shari'a-compliant; and the *waqf* emerges out of Shari'a law principles. The scope of the Shari'a, as well as its detail, is often staggering and there are other legal disciplines, from international law to environmental law (Khadduri 2002; Haneef 2002), which may be relevant.

While Muslims generally celebrate Islamic law as one of the important features of their faith and way of life, there are others who dismiss Islamic law as an ancient body of outdated rules that do not apply to present-day realities. Kuran (2003), for example, considers Islamic law as part of the problem which ails Muslim communities, arguing in particular that the Islamic laws of inheritance and the wealth tied up in the *waqf* have been barriers to economic development. Equally, there are commentators who hail the role of Islamic law in human development. Undoubtedly, care must be taken not to romanticize

'Islamic law'. The label is claimed for a range of political and ideological interests and, just as the Shari'a evokes images of justice and fairness, it is equally capable of distortion and excuse for unacceptable and discriminatory behaviour. There is no doubt that considerable power and legitimation flow from the classification of certain norms or practices as divinely intended or ordained. Why certain states or groups articulate or choose to adopt Islamic law to a greater degree or in a more stringent form than others cannot be attributed merely to pious intentions; there are political dimensions to be considered. As Peters (2001) found in the context of the reintroduction of Islamic criminal law in Northern Nigeria, the value in its adoption may be not real but symbolic. Despite these concerns, Islamic legal systems have a currency in contemporary Muslim societies and for this reason alone there is benefit in knowledge about the doctrines, methodologies and patterns of dispute resolution of Islamic law. It is a study which is critical in the attempt to understand issues of development and land tenure in Muslim communities.

Reasoning in Islamic Law

Islamic law is often distinguished from 'modern secular' law as a 'religious' law, given that its primary source is the divine revelation (the *Qur'an*). This in turn is expected to restrict opportunities for and means of interpretation (Hussain 1997). This is not entirely correct for several reasons. First, as discussed below, the *Qur'an* is only one of numerous sources of Islamic law and there are several mechanisms that provide avenues for flexibility and innovation. Second, not all Islamic law issues are considered 'religious' or equally resistant to reinterpretation. Broadly, matters within the field of Islamic law fall into two categories: *ibadat* (religious observance); and *mu'amalat* (social transactions). Much of Islamic law relating to land, property and housing would fall within the domain of 'social transactions' and therefore be open to a greater degree of interpretation than matters of religious observance. Third, Islamic law is not merely a set of prescriptions and norms. *Usul al fiqh* (Islamic jurisprudence) contains a highly developed field of methodology dealing with methods of reasoning and the rules of interpretation with regard to Islamic legal sources, also discussed below.

Perhaps more than any other set of legal norms, the Shari'a has been too easily perceived by outsiders as a set of rigid edicts. Bowen (2003: 9) comments:

> Far from being an immutable set of rules, Islamic jurisprudence (*fiqh*) is best characterized as a human effort to resolve disputes by drawing on scripture, logic, the public interest, local custom, and the consensus of the community. In other words it is as imbricated with social and cultural life as is Anglo-American law.

Despite its many clear and salient features, Islamic law is a contested zone. This arises not merely because specific provisions may be interpreted contextually but also because interpreters may disagree about the implications of the foundational principles. For example, Islamic law does not make sense without the ethical dimension of the divine revelation (Rahman 1983). There are certain basic Islamic concepts or 'golden threads' that embody the spirit of the Shari'a. They include: *haqq* (concepts of rights), *adl* (justice) and *qist* (equity). The importance attached to these principles is evident from the number of times they are reiterated in the *Qur'an*: *haqq* is used 227 times, *qist* 15 times and *adl* 13 times. Rosen argues that justice is the central feature of the religion, its laws and administration (2000: 74). Justice appears as the objective of Islamic laws and the ultimate goal of religion itself, making it a devotional act next to piety. Thus the *Qur'an* calls upon believers to deal with each other 'with justice' (4: 58). In a fuller invocation, the *Qur'an* demands:

> O you who believe! Stand firmly for justice, as witnesses to God, even though it be against yourselves, or your parents, or your relations, be they rich or poor; God is a better protector to both (than you can be). So follow not the desires (of your hearts), if it leads you to avoid justice; if you distort your evidence or refuse to give it, surely God is all knowing of what you do. (*Qur'an* 4: 135)

These notions of fairness and morality are intrinsic to Islamic legal tradition and theorization. Makdisi (1985) argues that 'equity' is a part of Islamic law and that Islamic law in turn had an influence on the evolution of common law during its formative periods. From Islamic human rights to Islamic finance, there is frequent reference to egalitarian principles, ethical standards and philanthropic expectation. Using a socio-historical approach, many contemporary Islamic thinkers seek to show that Islamic law in its ideal form is about instinctive justice. Yet the risk in using 'morality' as a yardstick is that it can be subjective and work both ways, depending on socio-cultural mores. For example, those who argue against the equal rights of women or migrants often do so convinced that the social order must be hierarchical. To argue otherwise (or hold any position) through logic and analysis is considered as mere *ra'y* (opinion) which is not persuasive. To make a valid argument in Islamic legal theory one must follow a well-developed methodology.

The distinguishing feature of Islamic law is that it was not born in a vacuum or constructed out of current needs and priorities. Rather it is the product of centuries of legal thought and experiences. This is often dismissed as the 'historical' Shari'a which is resistant to modern-day realities. However, Islamic law has to be appreciated in a socio-historical context and in terms of historical debates, even though it may have outgrown classical formulations (Starr 1992). The battle between 'tradition' and 'modernity' is not new, but evident throughout Islamic history and in Ottoman reforms (Messick 1993). What must be avoided is the adoption of an 'orientalist' approach of evaluating Islamic law against preconceived ideas about law (Said 1993). Contemporary Shari'a law is at the centre of debate not only from a Western perspective but within Muslim societies. As Arkoun notes:

> The so-called Islamic revivalism has monopolized the discourse on Islam; the social scientists, moreover, do not pay attention to what I call the 'silent Islam' – the Islam of true believers who attach more importance to the religious relationship with the absolute of God than to the vehement demonstrations of political movements. (1988: 205)

Islamic law is not God's law, a prerogative of jurists or a tool in the hands of fundamentalists or the state. It is about how Muslims are making choices about their legal and ethical framework.

Foundations of Islamic Law and Usul al Fiqh

*Usul al fiq*h is a science which deals with the methods of reasoning and the rules of interpretation when construing the *Qur'an* and *Sunna.* It is the methodology which determines the substantive rules of law through the practical application of Islamic law obtained from textual sources (*furu al fiqh*) and the foundations of Islamic jurisprudence, which is the search for essential and classical Islamic jurisprudential techniques. *Fiqh* is thus the end product of *usul al fiqh.* A freestyle Socratic deductive approach may be the mark of distinguished Western scholarship but, bereft of rigorous reasoning as recognized by Islamic sciences, it is merely *ra'y*, which is not formatted for 'in house' Islamic dialogue. An interpreter of Islamic law, for example one aspiring to conduct *ijtihad* or personal reasoning, would have to adjust his or her hermeneutics to traverse the narrow alleys of the highly developed and sophisticated jurisprudence that provides the theoretical and methodological base on which Shari'a law is constructed.

Although there are different ways in which Islamic law is interpreted, *ijtihad* is the best-known, being a well-established jurisprudential tool for seeking Islamic legal principles. Although it is not a magic wand or a smart weapon to validate premeditated conclusions or manufacture a new religious framework that mirrors particular expectations, it could well catalyse the discovery of a far more liberal, egalitarian, pro-poor, gender-empowering and innovative Islamic system than is presently conceded. Kamali argues that the 'principal objective of *usul al-fiqh* is to regulate *ijtihad*' (Kamali 1991: 3).

As discussed in the previous chapter, the foundational principles of Islamic law are known as *maqasid al* Shari'a (the objectives of Islamic law). There is juristic consensus that laws must serve the protection of, and desist from violating, these fundamental objectives. The three categories of rights which must be protected are the *daruriyyat* (essentials), the *hajiyyat* (complements) and *tahsiniyyat* (embellishment). The highest category, the *daruriyyat*, consists of five 'essential' interests: the preservation of *din* (religion), *nafs* (life), *'aql* (intellect), *nasl* (progeny) and *mal* (property). The implication of property rights being a priority is that no law can violate this essential and also that state policy through *maslaha* or promotion of the public interest must operate to promote it (Moghul 1999). Thus, property and land rights lie at the very heart of Islamic law but must be approached within the Islamic methodological framework, which is examined below.

Evolution of Islamic Laws Relating to Land and Property

As stated above, there exists no amalgamated or systematic field of Islamic land law or property law, even though it is an important branch of Islamic legal learning. However, classical jurists debated issues relating to property rights (see Khadduri and Lienbesny 1955: 179). It is worth noting that the Islamic (Hanafi) jurist Abu Yusuf is best known for his pioneering Islamic theory of taxation in his famous treatise *Kitab al Kharaj* (The Book of Land Tax). During the formative classical period between the seventh and the ninth centuries, institutions and doctrines relating to Islamic property law emerged (Yanagihashi 2004). In an influential legal analysis, 'The Case of the Land Rent', Johansen (1988) shows how Islamic conceptions of property rights adapted to their specific socio-economic and political contexts. Focusing on documents from the Ottoman period, he demonstrates that by and large the classical Hanafi notions of tax and rent did not hold for the Ottoman Empire, and that the jurists acknowledged the transformation.

The classical law relating to property and land rights underwent several periods of influence – Ottoman, colonial and postcolonial/modern. The Ottoman period saw the rise of legal enterprise when Suleyman, sultan from 1520, became known as the *Kanuni* (lawgiver). Among his contributions lay those in the areas of land rights, taxation and *waqf*. The Ottoman practice, which was rooted in part in traditional Islamic principles, although shaped by custom and specific socio-political contexts, is best known for efforts to codify the law. The 1877 Majalla or Ottoman Civil Code, dealing with commercial transactions, substantively codified Shari'a law, principally from the perspective of the Hanafi school of Muslim jurisprudence, but following Napoleonic form. In 1858 the Ottoman government consolidated various existing laws into a Land Code and it is from this, as will be discussed in more detail in later chapters, that most states in the modern Muslim world derive their land tenure categories (Owen 2000a; Jorgens 2000).

Colonial rule in Muslim countries produced efforts to 'simplify' Islamic laws relating to land and property or to adapt them to colonial conceptions, as will be explained in the next chapter. As Mitchell (1991) points out, '[c]olonial power required [colonized societies] to become readable, like a book'. Among the translations/codifications of Islamic laws from traditional sources are the works of Baillie, Minhaj, Khalili and Hedaya, which provide constructions from specific schools of Islamic jurisprudence, geographical areas or time periods. However, the contemporary structure of Islamic property law adopts much of the Western legal arrangement. It covers a wide range of topics such as leaseholds, joint ownership, pledges, bailment, lost property, licences, trespass, sale, gift, restraints on alienation, fixtures, pre-emption, mortgages, rights to water, wills, intestate succession, nuisance, and causation (see Makdisi 2004). Islamic laws relating specifically to the property rights of women are drawn from a variety of fields such as family law (marriage/*mehr*/*mahr*, inheritance, and guardianship), property law (gifts, *waqf*, sale and hire) (Shatzmiller 1995) and economic law (right to work, income), as well as public law.

Sources of Islamic Law Relating to Land

In Islamic law, there is a formal hierarchy of sources of law. The primary sources of Islamic law are the *Qur'an*, read alongside the *Sunna*. Muslims believe the *Qur'an* to be the literal revealed word of God and as such it is the primary material source of law, containing as it does God's plain and unambiguous commands and prohibitions. The *Qur'an* was gradually revealed to the Prophet, over a period of 23 years. However, it should not be regarded as a comprehensive Code of Law. Only a small proportion of the *Qur'an* is concerned with 'legal' matters and to the Western eye those matters are not presented in a systematic form (Esposito 1982: 4–5).

The Qur'anic stipulations on general aspects of property and land rights are significant and were discussed in some detail in the previous chapter. They are equally significant on gender rights – they recognize women's rights (*Qur'an* 4: 4, 4: 7 and 4: 32) – as well as in their fixed inheritance rules, which generally grant half the share of the male to women (See Awde 2000). Where an Islamic property regime, such as the compulsory inheritance rules, is dealt with explicitly by the *Qur'an*, most Muslims would consider the matter not subject to *ijtihad* or independent reasoning (Amawi 1996: 155). However, the *Qur'an* has to be interpreted as a whole and it is fertile ground for reappraisal of gender rights, as seen from the works of influential Muslim feminists (Hassan 1982; Barlas 2002; Wadud 1999; Al-Faruqi 2000). There are also renewed juristic efforts to interpret land, property and housing rights that remain heavily dependent upon the *Qur'an* in order to obtain pro-poor, flexible and inclusive land tools. In this regard, if one considers property rights under human rights documents such as the Universal Islamic Declaration on Human Rights (UIDHR), though divergences from a religious text more than 1,400 years old are to be expected, it is remarkable how many of the contemporary human rights standards with respect to property and land rights find resonance in the *Qur'an*.

The body of law derived from sacred sources was developed over a period of time in the hands of private scholars. Beyond the *Qur'an,* a further important source of law lies in the *Sunna*, the records of the words and deeds of the Prophet in the form of *hadith*, which are a diverse collection of narratives (Siddiqui 1993). Doubts over the authenticity of some narrations or their narrators led to the development of limited, well-acknowledged *hadith* reports. Where there is a conflict between the *Qur'an* and the *Sunna*, the *Qur'an* prevails. Problems can arise where the *Sunna* is extensive and the *Qur'an* is general and limited. For example, the basis of the Islamic law on maintenance is a verse in the *Qur'an* (4: 34), but there are also several *hadith* on the subject. Here the challenge is to weed out spurious gender-deprecating customary norms projected as Islamic truisms with reference to the gender-empowering Qur'anic stipulations.

There are two other main sources of Islamic law, first *ijma* (consensus) and second, *qiyas* (reasoning by analogy). *Ijma* is commonly taken to mean the unanimous agreement amongst those who are learned in the religion at a particular time on a specific issue (Hasan 1984). However, some scholars believe that the concept should be regarded restrictively and refers only to the consensus of jurists at the time of the first generation of Muslims. Others not only extend the concept to encompass consensus in each particular age or time, but also hold that it extends to the unanimous agreement amongst the *umma*. *Ijma* derives its authority from a *hadith* to the effect that 'My community will never agree on an error' (Esposito 1982: 7). Together *qiyas* and *ijma* bestow upon Islamic jurisprudence dynamism and scope for development. For instance, it is *ijma* which allowed guardianship over the property of minors; this allowance has been extended by *qiyas* to apply to the guardianship of minors in marriage (Moghul 1999). Reasoning by analogy arose because of concern amongst Muslim jurists and scholars on the need to maintain a close relationship to the major material and textual sources of law. *Qiyas* is the method of transposing a rule of law in one case to a new case that is under consideration, because of a similarity in the reason or cause on which the ruling was based. This form of reasoning by deduction in comparable cases links the reasoning back to the original sources of the *Qur'an* and the *Sunna*. For instance, the prohibition on the drinking of wine was extended by analogy to other alcoholic drinks which were not available at the time of the original Qur'anic injunction. Through *ijma* and *qiyas*, there are further possibilities for developing land and property rights.

Furthermore, there are supplemental law-generating mediums such as *istishan* (juristic preference) that enhance the flexibility and responsiveness of the Shari'a and demonstrate the plurality of method in Islamic law, since some of these tools are only closely associated with particular *Sunni* schools. The concept of *istishan* is linked with the Hanafi school of jurisprudence but is also used by another jurisprudential school, the Maliki. It arises in a relatively rare case where the application of *qiyas* gives rise to a harsh or unjust result and permits the exercise of discretion on the part of the judge to achieve a more equitable outcome. Discretion can only be so exercised when there is no indication in the *Qur'an* or the *Sunna* as to the appropriate decision (Kamali 1991). Additionally, Islamic courts could construe such mitigating factors as duress or necessity as grounds for voiding binding documents.

Another supplementary principle of law is *maslaha,* based on public interest and human welfare. It is a method associated with the Maliki school of jurisprudence and permits the jurist to find a solution using discretion that is based on determining and promoting man's best interest in a case (*istislah*), provided again that it is not a matter covered by any textual source of Islamic law. Several Qur'anic verses support this concept (10: 7, 22: 78 and 5: 6), though there is debate as to its nature and scope. Islamic scholars, including the influential jurist Al Ghazali, considered *maslaha* as applicable to secure a benefit or prevent harm. Generally three requirements for public interest (*maslaha*) have been stipulated. First, it must be for the benefit of the community and not the individual. Second, it must be a tangible benefit and not an illusory one. Third, it must not conflict in its essence with anything from Islamic law (Shari'a). Public interest or general welfare has had a wide and important role in the development of Islamic law, justifying Muslim rulers throughout history in interpreting and enacting laws on the grounds of justice. Protection of property interests is subject to public interest considerations as a matter of priority (Nyazee 1994). It is on the basis of *maslaha* that the companions of the Prophet decided to impose *kharaj* (agricultural land tax). The discretionary power of the *mutawalli* (administrator) of a *waqf* is governed also by the principle of public interest for the well-being of the endowment. However, as Esposito (1982: 9) warns, while this principle may add a flexible quality to legal interpretation, it should not be viewed as 'free-wheeling' but 'a disciplined principle of law with definite limits within which it is to function'. Moreover, it is concerned only with *mu'amalat* and not *ibadat.*

Islamic law itself, as it emerged from the Prophet's time, was built over pre-Islamic customary practices and as the faith spread it brought in various levels of symbiosis and amalgamation between Islamic legal theory and customary norms of the newer Islamic communities. Classical Islamic jurists actively engaged with the validity of *urf* (custom) in the Islamic context, and generally accepted the same unless it was in direct contradiction with Islamic principles (Omar 1997). In most Muslim societies, Islamic and customary norms have almost been fused together: a conscious effort is required to distinguish the two, as with land practices (Ziadeh 1960). Where there are injurious customary practices, positive Islamic principles can be used to weed out traditions that are unjust and unacceptable.

Ijtihad *(Personal Reasoning)*

Ijtihad is a well-established Islamic juridical mechanism to develop Islamic jurisprudence in the light of contemporary issues (Weiss 1978: 203) and like the principle of *maslaha* it is of some importance with respect to developing land and property rights. Strictly not a source of law but an interpretative methodology, it is literally 'an effort to find' the right principle. It is not confined, however, to the jurist, but is the *fard kifaya* (sacred duty) of every competent individual. A question may arise about a Qu'ranic text for which the jurist would apply personal reasoning to come to an interpretation. On the one hand, there are verses of the *Qu'ran* which are regarded as *muhkamat* (clear and unambiguous), incapable of interpretation and consisting of specific injunctions or commands. On the other hand, there are verses which are *mustashabihat* (capable of different interpretations) (Al-Nowaihi 1975: 175). Another principle that a Muslim majority accepts is the repeal of *naskh* (inoperative or contradictory Qu'ranic verses) when determining legal issues.

The idea that the 'gates of *ijtihad*' were shut in 1258 by a juristic consensus, which had led to the assumption that *ijtihad* is no longer possible, has been discredited (Hallaq 1984, Coulson 1969). Efforts of pioneers such as the Indian-born Muhammad Iqbal (d. 1938), Turkish Ziya Gokalp (d. 1924) or the Egyptians Mohammad Abduh (d. 1905) and Rashid Rida (d. 1935) to rethink Islam continue to resound. Far from being the prerogative of liberals or modernists, *ijtihad* has equally been a favourite with Islamic revivalists and conservatives. It is the *post facto* validation of *ijtihad* through *ijma* that converts the fruits of personal reasoning into a discovery or finding for the benefit of society. This is the internal Islamic authentic process through which Islamic land tenure and property rights can be more systematically clarified. It is also one of the keys to making Islam continuously relevant and also explains how Islam can be shaped by society. Since various aspects of land and property rights have not been fully thought out, such as access to land and security of tenure, there is considerable scope through *ijtihad* to develop Islamic thinking and legal theory in these areas.

Jurisprudential Schools or Madhahib

There is a plurality inherent in Islam and Islamic law, which is reflected in and shaped by the two major sects: Sunni and Shi'a. The Shi'a minority within the *umma* accepts the *Qur'an*, but consider the only acceptable interpretation as emanating from their Imam (spiritual leader). For Shi'a Muslims the Imam denotes both a religious and a secular leader. So far as the Shi'a recognition of *hadith* is concerned, only those which concern members of the family of the

Prophet and his descendants are acceptable. *Ijma* as a source of Islamic law too has to be validated by an Imam or his representative and *qiyas* is dismissed outright (Nasir 2002: 26–8). Among the Shi'a sect of Islam, as far as *ijtihad* is concerned the *mujtahid* cannot only make judgments and issue rulings on legal matters but also interpret the tenets of religion and the principles of the Shar'ia. Among the Ismaili branch of the Shi'a, there is a hierarchy of various degrees of knowledge and insight, distinguishing between the Imam 'endowed with perfect knowledge', his representatives (*dais*) and all other believers (Nasir 2002: 29). The main Ismaili legal text is the *Daaimul Islam* (Pillars of Islam).

Among the Sunnis, who constitute the majority of Muslims in the world, there are four main *madhahib* (singular *maddhab*, jurisprudential schools): Hanafi; Maliki; Hanbali; and Shafi'i. These *madhahib* were named after their leading jurists and each is the dominant authority in different parts of the world. The early jurists, through legal judgement and reasoning, justified their findings in terms of interpretations of the hierarchical sources and by paying attention to '*urf* (local customs), building the jurisprudence into a systematic body of texts and practices (Murad 1995). Anyone venturing to discuss Islamic law in a specific context must be aware of the prevailing jurisprudential school. A brief note on the geographical distribution of the Sunni *maddahib* may be useful.

The Hanafi and Maliki schools were the first to develop and correspondingly became the most geographically widespread. Hanafi originated in Iraq and spread from Afghanistan and India to parts of East Africa. As the official doctrine in the Ottoman empire, Hanafi jurisprudence is prevalent not only in Turkey but in other parts of the former territories such as Syria, the Balkan states, Cyprus, Jordan and Palestine. The Maliki school grew out of the city of Medina, spreading through North Africa and on to Sudan, Gambia, Ghana, Nigeria, Senegal and the Arabian Gulf including Kuwait. Maliki doctrine made extensive use of *hadith* and its reasoning was not confined to *qiyas*. Their use of *istislah*, though confined to social transactions as opposed to religious practice, furthered the pursuit of public interest (Esposito 1982: 9). Both schools, Maliki and Hanafi, tolerated divergence of opinion within their doctrines (Nasir 2002: 19).

The Shafi'i school started in Cairo, spreading to Yemen and then to parts of East Africa and South East Asia. It predominates in Indonesia, Malaysia, Sri Lanka and the Maldives. The father of this school – Muhammed ibn Idris al-Shafi'i – is sometimes referred to as the 'father of Muslim jurisprudence'. At a time of considerable conflict between different schools of thought, he laid down 'the basic structure and logic of legal epistemology and reasoning to be developed by subsequent jurists' (Zubaida 2003: 23). The Hanbali school is known for its strictness in terms of ritual. It did not prove as popular as other schools, but is most notably the official doctrine in Saudi Arabia. While some schools predominate in particular areas, or particular countries, adherents to more than one specific school may be found in a single country.

Recognition of the prevailing Islamic school of jurisprudence is necessary to engage with the Islamic legal discourses in a particular context. For example Hanafism, the most widespread of the four schools, is considered the most flexible and open to innovative interpretations of its core doctrines. However, even within schools there could be variations in practice (for example, in India and Afghanistan, where the Hanafi doctrine applies). Therefore, 'best practice' approach may lead to cross-fertilization and innovative approaches. In any case, there is the methodology of *talfiq* (patching), by which jurists may give authoritative support to the compilation of a legal regulation from the views of more than one *maddhab*, a method used more than once in the creation of modern legal codes (Sonbol 2003: 37; Esposito 1982: 69).

Islamic Law in a Pluralist World

Legal systems throughout the Muslim world exhibit considerable variety owing to their specific historical and colonial contexts, the state ideology and the extent to which Islamic law is able to trump secular or customary laws. The legal system of many a Muslim country has undergone extensive secularization to varying degrees, notwithstanding the principled irrevocability of its religious origins, owing to Western influences. This is evident not only in penal laws, where Islamic laws were considered harsh, but also in the commercial field. Muslim countries chose to reform laws relating to real estate, contract and tort laws which also impact on land, property and housing rights in the interests of international trade and business. However, one area where the Shari'a has continued to prevail is the body of personal status or family laws – including marriage, gifts, inheritance, maintenance and *waqf* – where property, land and housing rights are also implicated.

Saudi Arabia and Iran are exceptional countries which have largely resisted Western legal influences and profess exclusivity of Islamic laws (Vogel 2000). Other Muslim countries represent a greater hybridity of legal cultures. Even between the Saudis and the Iranians, however, there are substantial differences owing not merely to the Sunni and Shi'a Islamic ideologies, but also to the conservative Wahhabi tradition followed by Saudi Arabia, in contrast to other Sunni countries. Both countries often denounce each other as misconstruing Islam. Shari'a law thus emerges as a pluralistic framework, which offers choices and lends itself to a range of interpretations. The impact of different schools or sub-schools of particular Islamic jurisprudence can provide contrasts.

At the other extreme is Turkey, the seat of the Islamic Ottoman Empire, which has secularized almost its entire legal system, including personal status (family) laws. It derived its codes from various European legal systems, though Ottoman laws have persisted in many parts of the Muslim world. Yet, in

Turkey, Iran and Saudi Arabia, the relationship between religious and modern secular laws continues to be debated. Legal systems in Muslim countries are derived not only from the British or French systems but also from other colonial systems such as the Dutch (Indonesia), Spanish (Morocco) and Italian (Libya). In Central Asia – Uzbekistan, Tajikistan, Kazakhstan and Azerbaijan – the civil system is influenced to varying degrees by Soviet constructions.

Similarly, in some Muslim countries there is an amalgam of legal cultures from within civil law systems (as in Morocco) or a conflation between civil and common laws (Egypt). A comparison of Tunisia, Morocco and Algeria, despite the Islamic–French combination, yields interesting differences. For example, in Tunisia, family or personal status laws have undergone liberal reforms, applicable to Muslims and non-Muslims alike, while in Morocco certain family law forms are unfolding. This is equally true of Muslim countries from Bahrain and Brunei to the Maldives, Pakistan and Bangladesh, which apply British common law and where the extent to which Islamic law prevails varies and changes. In Qatar, the monarch's law prevails more than the formal, while the Yemenis and Indonesians are able to assert their customary laws despite Islamic, colonial and modern laws. Brown (2001) notes, however, that there are striking similarities between the judicial systems in the Arab world, although their varied histories and influences have given rise to a range of forms of government.

The primacy of Islam within Muslim countries is problematic, particularly where it is extended to non-Muslims and Muslim minorities, though many Muslim countries exempt non-Muslims from personal laws and offer extensive minority rights. Islamic law is not always uniformly applied within a state: there can be regional or local variations, particularly in response to customs or other religious laws. Further, the question of the application of Islamic laws to Muslims in non-Muslim countries such as India is controversial: there have been calls for the abolition of Islamic personal status laws presently applicable to Muslims. In several parts of Africa, from Eritrea and Gambia to Kenya and Tanzania, Islamic personal law generally applies to Muslims (Mamdani 1996). In Nigeria and Sudan, however, the application of Islamic law to all residents in regions of high Muslim concentration, regardless of their religion, is somewhat controversial.

Islamic Legal Pluralism

In attempting to analyse issues such as security of tenure, which is a meeting place of law, land, society and the family, one cannot consider law as 'exquisitely separable' (Rosen 1999: 89) from life. Law is a part of everyday lives in Muslim societies, where it is one of 'the diverse efforts to shape lives in an Islamic way' (Bowen 2003: 4) as a result of the formal inclusion of religious norms within legal systems. The practice of Islamic law in the Muslim world involves potentially complex and difficult relationships between particular brands of Islamic law and other forms of law, whether state or customary. The existence of a variety of different legal spaces and normative orders can be the cause of conflict; yet, as Rosen (1999: 93) suggests, that does not have to be the case. He points to the existence in Moroccan society of seemingly incompatible institutions, 'Maliki Islamic law, Berber and Arab customary practices, former colonial law, confessional laws, and contemporary Moroccan codes', which are not treated as mutually contradictory. Instead, individuals shuttle amongst them, making choices about forums and treating them as resources. As Bowen argues with reference to Indonesia, 'in the practice of reasoning about cases and justifying decisions reached, Muslim authorities and ordinary Muslims always have found themselves having to tack among competing values, norms and commands' (2003: 9–10).

Indonesia is an example of 'differing ideas of justice' or 'multiple norms', the site of long-standing, diverse efforts to shape lives in an Islamic way, but also of even longer-standing and more diverse efforts to shape them according to *adat* (local complexes of norms and traditions) (Bowen 2003: 4). Dutch colonial legal policy privileged the supposedly indigenous customary law, *adat* (or in Dutch *adatrecht*), utilizing the 'reception theory', which held that the Islamic rules only had the force of law where they had been received or integrated into the local tradition. Tensions about which regime should govern Indonesia's Muslims give rise to debates at all levels of society about the appropriate role for *adat*, Shari'a and state laws (Cammack 2000: 4). Thus debates regarding Islamic law are not always about Islamic law itself but about its relationship with other forms of law. This relationship is a product of historical, socio-cultural and political processes: particular countries or even local contexts can have their own legal dynamics and, equally, opportunities to mediate the outcome of such conflicts.

Similarly, Brown (1997: 202–9) considers the 'popular uses' of courts in Egypt, arguing that, at least where housing and real estate are concerned, people choose between formal and extra-legal bargaining opportunities, deploying tools offered by law as a complement to a range of problem-solving strategies. However, rather than this seemingly passive legal pluralism, 'Abd Al-Fattah (1999: 161) finds Egyptians confronting legal dualities, contradictions and shortcomings, with the confluence of Islamic, customary and state laws yielding wider choices and possible strategic use:

> Conflicts stem from many sources ... [such as] historical shifts between modern and traditional modes and between secular laws and customary laws, to the nostalgia for Islamic law, and to the rift between meta-positive laws and religious laws....

This is not the metaphorical yacht skimming gently across the waves, but 'psychological rifts and rifts of misunderstanding between the majority of Egyptians and the modern legal system' ('Abd Al-Fattah 1999: 161). Thus

Islamic law cannot be studied in isolation. It is continuously mediated by the state, the community and individuals in response to specific situations. Choices made regarding Islamic law are not purely religious or juristic but need to be appreciated in their political milieu. Ayubi, in discussing the debate around the 1971 Egyptian Constitution (relating to the Shari'a) notes how the political dimension can dominate: 'Because of such politicization, discussion of the law does not rise above the level of political agitation and superficial reflection and feelings. This politicization is to the detriment of serious approaches which seek to be impartial' (Ayubi 1991: 203).

Paying attention to 'legal pluralism', or legal dualities/contradictions, may enhance our legal understanding of both Islamic law and the complex, overlapping and competing norms to be found in Muslim societies. Woodman (1999: 14) suggests that it enables us 'to see more clearly situations, and to clarify the possibilities open to [those] who seek to redesign the legal environment'. In those times or places when individuals do not tack between legal norms, but seek either to manipulate or altogether ignore the formally recognized laws, 'extra-legal' norms are adopted. This is often the case with respect to property rights, particularly in the context of the informal squatter settlements of the world, including the Muslim world. It is well-known that in such settlements one finds, for instance, well-developed land markets, which are enforceable and legitimate from the perspective of the participants, but which nominally exist outside established legal authorities (Razzaz 1998). These normative systems are sometimes referred to as quasi-legal or informal, but their legality and illegality are not so clearly delineated. However, the full picture of law emerges from engaging with both internal and external pluralities, or what Bowen calls 'normative florescence' (2003: 4).

Islamic Law in Action

The scope of Islamic law (Shari'a) relating to property law emerges from its main textual sources, generally applied in Muslim societies. However, it equally flows from state policy and legal practice through land registers, court records, religious advisory opinions (*fatawa,* singular *fatwa*) and laws. Messick (2003) identifies a hierarchy of legal texts with respect to property law, with Shari'a doctrine at the top, Shari'a court judgments in the middle and, at the bottom, the 'day-to-day' documents such as marriage contracts, wills and leases. However, there has always existed, since the Islamic Ummayad and Abbasid empires, a dichotomy between Islamic law and secular law. It was during the Ottoman period that, while Islamic law was codified and promoted, a series of secular laws referred to as the *qanun* and *qanunname* were also promulgated. The Ottoman judicial system was thus a dual one. On the one hand the Ottomans kept the Shari'a with all the interpretations that followed, those of the four orthodox Sunni schools, with the Hanafi school of thought occupying a privileged position as the most flexible of the four. On the other hand, and because of the limits and lacunae found in Shari'a law, the Ottomans had to devise secular codes and laws. The Ottomans, however, heightened and seriously worked out this distinction between the religious and secular laws. These *qanun* were extracted from *urf*, the customary law and practice, as far as they did not contravene Islamic laws.

Even within Islamic legal systems, there exist numerous institutions or personnel that implement the range of laws and interests. These include not merely the *qadi* or judge within an Islamic jurisdiction but also judges dealing with secular matters. There could be administrative offices such as the *Muhtasib* (ombudsman) as well as those in the informal legal business such as *muftis* who issue *fatawa* and the *mujtahids* (those exercising *ijtihad*). The *qadi* is only one of the authorities for implementation and dissemination of the laws. The *qadi*'s role often overlaps with that of the *mufti* or other legal offices, sometimes leading to tensions over who trumps (Vogel 2000: 13–32). *Fatawa* are a distinct Islamic phenomenon. They consist of formal advice or responses to a question, usually asked by lay persons, from a person considered knowledgeable on a point of Islamic law or dogma. *Fatawa* from virtually all periods of Muslim history have been influential and in engaging directly with the challenges of new realities have been catalysts for social and legal change (Masud 1996). The state seeking religious endorsement of a controversial position can seek ratification from a well-regarded authority. Since there is no formal priesthood or hierarchy in Sunni Islam, the *mufti* may be drawn from a range of religious backgrounds and provide different conclusions. They are not binding as such and depend on how the questioner receives the *fatwa*. However, either by choice or through ground realities, land disputes are often settled by those who have the power or muscle, whether financial, political or physical. Ghazzal (2005), writing in the context of Ottoman Beirut and Damascus, refers to the existence of *de facto* systems or tribunals, under the aegis of local notables, settling matters in relation to state land, taxation and disputes arising from tax farms.

The role of the *qadi* is relevant in understanding how the system of administration of justice has evolved. First, the *qadi* often had to deal with non-Islamic law or a combination of Islamic and non-Islamic norms. Without examining the judge's legal reasoning one cannot assume that a judge in an Islamic court was invoking an Islamic legal principle or even interpreting a statute through Islamic justifications. Vikor (1998) argues that while, as in any other legal system, the issues were secular and were dealt with in a secular manner – whether a crime or a contract for the sale of land – what makes Shari'a law religious law is that it is legitimized from its source in the revealed word of God. Though Islamic law emanated from textual authority, Weiss argues that Muslim judges were generally conscious of moral contexts, social visions and the need to garner legitimacy across multiple schools of legal thought (1998: 185). The *qadi* balanced the 'rights' or duties owed to God with the rights of individuals through elaborate procedural guarantees. In addition, the judge was generally conscious of determining the role and limits of the state. Islamic courts have emerged as key sites in struggles involving ethnic and religious groups, social classes, political parties, and others with a major stake in defining Islam's role. However, Rosen argues that 'in Islamic law ... the courts have long operated not as a counter-balance to the state but as a stabilizing device among contending persons' (Rosen 1989: 61). Sherif and Brown (2002) point out that judicial independence is an important and well-established feature of Islamic legal systems. Classical jurists devoted much attention to the *qadi* and his qualifications. A genre of legal literature, the *adab al qadi*, expresses the model behaviour of the judge and the procedures in a courtroom.

One of the significant questions regarding the operation of Islamic courts is how women are able to access justice. Recent debates, from those in Canada over the introduction of Shar'ia family courts to the Kenyan constitutional referendum campaigns over the status of Islamic courts, demonstrate this concern. Some of these problems are inherent in the gender-discriminatory attitudes of court personnel arising out of patriarchal social structures in most societies, in varying forms and degrees, whether they are Islamic, secular, custom-based or of any other orientation. Historically, there is evidence that Islamic courts were able to dispense justice across gender and religious lines, and that all members of society were generally protected by the law. Ottoman court records show that 'no one, including the husbands or even fathers, could make use of women's property without their consent, and women appealed to the courts when anyone tampered with their assets. The judges consistently upheld women's property rights' (Jennings 1975). Sonbol also notes that '*Qadis* and courts treated women the same way as they treated men when it came to all types of transactions. A woman's word in the court did not need corroboration any more than a man's' (Sonbol 2003: 73). Women's experiences with Islamic courts often vary but women are not passive or powerless stakeholders (Mir-Hosseini 1993). Hirsch (1998) finds that Swahili Muslim women in coastal Kenya, despite the usual attitudes, initiate and win the majority of marital conflicts handled by the local *qadi's* court.

Contrary to general assumptions about 'summary' Islamic justice, procedural guarantees are elaborate within Islamic legal systems. Powers (1992) argues that Islamic legal systems, on an analysis of fourteenth-century Islamic court practice, also acknowledged that a judicial decision was reversible by the issuing judge himself, albeit under limited and precisely defined conditions; that hierarchical organization was a regular feature of Muslim polities; and that the court of the chief judge of the capital city served as a court of review for the decisions of local judges. There is no doubt that in most cases Islamic courts have adapted to both modern constitutional legal frameworks and current methods of legal thinking and decision making. Brown (2001) makes a positive assessment of reforms in the Arab legal systems, arguing that even in the face of political and economic problems the judiciary are in the main a respected group in the majority of Arab countries, known for dealing professionally with disputes. Moreover, in many countries efforts have been made to enhance the training and independent standing of judges. Nevertheless, there are endemic problems relating to the rule of law as detailed by the *Arab Human Rights Development Report 2004*, which argues that legal institutional reforms as well as steps to further the independence of the judiciary are overdue in many parts of the Muslim world. These problems cannot be seen in isolation from general issues of corruption, freedom of speech, democratization and the role of civil society.

Alternative Dispute Resolution and Access to Justice

Historically, the part lawyers have played in an Islamic legal system has been different from their adversarial style in the Anglo-American legal tradition. The legal system did not require any lawyers since the litigants themselves generally pleaded their own case. Rather than a 'winner takes all' approach, Islamic legal processes seek to address the needs of all parties within an Islamic framework. Disputes are often settled through the community as well as formal processes. Muslims are seeking not only their material interests but also to establish what would be acceptable in accordance with God's objectives. There is an element of the spiritual in the legal advice and proceedings. Even the *qadi* is more personal and engaged with the parties to the conflict, as opposed to the more technical approach often in evidence in non-Muslim contexts (Rosen 1989: 27). It is not surprising, therefore, that the concepts of mediation and conciliation are found in the *Qur'an*, as well as in the practice of the Prophet's generation. For example, in relation to settlement of marital disputes, the *Qur'an* (4: 35) states:

> If you fear a breach between a man and his wife, appoint an arbiter from his people and another from hers. If they wish to be reconciled God will bring them together again. God is all-knowing and wise.

Solh (the doctrine of conciliation) appears in seven verses of the *Qur'an* where the believers are called upon to settle their disputes amicably and through justice. The Ottoman Code, the Majalla, which attempted to codify Shari'a principles, referred to conciliation in contracts. When compromise is impossible, *wasta* (mediation, collective *waseet*) takes place, where one or more persons intervene in a dispute, either of their own initiative or at the request of one of the parties. Makhoul and Harrison (2004), studying the role of *wasta* in contemporary local development projects in Lebanon, discuss the 'intercessory *wasta*' as a continuing practice of social exchange in dispute resolution. Joseph points out that 'the urban working class experienced the law as a series of face-to-face relationships built from *wasta* connections. They learned about the law through kin, friends, neighbors, and associates' (Joseph 1990: 153). Biezeveld (2004) refers to the example of a conflict over land in a Sumatran village in Indonesia as 'discourse shopping': 'Every actor in the dispute makes his own choice of argument, and creates his own interpretation of facts, rules, and norms. Not only do legal arguments play a role, but political, cultural, and historical arguments are used.' Antoun (1990), discussing litigant strategies in a part of Jordan, posts similar experiences. He finds that 'the families still lived in close-knit villages in which kinship ties remained close and still regarded the village guest house (*madafa*) and not the court as the primary arena of conflict resolution, and still operated in an arena in which economic opportunities outside the sub-district and outside the country were limited [but] women's major role and women's recognition is nonetheless reflected'. Conciliation and mediation are distinguished from *takhim*, which is a more formal process of arbitration. The *qadi* himself would encourage parties to exhaust these options (Kemicha 1996).

The advent of colonial influences saw the rise of the legal profession but it did not extinguish informal legal practices and local methods of conflict resolution (Irani and Funk 1998). Given that land disputes are considered a family and community matter and court legal proceedings are viewed as uncivil and distasteful in many Muslim societies, there is frequent recourse to informal negotiated fora. In Afghanistan, for example, while parties to land disputes do file land rights claims, which add to the existing backlog of court cases, they frequently rely on informal means of resolving their disagreeements (d'Hellencourt *et al.* 2003). The filing of court cases is often either a safety net (in case the formal process intervenes) or a bargaining tool. Elaborating on this phenomenon, Wily (2005: 30) identifies three mechanisms for community dispute resolution in property cases: neighbours and elders; the local mosque council; and the *wakil-e-gozar* (chairperson of the council). In many instances all three will be used in the same case. To ignore these community-based procedures in most Muslim countries is to miss out on the totality of land law in action. At the same time such informal processes, whatever their popularity and efficiency, while left to indigenous values, must be tested for certain basic human rights standards of fairness, impartiality, honesty and inclusivity.

Among the duties of the Muslim state, and of dutiful members of the society, is the promotion of *ma`roof* (good) and the prevention of *munkar* (wrongdoing). These are public duties contained in the *Qur'an* to create the institution of *hisba*, promoting both a just society as well as an efficient market economy. This is evident, for instance, in the Universal Islamic Declaration of Human Rights which adds a twist to the 'right of free association' in Article 14:

> Every person is entitled to participate individually and collectively in the religious, social, cultural and political life of his community and to establish institutions and agencies meant to enjoin what is right *(ma'roof)* and to prevent what is wrong *(munkar)*.

The institution of the *muhtasib* – which emerged from the first generation of Islam and developed through Islamic history with (among others) the Abbasids, Fatimids and Ottomans – is connected to the notion of public duty. The mandate and influence of the office varied, but it combined the functions of a market inspector, chief public health officer, receiver of complaints generally and land use enforcer. There are fears that using this Islamic 'public duty' paradigm could lead to an extra-legal and omnibus authority serving as a vigilante force. However, the idea of an ombudsman having a broad oversight has worked in many modern contexts with a defined mandate. Khalid (2002), noting the decline of the institution in the past two centuries, argues that it could be used effectively in contemporary Muslim societies.

Conclusions

Islamic law is not monolithic, static or autonomous. It is a field that is developing, receptive and amenable to competing ideologies and interests, and has been shaped by human interpretation of divine intent. Islamic law has a well-developed field of *usul al fiqh* which deals with the processes of reasoning and interpretation. The primary source is the *Qur'an*, which has a limited number of 'law verses' – some of them being explicit, others general. These are interpreted in their context alongside the *Sunna*. The two other sources, *qiyas* and *ijma*, need to be appreciated. A major avenue for exploring the true spirit of Islam is *ijtihad*, a well-recognized Islamic jurisprudential tool, and there are other supplemental, law-generating mediums such as *istishan* which enhance the flexibility and responsiveness of Shari'a law, as do *maslaha* and *istislah*. The deployment of these mechanisms and tools could well enable the emergence of inclusive, innovative and empowering land management tools.

There is considerable divergence among Muslim countries with regard to the form and extent of Islamic law in their legal and political systems. This may have to do with whether the Muslim community in question follows the Sunni or Shi'a creed of Islam, or a particular *madhahib*. In addition, legal systems throughout the Muslim world exhibit considerable variety owing to their specific historical and colonial contexts, the state ideology, and the extent to which Islamic law is able to trump secular or customary laws. To consider a particular brand of Islamic law as generally applicable to all parts of the Muslim world would ignore the specific national or local contexts. In most Muslim societies, complex and contentious relationships exist between particular conceptions of

Islamic law and other forms of law – state or customary law. They may be visible or understated but these legal, quasi-legal or informal systems are equally important for Muslims and represent choices that Muslims clearly make between competing options. Islamic law, in fact, recognizes *urf* unless it directly contravenes Islamic principles. Paying attention to 'legal pluralism', or legal dualities/contradictions, may enhance our legal understanding of both Islamic law and the complex, overlapping and competing norms to be found in Muslim societies. In some cases, it may be necessary to differentiate Islamic and customary practices in order to weed out discriminatory practices.

In the implementation of Islamic law there is a whole range of state, independent judicial, religious, customary, extra-legal and civil society mediums. They serve to deliver justice in various ways and impact on Muslim societies differently. Seeking to promote access to land and security of tenure, therefore, is a multidimensional enterprise in Muslim societies. Islamic history, particularly Ottoman experience, is instructive and demonstrates that these matters were considered amenable to secular and efficiency approaches, albeit cast in Islamic language. For instance, Shari'a courts across the Ottoman world used the traditional method for registering property transactions and demonstrating ownership by means of a document, the *hujja*, literally translated as 'proof'. The *hujja* was sealed by the court and was, in theory, the only means for effecting land transactions between buyers and sellers. However, where no such documentary proof existed, the prospective seller could fall back on witnesses prepared to confirm both continuous possession of the land in question and also the absence of any other contenders as to its ownership. As explained in the previous chapter, though no modern surveys or maps were available during the Ottoman period, land was registered according to description, which was verified. Wherever disputes arose and were brought before courts they were decided on the basis of registration deeds. The courts as well as other legal institutions and alternative dispute resolution mechanisms used both the Islamic legal framework and the documentary evidence to decide claims. Land and property transactions were regulated within defined legal parameters.

There is a need to enhance our understanding of how courts and other legal institutions deal with property rights. Whether the *qadi* or a judge with secular jurisdiction is dealing with property or land issues, use of Islamic foundational principles such as *adl* or *haqq* could promote inclusive, pro-poor and innovative legal solutions. Judicial independence and procedural guarantees are well established in Islamic thought, but in general courts lack organization, resources, training and a human rights perspective. In all parts of the Muslim world, efforts are under way to modernize and streamline the judicial system. Support for capacity building and a more efficient mode of justice delivery is needed, while the particular contexts and needs of courts in the Muslim world must also be recognized. Islamic law is not, however, a prerogative of the state – as seen in the existence of mechanisms from the *mujtahid*, who could be anyone, to the *mufti*, who may or may not be 'officially' recognized. Islamic law is not a centralizing force but rather one that manifests itself through a range of stakeholders, including the lay persons themselves. The Muslim world demonstrates not merely distinctive formal legal systems but also a wide array of alternative dispute resolution mechanisms. Concepts of mediation or conciliation are found in the *Qur'an*, as well as in the practice of the Prophet's generation. In assessing the applicability of Western-based conflict resolution models in non-Western contexts such as the Arab-Islamic culture area, theoreticians and practitioners alike have begun to recognize the importance of indigenous ways of thinking and feeling, as well as local rituals for managing, reducing, and resolving conflicts. Access to justice implies not merely the existence of *any* mechanisms, but of those that consumers are able to relate to and use efficiently. Informal dispute resolution mechanisms therefore need to be recognized and, where beneficial, promoted.

The modernization of Muslim legal systems has been facilitated in part by colonial encounters, usually involving the importation of Western legal structures. However, even where an existing system of property rights is judged inadequate, one must replace it with due care, especially if it is culturally embedded. Attempts at reform of customary systems that do not succeed in changing behaviour can create confusion and conflict between claims based on custom and others based in national law. Thus, in adopting legislation and policy to 'create' new frameworks or norms, the state may not be expressing the legitimacy or ownership of the masses. The lack of a unified system of Islamic law relating to property and land rights and the absence of implementation mechanisms have given rise to a plethora of avenues and opportunities. Land and property rights, as part of the Islamic legal sphere relating to *mu'amalat*, are inherently more susceptible to flexibile and innovative tools, though egalitarian Islamic principles apply. Yet the fertile Islamic rights literature supporting a pro-poor and inclusive land and property regime fails, as later chapters argue, to deliver fully on its promise. For example (see Chapter 6), a 'compensatory regime' for women which balances the various property flows is envisaged in Islamic law but is not fulfilled in practice. Though Islamic legal raw materials, concepts and individual doctrines exist, more juristic work needs to be done to systematically develop equivalent doctrines of access to land, security of tenure and protection from forcible eviction. In taking forward that venture it is important to appreciate the Islamic contribution to land categories and the web of tenure regimes in the Muslim world.

3

Islamic Land Tenures and Reform

> Every aspect of land tenure is intricately connected with the socio-political life of the community. Most conflicts seem to arise over access to land or rather the abuse of perceived rights to the land. Land issues in the Middle East are complicated because of the vast variety of forms of landholding – *Al-ard btifriq bi-l-shibr* (land differs from one foot of ground to the next). (Schaebler 2000: 242)

Land tenure concepts in Muslim countries have to be understood within the complex, dynamic and overlapping weave of Islamic legal principles, state and international legal frameworks, customary norms and informal legal rules. The term 'Islamic land tenure' is more appropriate than 'Muslim land tenure' because the foundation of these systems is ultimately religious, even though there are considerable variations in the doctrine and practice of land tenure across Muslim countries. Modern land regulation laws in most parts of the Sunni Muslim world are derived, at least in part, from categories of land in classical Islamic law and Ottoman land law culminating in the Ottoman Land Code of 1858, which were further shaped and distorted by the colonial encounters. As already argued, historical narratives and categories remain important despite the waves of land reform and regulation, particularly across the Arab world, in the late nineteenth and twentieth centuries. These included efforts to redistribute land, the reorganization of existing principles into a variety of state codes in many countries, and eventually privatization and market-led changes. Land tenure arrangements are driven also by local socio-economic, cultural and political factors, which in turn affect the choice of Islamic proposals for land tenure. It will be suggested that what has emerged is a web of tenures, frequently with a local distinctiveness. These 'web of tenures' regimes are often dismissed as intractable, inscrutable or outdated, but the lack of adequate systematic research hampers understanding of the current manifestations of Islamic land concepts.

The main objective of this chapter is systematically but generally to outline the development of Islamic land tenure regimes, rather than to offer present-day country case studies. Though the histories of individual Muslim countries vary, the contemporary land tenure regimes have evolved from, or have been influenced by, a variety of historical periods or episodes. To unravel or effectively engage with these complex and overlapping land tenure forms requires a sensitivity to land history, which often takes the form of local or communal narratives. These include the impact of distinctive pre-Ottoman Islamic land conceptions, the Ottoman land administration and regulatory framework, the colonialist modifications or extensions of land tenure practice and the post-colonial and modernist land reforms. The evolution of Islamic land tenure regimes from the classical and Ottoman periods to colonial and contemporary times provides vital insights into the dynamics of Islamic land. Historical narratives with an impact on the development of contemporary land tenure regimes in Muslim countries not only provide an appreciation of why such classical concepts persist in their present manifestations, but also offer insights into how they may be traded for innovative tools for enhancing access to land. An awareness of the historical and social context of land tenure in Muslim societies also permits a consideration of conventional approaches to land regularization through methods involving land registration and land titling. It will be argued that, in the context of Muslim societies and Islamic land tenure regimes, such approaches are not necessarily possible or appropriate. However, other authentic pro-poor strategies may be available which make use of the flexible tenure web.

Contextualizing Islamic Land Tenure

Land tenure concepts are not a modern phenomenon: they have existed in several ancient civilizations, from parts of Africa to China. This is equally true of the Muslim world, where formal land management systems were found in ancient Syria, Egypt and Saudi Arabia (El Ayachi *et al.* 2003). Given the synergy between Islamic and Western civilizations, further research might well show that Islamic land tenure regimes could have influenced Western land systems. On the more modest proposal that Islamic land tenure concepts influenced Muslim countries, there is no doubt. Lambton (1953: 393) writing in the context of Persian/Iranian land reforms, notes this enduring connection:

> There has been a striking continuity of tradition over a period of some 1,200 years, and some features can be traced even farther, to pre-Islamic times. It is true that in law the traditional forms were from time to time virtually suspended, but they have repeatedly reasserted themselves, modified, it may be, by the incorporation of new customs and theories ....

The Islamic content in the modern land tenure regimes of many Muslim countries, particularly outside the Middle East, is sometimes not easily perceived. However, it exists even in countries like Malaysia where land law is driven largely by the seemingly wholly secular demands of the strict 'Torrens' registration system (Haji Buang 1989). In the small number of established Islamic states like Saudi Arabia, where the legal system is based on the Shari'a, the Islamic dimension is more explicit. However, the Islamic contribution to land tenure forms in other countries is perhaps best explained, adopting Forni's (2005: 2) description, as 'subjacent' or 'indirect'.

Contemporary debates surrounding security of tenure assume that 'efficient' land titling infrastructures and legal systems are Western constructs that need to be imported into the developing world. Yet, as argued above, Ottoman practice suggests that there is nothing peculiarly Western about land registration systems, land information records or centralized land management regimes. Furthermore, this history demonstrates that there is also nothing inherent in Islamic principles to inhibit the development of such systems. This is important given that there is a growing call today for 'authenticity', to ensure that modern land reforms are in conformity with Islamic principles. Further, there are demands at all social levels to reintroduce Islamic precepts into property law in a more systematic manner (Haji Buang 1989; Saad 2002). Forni (2005: 2) recounts, for instance, the religious dimension to debates around Law 96 of 1992 in Egypt, which repealed most of the agrarian land reforms introduced by Nasser in the 1950s and changed the relations between landlords and tenants to provide for a free market. The government sought and received confirmation from the established religious authorities that the proposed law did not violate Shari'a law, while at the same time some groups which opposed the legislation argued their position on the basis that it was un-Islamic (Saad 2002). Forni (2005: 2) concludes that this example also demonstrates that Islamic interpretation is by no means 'univocal' and the debates over the Islamicity of land tenure initiatives continue.

Security of Tenure in the Muslim World

The challenges of urbanization, population and poverty, together with increasing pressures on land and environment, arise throughout the Muslim world, although with variations between countries as elsewhere across the globe (Bonine 1997). Of particular concern is lack of secure land tenure for significant proportions of people. For example, many inhabitants of Muslim countries, particularly in the cities, live in settlements where they enjoy at best only limited security and protection from eviction. Often they reside in areas that are not recognized by public authorities and without any formal title to the land on which their homes were built. In predominantly Muslim West Asia alone there are estimated to be 41 million residents of informal settlements, amounting to 33 per cent of the population. In North Africa the figure stands at 21 million, comprising 28 per cent of the population (UN-HABITAT 2003). Across these regions the scale and the rapidity of growth in cities over several decades, in the context of increasing globalization, has placed demands on urban and peri-urban land of which the illegal settlements are perhaps the most visible part.

Secure tenure is the fundamental right of every individual but it is particularly important for the poor, whose access to land is often their only form of security. As the Universal Declaration of Human Rights (UDHR) of 1948 recognizes, the right to adequate shelter is an element of the right to an adequate standard of living. Security of land tenure for all is in turn a component part of the right to adequate shelter and a salient condition for sustainable human settlements in a rapidly urbanizing world. For example, the New Delhi Declaration which emanated from the Global Conference on Access to Land and Security of Tenure in 1996 calls upon public institutions to embark on regularization processes, using a range of options for tenure security. Payne (2001) argues that research indicates the widest range of options should be considered in attempts to enhance security of tenure, bearing in mind local conditions and contexts. Intermediate forms of tenure – certificates of use, comfort or occupancy; communal landholdings; land trusts – all have a role to play, where they have social legitimacy. It is in this context that Islamic land tenure systems have to be explored.

In the Muslim world, debates about the development of policy towards informal settlements often take a religious dimension, articulated through the desire to introduce or reintroduce authentic Islamic approaches to property systems and land regularization programmes. Vasile (1997) argues, in the context of Tunisia, that the turn more generally towards religion as an answer to contemporary problems is linked to the character of 'illegal' urban settlements. She contends that 'it is here that religious practice has grown' in response to conflicts that arose from the failures of official systems. Postcolonial Tunisia, in particular, was determinedly secular and based on the civil law model of the French system. However, as Vasile (1997) explains, it has not delivered 'decent, affordable housing' but 'locked [settlers] ... into a spatial Other'. This raises a question here considered more broadly: whether the Islamic framework contains the concepts, mechanisms and legal infrastructure capable of addressing current land issues in Muslim countries.

Islamic Webs of Tenure and the Tenure Continuum

Documented titles, particularly freehold titles, secured through the formal legal structures common in the West, have been projected as the best tenure option and goal for all states (de Soto 2000). It is de Soto's (2000) influential argument that the hidden infrastructure of a modern land titling system will transform the assets of the poor in the informal settlements so that they can be used productively as capital. As opposed to loosely managed and 'cloudy' ownership rights, the integration of dispersed information into a single property rights system builds 'a bridge' across which the poor who inhabit the informal settlements will walk 'to enter [a] a new, all-encompassing social contract' with the relevant state and its institutions. For de Soto (2000) property rights systems are, therefore, the key to sustainable development. However, as has already been mentioned, de Soto's proposals have not engaged with Islamic land theories, although his recipe for poverty alleviation has been formally welcomed by some Muslim governments.

Tenure regularization of the kind envisaged by de Soto (2000) includes 'registering all plots and occupiers, providing basic services, resolving land disputes and allocating property rights to recognized claimants' (Home and Lim 2004: 150). The costs of land survey and record keeping for such sophisticated upgrading programmes are high and usually too high for countries with limited resources, including shortages of skilled personnel. There may be a gap between the intention of the state and the reality on the ground (Home and Lim 2004). Home and Lim (2004: 151) conclude that where 'the "modern" land titling system struggles to maintain itself, even when pursuing intermediate or incremental tenure regularization, then a more localized land tenure arrangement may fill the gap'. They point to examples of the enduring quality of family land outside the official system in the Caribbean and tribal land tenure protected by the 'underground resource' of customary or communal law in Botswana and Zambia. The 'webs of tenure' relations in the Muslim world, where categories derived from religious law are shaped by local custom and history, also provide an alternative framework for addressing land rights.

Payne argues (2001: 1), that 'current research on innovative approaches to tenure for the urban poor has demonstrated that many other tenure options have proved equally effective in meeting people's diverse shelter needs'. He comments that while for an individual household the lack of official documents may engender insecurity, tenure does not necessarily concern the inhabitants of informal settlements who live surrounded by thousands of similarly placed people. Payne (2002: 6) cites a case in Karachi, where the offer of freehold titles to 100,000 households living in informal settlements was taken up by only 10 per cent of households, who appear to have wanted to avoid the administrative costs associated with title deeds and subsequent taxation. However, the mere *offer* of the titles seems to have inspired in the residents a belief 'that they would be free to enjoy permanent occupation of their plots'. In a similar case in Cairo (Payne 2002) the provision of services by the state, rather than freehold titles, which were again rejected due to their associated costs, led to improvements and investment in their homes on the part of the inhabitants of so-called 'squatter' settlements.

As discussed further below, Islamic land tenure systems can be complex and overlapping, defying neat categorization. Urban land tenure cannot be understood through simple and conventional binaries of legal/illegal, formal/informal or even secure/insecure. As Payne (2001) suggests:

> The reality is that tenure systems exist within a continuum in which even pavement dwellers may enjoy a degree of legal protection and there may be many gradations or sub-markets between those at the lowest level of recognition and the fortunate minority at the top. The vast majority in between live in a grey area whereby they can claim some degree of *de facto* rights through adverse possession, legal ownership of land, if not the buildings on it, or the acquisition and development of land in areas not recognized by authorities.

UN-HABITAT also deploys a continuum of rights in its general strategy on security of tenure, particularly in relation to informal settlements. What will be termed here the Islamic 'webs of tenure' could be mapped on a continuum that is neither hierarchical nor universal but adjusted to local contexts and choices. At one end of the continuum lies land provided with services where the occupants have no legal protection for their possession, through customary tenure, intermediate protection such as certificates of comfort, adverse possession, group and collective tenure to registered freehold. At each stage it is possible to improve the rights of vulnerable social groups in unauthorized settlements, although only towards one end of the continuum does that involve tenure security in law.

The residents of informal settlements in Muslim countries also exist on the tenure continuum, as explained by Abu-Lughod (1980: 329–30) with reference to those in Rabat, Morocco. She speculates on this 'Other space':

> What shall we call them? The term 'squatter settlement' will not do, since most land is occupied with the compliance of the owners (whether private, public or *hubus* [endowment]); indeed residents often pay for their tiny plots. Illegal settlements may be a more descriptive term, since house construction has taken place without building permits, and is often in zones expressly forbidden for residential use. And yet, there are parts that are clearly legal in the sense that occupancy rights have been 'regularized' by government action – whether by public construction or by the installation of utilities and ... communal facilities ... Clandestine subdivisions and/or clandestine permanent structures are terms that apply to some .... The lack of a single term to encompass all these structural and legal variations suggests that, if they have something in common, we have not yet captured it.

The construction of appropriate urban land policies depends in the Muslim world, as elsewhere, upon their ability to respond flexibly to the local context. This includes assessing the extent to which existing options have provided the inhabitants of informal settlements with the means to protect their possession of land. However, attention must also be paid to innovations that employ indigenous law and legal concepts, which are embedded in customary local structures.

Categorization of Land

A multiplicity of types of land tenure emerged from different parts of the legal texts, whether dealing with contracts or conquest, combined with taxation systems ('Abd Al-Kader 1959). However, as explained in Chapter 1, there are widely thought to be three broad types of land and land tenure in Islamic theory, which continue as categories into modern Muslim societies. These are first, *mulk* or land in full ownership, second, state-owned land and third, *waqf* land. As has also been previously explained, fundamental to these categories is the traditional Islamic theory of taxation, with a classical Islamic division between Muslim-owned land on which a tithe is paid (*'ushr*) and land under state control upon which a tax is paid (*kharaj*) by those in possession. As Ziadeh (1993: 4) has argued: 'terms of revenue like *kharaj* [and] '*ushr* … predominate' in the Islamic system of land tenure, as opposed to those terms 'which denote rights of property'. The tax was charged at a much higher rate than the tithe.

Mulk or *milk* land, which is sometimes translated in Western terminology as freehold, was essentially that on which *'ushr* (a tenth), a religious land tithe, was collected. This was part of the more general payment of *zakat*, levied on property such as gold, silver, merchandise and income-producing animals, as well as land, required of all Muslims to purify both themselves and their wealth. *'Ushr* land was land owned by Muslims and regulated by Shari'a law. Ziadeh (1985: 94) describes *'ushr land* as:

> land belonging to a Muslim at the time of his conversion or distributed to a Muslim soldier as his share of the spoils of war. All land in Arabia proper was considered as *'ushri*, since the inhabitants were converted in the first stages of Islamic history.

State land is a useful and widely deployed umbrella term for 'a complex set of different kinds of estates in land' and 'subject to different conditions of tenure' (Ziadeh 1985: 94), which was to become *miri* land. This was the most important form of landholding in Islamic history. Care must be taken with respect to generalizing about this form of tenure, but most land subject to state taxation (*kharaj*) – essentially, land upon which a tribute was paid by those with possession – fell within this category. Both the tax and this land itself were known as *kharaj* (Modaressi 1983; Jorgens 2000). It consisted initially of land where the inhabitants after Islamic invasion were, under Islamic legal principles adapted around existing systems, as agreed upon by early Muslim jurists, permitted to retain possession of their lands in return for paying *kharaj* (Jorgens 2000: 111). It should be noted that some land upon which this tax was paid, where it was surrendered peacefully or by agreement, was considered by some early Islamic jurists to be held like *'ushr* land in full ownership (*mulk*) title, but this theoretical distinction appears to have faded (Ziadeh 1993: 5). Certainly, *kharaj* land formed the greater part of state-owned land, the details of which were not defined or regulated by the Shari'a but were a matter for state administrative law. There was also *waqf* land, whether a family endowment or one which was purely religious, although some jurists did not strictly conceive of it as a type of landholding (Ziadeh 1985). The importance of *waqf* land, the extent of which historically was vast and remains very large in the contemporary world despite reforms, is such that it is the focus of Chapter 7.

In addition to the established categories, as discussed in Chapter 1, individuals also have a right to reclaim *mewat* land, based upon the *hadith* that 'he who turns dead land into life becomes its owner' (Bukhari 1982: 555). There was some dispute between Muslim jurists of the classical period, and between different schools, as to whether it was the capacity to work the land, the length of time the land was cultivated, or some other indication such as the placing of a stone or some other mark of ownership, which would suffice to demonstrate reservation of *mewat* or *mawat* land. There are also some differences concerning the requirement, or otherwise, of the permission of the relevant Imam ('Abd Al-Kader 1959). However, there is no dispute as to the overall view that since land was given to the whole Muslim community by God, if a Muslim can actually cultivate empty land he may continue to use it productively, provided it does not harm others or the community at large. The dead land (*mewat*) concept is important in the material sense, but also in the manner in which people 'think through' their relationship with land. Bukhari (1982: 555) points out that large-scale modern 'squatting' in Al-Madinah in Saudi Arabia in the 1970s was 'viewed by the squatters as a continuation of their traditional and legal rights' (Bukhari 1982: 555). He recounts that squatters occupied 'virtually dead' land, building a fence, putting up a shelter and then took 'their case to the religious court for legalization of their possession' (Bukhari 1982: 556). Provided the court deemed the land to be 'useless' and unclaimed, after investigation, it was registered in the name of the occupier. Later the occupants invested in the property and erected permanent homes. Despite his use of the term 'squatting', Bukhari records that no such 'popular' word was used to describe these occupations, because they were part of the legal and social tradition.

Acquiring Individual Ownership of Land

In the *Qur'an* it is clear that 'the earth belongs to God. He provides to whom He chooses' (7: 128). However, this has not precluded either the individual ownership of land or the legal protection of individual property rights, albeit subject to an overall social responsibility. It is widely held amongst Islamic scholars that plain land (in its natural state) is under state ownership. Here, the state, representing the will of God, holds the land in trust for the *umma*, with powers to alienate use of the land to deserving grantees. But rights of possession are conditional upon the continued use of land and the proscription of hoarding. A landowner who neglects to use land and leaves it uncultivated will lose the right to retain it, as in the *hadith* that: 'Land belongs to God, whoever leaves it uncultivated for three consecutive years will have it taken away and given to someone else' (Weeramantry 1988). There is an example of the Prophet taking away land from some of his companions when they ceased to cultivate it.

Private ownership may be obtained through either transaction, such as *bay* (sale), or *hiba* (gift), including the revival of *mewat* land and inheritance (Hamza 2002: 33). Islam recognizes contractual rights and the *Qur'an* commands followers to fulfil their contractual promises (4: 33; 16: 91–2) and obligations when dealing with each other (5: 1). It is stated: 'Keep your promises; you are accountable for all that you promise' (*Qur'an* 17: 34). This command is relevant to the modern debate about the extent to which the state may intervene in contracts, for instance in order to control rent. Some scholars would suggest that the high esteem given to sanctity of contracts and the promises within them preclude such intervention other than in limited circumstances. However, at a recent meeting of scholars at the Sixteenth Session of the Islamic Jurisprudence Council in Dubai, there was broad agreement that government could intervene in order to prevent exploitation: it should set a rent affordable by the tenant while also permitting the landlord a reasonable profit (Za'za 2005).

Hamza (2000) describes the key elements in land transactions that he discovered in Bahrain before 1924, which reflect the requirements of Islamic legal principles (Rayner 1991). Most contracts included details of the following: the names of the two parties, and in some cases their occupations, village or town of residence; their capacity and responsibility to contract; the existence of the property and the awareness by both parties of that existence, including some form of description such as its name or other defining attributes; in some cases the source of ownership of the vendor; the value of the property and that the purchaser has given the money to the vendor; irrigation rights, if any; the day and date of the contract, the town and village where it took place; and the names of two witnesses with their signatures or ring seals. Hamza notes that in Bahrain, unlike Palestine for instance, the Shari'a judges did not keep a register of such documents (2002: 78). Islamic contracts for the sale of land in the Sudan analysed by Bjorkelo (1998) mirror in most respects those studied by Hamza in Bahrain. He emphasizes that these documents, known as *hujjas*, were written largely in the past tense and acted as both a record of the contract of sale and the deed of ownership, confirming the purchaser's rights for any future transaction. He stresses also that while he studied documentary evidence, a perfectly suitable legal transaction could be effected even in eighteenth-century Sudan by means of a sale conducted in the presence of witnesses, who could then give oral testimony if required to the local Shari'a court by way of confirmation.

Shuf'a (pre-emption) does set a barrier in Islamic law upon the free disposal of *milk* land. It is the means by which a co-inheritor or neighbour may use a privileged option to purchase land when it is for sale. For instance, the application of Islamic inheritance rules to a deceased's estate will in general lead to property, such as a house, being owned in fractional shares by two or more co-owners. When one of those co-owners sells his or her share to a third party who is not one of the joint owners, the sale can be pre-empted by another co-owner (Messick 2003). The co-owner will receive the share after compensating the third party buyer for the price paid. *Shuf'a* is a process capable of keeping strangers to communities on the outside and thereby placing limitations upon certain kinds of economic development (Ziadeh 1985). Different schools of law take different approaches to pre-emption, with the Maliki and Shafi'i schools limiting its scope to co-owners, while the Hanafi school extends the right to an adjoining neighbour.

The legal prohibition against hoarding has led to considerable debate amongst Islamic scholars concerning the appropriate utilization of land, particularly with respect to the question of rent and the related issue of sharecropping, with different *hadith* quoted in support of each position (Behdad 1992: 88–9). Some Islamic economists argue, for instance, that land rent is always unlawful. This argument relies on the *hadith* to the effect that ownership beyond what one can cultivate is surplus and should be distributed free to other Muslims or surrendered to the state, not leased out to others. On the other hand, a larger group of Islamic scholars hold that the tradition prohibits only the payment of rent on land which has not been improved in some way. In this case rent is a rightful return on the inputs into the land in terms of labour and capital (Behdad 1992: 88). A similar debate has taken place concerning sharecropping. It seems that there is a distinction between sharecropping where the owner provides only the land (*mukhabara*) and the more common form of sharecropping in much of the Muslim world, where the owner provides both land and seed for the crop (*muzara'a*). The former may not be permitted, unless perhaps the owner is engaged with non-Muslims, but the latter appears to be widely regarded as sanctioned.

Land Tenure Regimes in Ottoman Practice

Islamic land tenure models, diverse in themselves, were not seen as static or formulaic arrangements but rather as driven by principles and ideas, which in turn were debated. As discussed in earlier chapters, Islamic land tenure concepts were rooted in strong theoretical and theocratic foundations. They were also realized from the first generation of Muslims through to the end of the Ottoman Empire in 1916, and beyond. However, modern land tenure regimes in the Muslim world owe much to the longevity of the Ottoman Empire. Through much of its 600 years an extensive land administration system developed, based on Islamic and local principles, involving elaborate record keeping and statistics (Crecelius 1995). Rules governing landholder–state, peasant–landlord and peasant–state relationships, as well as the cultivation of *mewat* lands, were inspired by Islamic principles, but driven largely by the need for revenues through tax and for stable food production for the urban classes. The elaborate network of laws, guidelines, categories and records which developed in the Ottoman period continues to inform contemporary land classifications in many of the successor states, despite colonial and postcolonial modifications. Most crucially, although there is a rich variation of custom which shapes land tenure concepts in particular social and political contexts, throughout much of the region there is a common derivation from the Ottoman Code of 1858, which was based on Ottoman practice and Islamic law.

Ottoman land law was not a blanket imposition producing a homogeneous system across the entire Ottoman world or throughout the lengthy period of Ottoman rule. Each area, or more correctly each province, had its own system of land law that preceded Ottoman rule, and to an extent at least continued to be applied after occupation (Udovitch 1974). As time passed some amalgamation or unification of principles and legal categories took place, but this was never complete and was almost invariably contested (Gerber 2002). The categories of land and land tenure were not derived simply from the nature and quality of property rights or Islamic legal theory, but owed much to the demands of the state in the Ottoman world, particularly the army (Ziadeh 1985). Land was also used by the state as a means for securing the allegiance of different individuals/groups (Islamoglu 2000) and maintaining supplies of food for the urban élite. This objective required that the state, that is the ruler or *bayt-al-mal* (the treasury), while retaining *raqaba* ('ownership') of most agricultural land, defined the cultivators' use rights, possession and access to the land on the basis of conditions which varied from locality to locality. Ziadeh (1993: 6) comments that the 'Ottoman system of land tenure was based on the assumption that arable land was state property' and therefore subject to regulation by state administrative law, by means of *qanun*.

Complex power relations shaped the forms of tenure that emerged and, as Islamoglu (2000) has argued, property rights in land in the Ottoman world should be viewed as a 'bundle' which was subject to a dynamic process of negotiation, renegotiation and resistance. The result was conveyed in the oft-quoted phrase with which this chapter opened, that 'land differs from one foot of ground to the next' (*Al-ard btifriq bi-l-shibr*). Moreover, it should be emphasized, as Islamoglu (2000: 18) has further argued that the various types of tenure that authorized land use or rights to revenue 'did not correspond to an understanding of ownership', whether state or private, at least in the Western liberal sense of the word. The emphasis upon 'possession' and 'use of land', as opposed to ultimate ownership, remained and remains an enduring feature of land tenure in the Arab world.

The Islamic tradition that distinguished between *mulk* land on which a tithe was paid and land on which a tax was paid was followed by the Ottomans, and all land conquered by Muslims was deemed to be *kharaj*. *Mulk* land was found principally and with only limited exceptions in towns, or close to towns, consisting of land with buildings on it, whether houses, commercial premises, or fruit and vegetable gardens. Marcus (1989: 111) determined that 80 per cent of the real estate in the Syrian city of Aleppo in the eighteenth century, for example, was *mulk*, the remainder being *waqf*. His analysis also shows that there was a highly active real estate market in Aleppo. Trading in houses and to a lesser extent shops, coffeehouses, bakeries and bath houses took place on an almost daily basis, as evidenced in the city's Shari'a court records of the *hujja*, which were formally sealed by the court. Marcus also identified a high degree of fragmentation in ownership as a consequence of Islamic inheritance rules, which led to property being held in undivided shares by several co-owners, but also because of joint purchase, as between husband and wife. Under the Ottomans (1299–1923) virtually all cultivated state land in the possession of individuals became known as *miri*. *Miri* is a term which derives from, or is a shortened version of, the literal explanation that it was land under the control of the *Amir-al-Muslimin* or leader of Muslims (Wilkinson 1999). The conditions placed on what effectively became state grants of possession to individuals varied and were very far from being uniform, sometimes giving very limited and at other times quite extensive rights. Bunton (2000: 126) warns of falling into the trap of envisaging Ottoman land tenure concepts through the Western and colonialist lens. He makes the point that the term 'state land' is perhaps an unfortunate translation and that it should not be confused with the British concept of crown land/public domain.

State land developed in part through a system devised for military reasons, which was a feature too of regimes that preceded Ottoman rule, by which an army of cavalrymen was given an income from land subject to taxation so that they could be in readiness for war. Ultimate title to land lay with the state or *bayt-al-mal*, which distributed through a *timar*, an Ottoman equivalent of the *iqta* (Islamic grant of land) (Lewis 1979: 122), the right to revenue of a *sipahi* (individual cavalryman). The subsistence farmer or cultivator of the land had *tassaruf* (possession) vested in him. The farmer paid *kharaj* for the rights of possession in the land to the *sipahi*. The *timar* could and quite often was revoked by the state and transferred to someone else. Equally, while there was no right of inheritance the *timar* could and quite often was reassigned by the state to the son of the *sipahi* or another male member of the family. For a variety of reasons, including changes in the make-up of the Ottoman military and commercial expansion in agriculture, by the seventeenth century the system of revenue grants had been replaced by *iltizams* or tax farms (Isamoglu 2000). The tax farmers acquired life-interests over their tax farms; their children gained prior rights to acquire their father's interest upon his death; and in some areas the tax farmer even obtained some local political power, thereby weakening the distinction between state land and *mulk* land. However, the tax farms continued to be designated as *miri*.

Ottoman land strategies ranged from realizing Islamic first principles to openness towards customary practices. This is well evidenced by Ottoman approaches to empty or *mewat* land, which exhibited both creativity and flexibility. In contrast to the modern situation in many Muslim countries, the Ottoman state was not concerned with any 'shortage of land'; rather, it was keen to encourage the cultivation and use of land (Lewis 1979) to ensure the continuance of subsistence farming and a regular supply of provisions to urban dwellers. In the Ottoman world *mewat* land, that is undeveloped land at a distance from any town or village, in accordance with Islamic legal theory could be 'enlivened' through cultivation or other acts such as irrigation. The occupier who reported effective use of such land and received the permission of the state would be granted rightful possession (Altug 1968: 165). Pastoral lands, as opposed to cultivated land, were held as the traditional communal domain of particular tribes both for residence and herding, according to local custom (Razzaz 1998; Forni 2005).

In some rural parts, predominantly on the frontiers of the Ottoman Empire, in highland regions or those occupied by non-Sunni communities such as the Druze, but also in Palestine, there existed also the phenomenon of '*musha*. It has been described as 'still the most puzzling and confusing form of land tenure in the Middle East' (Schaebler 2000: 241) – presumably to outsiders. At village level '*musha* denoted either common undivided land or communal grazing land. However, it was used by colonial officials during mandate rule in the Middle East to describe the system by which most of a '*musha* village's arable land was held in common and in shares, generally known as *sahms*, giving the villagers access to the land. Each share gave access to different sections of cultivated land, with a range of methods used to determine the number of shares, although the fixing of the shares did not necessarily lead to their attachment to fixed lots of land. The most important aspect of the practice of '*musha* was 'the periodic redistribution of lots' (Schaebler 2000: 244). Schaebler (2000) explains that some of the confusion and mystery surrounding this form of tenure is due to the fact that this communal land existed '"below" and "beyond" Ottoman law' (2000: 243) – outside the court records and other documents that provide the usual historical source materials for other forms of tenure. However, she describes also the importance of owning a share for the villagers in question, in terms of confirming a sense of belonging and social status within the community. While recognizing the danger of placing an over-romantic orientalist gaze upon the *'musha* system, it did reflect in many ways the egalitarian principles and respect for equity that are integral to an Islamic way of life.

The Ottoman Codes and Land Regulation

The Ottoman Land Code of 1858, consisting of 132 articles, was based upon both Ottoman practice and Islamic law. It defined (articles 1–7) five categories of land: *mulk, miri, waqf, mewat* and *metruke* – the last being public land for general use: pastures for the use of towns and villages, markets, parks and places to pray. The Code has been seen as the basis for modern state legislation and the division into these forms of land tenure remains in place today. However, the Code particularly regulated state land, as Altug (1968: 155) explains:

> The underlying principle was that state lands were once and forever state property, but could be handed over, by means of a particular title deed, called *tapou*, to private persons for their use and that of their children and parents, but that if the holder wished, during his lifetime, to convey it to others or change its character by building upon it or planting orchards ... a special permission had to be obtained from the state.

The Majalla (Ottoman Civil Code), issued between 1869 and 1878, which was based entirely on Islamic law, dealt specifically with *mulk* land. It adopted the Hanafi view and included for instance its wide scope for the doctrine of pre-emption. The privileged option to purchase land applied not just to a co-owner of the land, as with some other schools of law, but also to the adjoining neighbour of the land in question. In practice, the differences between *miri* and *mulk* were fairly narrow and the grant of the usufruct rights (*tapou/tapu*) on state land could be inherited, although according to the principles of the 1858 Ottoman Land Code and not as stipulated in the Shari'a. A person who possessed state land and paid the relevant taxes for five years secured the land against confiscation and the individual in possession could lease land held as *miri* to another for cultivation (Jorgens 2000).

Ziadeh (1985: 98) suggests also that the prescribed permission to sell the rights in state land by the government to a private individual became little more than a formality. Later, in the Provisional Law of Disposal of 1913, the absolute requirement of consent for validity of the transaction would be abolished (Bunton 2000: 125). The remaining limitations on the title granted by the state were that the title-holder could not create a true *waqf* from his holding and could not dispose of his interest in a will. Further, if the holder of title in state land left it uncultivated for a period of three years (Article 103 on *mehlul/mahlul* land), the state could deprive the holder of possession. The private owner of land (*milk*) suffered no such deprivation for non-cultivation. One of the Code's general aims was to ensure that land was cultivated. It provided for bringing *mahlul* and *mewat* land into use. An individual in possession of such land could notify the authorities and receive a *tapu*. The Ottoman Code was mirrored and in many ways exceeded by similar legal and administrative innovations in Egypt, notably through Khedive Sa'id's law also of 1858 (Jorgens: 2000). Looked at in retrospect, while these reforms were initiated as a means of securing land as a tax-producing asset and retained the basic principle of state-owned agricultural land, they may also be regarded as the start of a considerable push towards greater individual property rights (Cuno 1980: 245).

As argued in Chapter 1, the records and laws from the Ottoman period reveal a highly developed land tenure regime, flourishing land management systems and sophisticated land registration specifically with respect to state land (Islamoglu-Inan 1987). As Jorgens comments (2000: 112), 'article after article of the land codes reiterated that government officials must record land transfers of whatever kind'. Owen (2000b) suggests that the public nature of registration and the authority given to state agents (*memuru marifetiyle*) in the Code, for instance with respect to denying access to uncultivated land (*mehlul*), combined to underline central state power. The control of the central government of the Empire was cyclical, at times strong and in other periods allowing local élites to dominate social and economic life. It is thought that renewal of the cadastral registers, both central and provincial, through a new survey was usually evidence of an upswing in the central government's power (Wilkinson 1990: 57–8). Forni (2005) thinks that general registration was not achieved because the concept of individual title was not consonant either with prevailing land use, organized around the group or clan, or with the manner in which land tenure was 'thought through' on the ground, which was communal as opposed to private. The Code was, in Owen's words (2000b: 35), 'continuously contested, resisted, negotiated, and renegotiated in different contexts'. This was the case particularly with respect to *'musha* lands, where resistance to cadastre and registration was frequently violent and met with a brutal response from Ottoman troops seeking to enforce state power (Schaebler 2000: 241). However, these systems served to clarify legal rights and the land registers continue to be used to resolve contemporary disputes in some countries whose territory was once under Ottoman rule.

Impact of Colonialist Land Administration

The nineteenth century witnessed a series of legal and administrative reforms and innovations in an attempt to reassert state rights over state arable land and to secure land tax revenue. These changes often took place under European -

pressure and economic influence, although the logic behind them was as frequently different, depending on whether the Ottoman Empire proper or Egypt was in question. At their heart lay fiscal reform, the elimination of the local tax-farming middlemen and the implementation of a direct tax system between the state and the peasants who cultivated the land, with tax collected by salaried state agents. The process of codification which was an integral part of the reform aimed at preserving the authentic Islamic content of the law, but placed it in a European, specifically French, form – the Code.

The period of direct colonial engagement had a particular impact on the conceptualization of state land in Islamic countries and further complicated land tenure regimes. As already outlined, the rights and interests in state land were never defined in Shari'a law and gave rise to a diversity of landholdings by individuals throughout Muslim history. Ziadeh (1985) has warned against generalizing about state land given its Ottoman and colonialist constructions. He notes the efforts by some colonial administrators to construe land held as *miri* within a wider definition of state land than that envisaged within Islamic legal principles, or indeed even that pertaining under Ottoman rule. To many officials of colonial powers like Britain in Palestine, state land denoted crown land or land in the public domain. As Bunton has commented (2000: 126), colonial bureaucrats 'were keenly aware' during the early period of mandate rule in the 1920s 'that the mass of agricultural land fell into the *miri* category and was therefore held on something less than freehold terms'. He describes the Palestine government taking 'assiduous steps' to try and maintain or gain control over land which was perceived to be under the control of the state. Bunton provides evidence to suggest that confusion as to the precise nature of usufruct rights in *miri* land came at least in part from the translation of this category as 'state land', a term which persists today and is also used in this book for convenience. This confusion was fuelled, no doubt, by a desire on the part of the colonial power to justify extensive government management of agricultural land. In effect, the British administration in Palestine created a new land category, state land or public domain: it is questionable, however, whether *miri* land should ever be placed in this category, except where it has been left uncultivated and become *mahlul* land. For under Ottoman law *miri* land could not be taken back under state control, provided the relevant tax was paid and the individual with usufruct rights continued to cultivate it.

This confusion over the character of usufruct rights was responsible for the Mahlul Lands Ordinance of 1920, under which anyone in possession of uncultivated land was obliged to inform the state (Bunton 2000). As discussed above, under Ottoman law a person who possessed *mahlul* land and who informed the state would be able to obtain a grant of title. However, under the Mahlul Lands Ordinance of 1920 the best that he could hope for would be a lease. The colonial powers were also anxious to limit rights over *mewat* land, which could be drawn into state control. The Mewat Lands Ordinance in Palestine of 1921, for instance, removed the right of the occupier who cultivated dead land to a grant of title, thereby creating what Bunton (2000: 127) describes as 'a new juridical creature' – squatters. Under Ottoman law the person who occupied and cultivated either *mewat* or *mahlul* land was not a trespasser, provided that occupation was reported to the state authorities. Under colonial rule such individuals became trespassers on state land.

The approach of the colonial administration to the phenomenon of lands in particular villages in Palestine, known as *jiftlik* villages, gives a further indication of its acquisitiveness in terms of drawing as much land as possible into the public domain. This land had been registered personally in the name of Sultan Abd' al-Hamid and was 'turned over' to the Ottoman Treasury in 1908, but its occupants regarded themselves as having full ownership. Given that there was no particular category of *jiftlik* land in Ottoman law, the colonial administration had to find a means to address this customary form of tenure and rationalize it within existing classifications. As Bunton (2000) indicates, 'the Palestine government's immediate attempts to define its position regarding *jiftlik* land closely followed the pattern established for *mahlul* and *mewat* land – that is, to guard jealously whatever control over land they thought they could'. The response in Palestine did not amount to a coherent policy, with *jiftlik* cultivators dealt with differently at various times. Ziadeh (1993: 10) indicates that in Syria, under the French mandate, 'turned over' lands, known there as *aradi mudawana*, were dealt with more systematically and registered as the property of the state 'in its capacity as a juridical person' and 'entrusted ... to a special department, the Directorate of State Domain'.

The early period of British mandate rule in Palestine saw also the 1921 Land Transfer Ordinance, which deemed that all land transactions, with the exception of short leases, would require consent from the High Commissioner, who was not obliged to supply any reason for refusal. This was designed to address unwanted speculation in land and there was specific provision for consent to be refused if the vendor did not retain sufficient land to maintain his family (Bunton 2000: 124) – a stipulation designed to protect agricultural tenants and prevent the creation of large estates. Resistance to the limits placed upon Palestinian landowners, which were formulated in terms of the Ordinance's non-compliance with Islamic law (Shari'a), led to amendments in 1921, which shifted authority from the High Commissioner to the Director of Land Registries, as well as removing the protective restrictions on size and value.

Under mandate rule there was also a 'rush to reestablish the land registration system' (Bunton 2000: 123), in order to facilitate land transactions and stimulate the land market, albeit under the surveillance of the administration. A topographical land survey was conducted in Palestine in 1933, which is still in use today in East Jerusalem. Three years later a block survey of the main cities, including Jerusalem, was carried out. Later, under Jordanian rule, the survey would be tied to ownership in a modern land registration system for East Jerusalem, although the limited progress in registering titles was brought to an abrupt halt in 1967. In Bahrain, fuelled by oil exploration, the colonial administration conducted a survey of agricultural land in 1926–37, using Indian land surveyors, and recorded land parcels and agricultural plots with an index of the names of occupants (Hamza 2002: 92). But some people resisted registration of their plots, believing that it was simply the forerunner of expropriation.

In countries that fell under the French mandate, and specifically in Syria and Lebanon, both land survey and registration were implemented in the 1920s. Land tenure reforms were carried through in both countries at the same time and using the same legal decrees. In Syria almost all arable land was, as elsewhere in the former Ottoman Empire, categorized as *miri*, but because of its particular history of relative autonomy from Ottoman rule, large areas of cultivated land in Lebanon were unusually held as *mulk* and subject to Shari'a law. Ziadeh (1993: 10) comments that one of the benefits of registration was that it brought to an end the key element of the *'musha* system of communal landholding, that is the periodic reallocation of shares giving access to the land amongst members of the community or village. In his opinion this was a practice which had 'deleterious effects on the land'. This opinion echoes the standpoint taken by colonial officials in the 1930s who denounced the *'musha* system as an inefficient form of farming, due to over-seeding, loss of time in moving between strips of land and loss of land to cultivation (Schaebler 2000: 283). In Syria the Cadastral Department (Bureau de cadastre) adopted a system whereby it registered the share of each villager in the communal land as a fraction of the total, but did not attach title to an individual holding of land. Even in Ottoman times, in northern Iraq village headmen had taken the opportunities provided by the Land Code of 1858 to register title to land worked by entire communities into their own names, a process which intensified under legislation in the 1930s. The effect of this legislation was to replace the semi-communal, relatively egalitarian system with a small number of large landowners and a large group of tenants and sharecroppers.

Najjar (1999) states that there has generally been resistance to 'most Western ideas, ideologies and institutions as a threat to Islamic law, values and culture. Among these foreign imports, secularism seems to represent the greatest danger.' However, colonial land measures were internalized and the dual track of part secularization/modernization (arising from the colonial heritage) and part Islamization (from the Ottoman experience) did take place through codification. The late 1940s and 1950s brought to much of the eastern Arab world modern civil codes that owed a great debt to the work of Dr 'Abd al-Razzaq al-Sanhuri. His influence was seen in the Egyptian Civil Code of 1949, the Syrian Code of the same year, the Iraqi Code of 1953 and, though not directly and much later, the Jordanian Code of 1976. These codes preserved, either explicitly or implicitly in the case of Iraq, the basic and traditional categories of *mulk*, *waqf* and *miri* land, although the emphasis varied with the particular histories of different countries and earlier reforms (Ziadeh 1985). The Egyptian Code also preserved to a degree the doctrine of pre-emption, although with restrictions to prevent attempts at extortion between neighbours. A similar position was adopted in Jordan and Iraq, although in Syria *shuf'a* was abolished.

However, the 1950s were also marked by land reform, in the sense of imposed redistribution of agricultural land to the landless and poor farmers. Again Egypt led the way in 1952, giving the state authority to seize the holdings of large private landowners, who in the main were the descendants of individuals who had received land as a reward for their services or loyalty in the Ottoman period (Bush 2004: 11). Bush indicates that the seized land was designated as state land, to be redistributed to poor tenant farmers, smallholders and the landless. He suggests also that the large estates, over 200 *feddans* in size, at which this reform was directed, disappeared, while the holdings of the poorest farmers increased quite dramatically. Forni (2005) explains that the private owners retained ownership, but the small farmers became tenants, 'farming the land as if it was their own', paying fixed rents and with considerable protection from eviction for both themselves and their heirs. Saad (2002) describes the relationship as one of 'permanent tenants' occupying land upon which the owners 'were unable to practise their *ownership rights*' (2002: 105). In 1961 further reform saw the ceiling for expropriation reduced to 100 *feddans*, albeit with some exemptions. There is evidence that in Egypt these reforms did help to reduce poverty levels, and that farmers benefited from government aid in the form of subsidies, seed and so on (Bush 2004; El Ghonemy 2005), despite the fact that large landowners developed strategies to avoid the landholding ceilings. The economic effects of similar reforms in Iraq, where much of the land came under government control, seem to have been more disappointing (Forni 2005).

Postcolonial 'Land Tenure Webs'

Islamic land tenure systems, which were filtered through Ottoman administration and then colonial constructions, have endured into the postcolonial world (Anderson 1996). At least in most of the Middle East, the Islamic tradition is relatively easy to detect in official land law systems, albeit overlaid in many countries with secular codes. The distinction between the land itself and its usufruct, the principle that ownership of land lies with God but is held in trust by the state for the community of Muslims, still underpins categories of land used today. The most basic categories of land tenure resonate through Middle Eastern land law, as do their separate histories and consequent distinctiveness.

Miri and *mulk* land tenure may for many purposes now be virtually identical. However in terms of inheritance the difference between these two concepts has some significance and inheritance may for many people in the Middle East be the most important means of access to land. Processes such as the enlivening of *mewat* land and the practice of the state taking back *mehlul* land which the occupier failed to cultivate resound in contemporary normative thinking and legal systems, although sometimes manipulated for political or ideological purposes. It is pertinent to note that in its curious and more recent manifestation, the Israeli government has used the *mewat* land concept to acquire most supposedly uninhabited and uncultivated Palestinian land (Kedar 2001). State land deemed uncultivated for three years has also been requisitioned by the Israeli state, with 40 per cent of the West Bank declared as state land by 2002 (Forni 2005: 12).

Property and land law in most of the Muslim world straddles the 'public'/'private' divide. Land administration, management, regulation and conflict resolution are necessarily a part of the public sphere. Land registration, which has a relatively long history across the Middle East, is embedded in some parts of the region. It carries with it at least a veneer of secularism, although it bumps up against the Islamic legal framework and customary/unofficial tenure. In the Gulf States, cadastral and land registration records are relatively systematic, providing a legal basis and protection for land tenure, integrated with sale transactions and the provision of mortgages (Hamza 2002). However, *waqf* lands frequently remain unregistered, as is the case with respect to government land. In Oman, where the central registration system was not introduced until 1972, later than most of its neighbours, many properties or plots are still unregistered (Hamza 2002). Egypt has some elements of a fairly sophisticated and mature institutional framework for dealing with registration and land transactions, although this has limited coverage. Moreover, there is evidence that Egyptians seek to avoid the registration system (Bahaa-Eldin 1999). There are several reasons for this, including the avoidance of tax and transaction fees, but, as will be discussed in Chapter 5, the effect of inheritance rules – leading to fragmented ownership through compulsory shares in estates – also accounts for this lack of engagement with the registration process (Bush 2002). Speaking in the Egyptian context, 'Abd Al-Fattah (1999: 161) makes the general point that 'the ineffectiveness of modern law … is losing its credibility within vast social groups of people who are subjected to its provisions'.

The impact of land reform in terms of land redistribution, land administration and management with respect to access to land is generally evaluated as limited. Access to land in much of the Muslim world, as in other parts of the world, is considered to be considerably worse in comparison to the situation several decades ago. Some states have responded by attempting to reverse earlier land reforms, introducing privatization or re-privatization schemes built around a neoliberal economic paradigm designed to 'free' the market.

Perhaps the most visible of these legislative interventions is Egypt's 1992 Tenancy Act, fully implemented from 1997, which revoked much of Nasser's agrarian reforms of the 1950s and 1960s. The Act deregulated tenancy agreements leading to a rise in rents and the removal of security of tenure, shifting power from tenants to landlords. Landowners could take back their land, charge market rents, sometimes 300–400 per cent higher than in the past, and tenancies became annual contracts which could be renewed at the option of the landlord. However, Bush (2004) indicates that 'it is rare for an actual contract to exist'. He points also to the web of tenure arrangements that may exist for each rural household:

> Perhaps as much as 15 per cent of Egypt's agricultural land is tenanted, and tenants may have access to their own family land as well as renting in land – some may also rent out land. This means the relationships of tenancy are complicated, and they vary from household to household, but no allowance was made for this in the drafting of the legislation.

It appears that many small farmers did not know about the legislation, or did not actually believe that it would ever be implemented (Saad 2002). There is evidence that the Egyptian countryside has experienced a marked increase in land-related violence, both in terms of tenants who contest the application of the legislation and landowners seeking to dispossess tenants by force (Saad 2002: 120). Forni (2005) suggests that the Tenancy Act may have laid the basis for stimulating and improving the land market, but significant progress in market development remains unlikely while landowners fail to register title to their land. At the same time both Forni (2005) and Bush (2004) suggest that the tendency of the Egyptian government to focus upon land titling takes away from the arguably more important questions of landlessness, dispossession and access to land.

The 'web of tenancy' (Forni 2005: 9, quoting Bush 2002 in the context of Egypt) is a term used to denote the 'multiple interrelated tenancy relationships in which the landholder accesses land through combinations of more than one pattern'. It echoes the opening quotation of this chapter to the effect that the great variety of landholdings meant the 'land differs from one foot of ground to the next' (*Al-ard btifriq bi-l-shibr*). The convergence of Islamic principles, Ottoman law, colonial interventions, custom and unofficial norms may have led not merely to a 'web of tenancy' in some households, but to a broader 'tenure web' (Forni 2005: 8). Forni (2005: 8–9) argues that in Syria:

> field investigations have demonstrated the existence of a substantial overlap of different types of tenure within one farm household, where a land reform beneficiary may also manage other operations under a different title i.e. as owner-operator, squatter, sharecropper or any combination of these.

There are, she suggests, no 'clean patterns' or 'neat categories', but multiple combinations of relations which give access to land. There 'is also a tendency for those with multiple tenures to hold highly fragmented parcels' of land (2005: 9). This is true also of the urban environment in many Middle Eastern cities, although with different combinations of relations. Bonine (1997: 329) notes that:

> The Middle East is one of the fastest-growing regions in the world, and growth is especially concentrated in its cities. Not only will this tremendous population increase make it difficult to correct most of the urban problems but there is also the distinct possibility that the situation will worsen and that the living conditions and environments of the cities in the Middle East will deteriorate considerably. The question, then, must be posed: Are cities in the Middle East sustainable?

Inside those cities are the informal squatter settlements, some well established over many years. The city is also the location of other particularly vulnerable groups, including street children and widows – who, as a consequence of war or other disaster, no longer have a supportive safety net from kin – together with migrants, religious minorities and internally displaced persons. Razzaz (1998) demonstrates that in the so-called informal or squatter settlements the web of tenure relations is shaped in part by norms that exist 'beyond' and 'below' the formal legal system and informal land markets. But 'governmental law [still] plays a major role in formulating people's claims and bargaining strategies as well as their expectations, even when disputants do not resort to it directly' (Razzaz 1998: 85).

Research conducted by Razzaz (1998) into Yajouz, a low-income suburb of Amman, Jordan, which was formerly the communal pastoral land of the Bani Hassan tribe, yields interesting dynamics. Tribal members were denied the right to register the land or to acquire 'official' recognition by the government, which wished to exploit it as state land. However, tribal members sought to 'cash in' on the land, which they held in *de facto* possession. They did this through a process of 'illegal' subdivision and sale to lower-income groups. Razzaz found a functioning informal market, using *hujja*, the traditional documentation, as evidence of the legitimate transfer of property interests. The documents were increasingly produced on standardized forms, resembling 'official' contracts recognized by the state and even including the state logo, stamps and so on. The documents are not recognized by the courts of law as valid, since the tribal members do not own the 'state' land and the transactions are not recorded in the Land Registry. However, in the local community of Yajouz the *hujjas* acquire their legitimacy in part from association with traditional, pre-Ottoman, symbolism and terminology.

Nevertheless, unofficial land transactions exist also 'in the shadow of the law' (Razzaz 1998: 74). Buyers of illegal subdivisions regard this shadow as an assurance that vendors will fulfil their obligations in relation to the 'unofficial' land transactions as set out in the *hujjas*. The well-articulated opposition of the state to what it regards as the 'lawlessness' of the tribal members and its attempts at times to stamp out unofficial subdivision and sale are viewed as a deterrent to fraudulent or unworthy behaviour. Tribal members do not wish to do anything that would lead buyers to complain to the authorities, thereby encouraging state intervention against the tribe's activities. The local documentation is not recognized by the courts as legitimate, but in a limited number of cases the courts have ruled that buyers have a right to what in the common law world would be termed rescission. In other words the buyer's position prior to the illegal transaction is to be restored. Thus a disgruntled buyer may be able to use the authority of the court to avoid a contract for an unwanted plot and to gain the return of any payment (Razzaz 1998: 81–2); and such a process provides the informal and unofficial transactions with a form of official validation.

As evidenced in Yajouz, communal elements form part of the web of tenure in some contexts. Issawi (1966: 9) has warned about the impact of the 'breakdown of the system of communal or tribal ownership of land and its replacement by individual ownership', as a result of the shift in economic and agricultural patterns. However, communal approaches to landholding, including the tenure categories and concepts themselves, remain important, as do their roots in Islamic principles and Ottoman history. Several of these phenomena have proven highly resilient and resistant to the efforts of reformers, continuing to play a role in the lives and the minds of postcolonial actors. For instance, the *'musha* land system – communal land held in shares and involving the periodic redistribution of lots – survived the demise of the Ottoman Empire and the colonial mandate authorities that followed, despite attempts at abolition and land registration. The *'musha* system has declined only because it has become less crucial as a means for an individual to identify with a community (Schaebler 2000).

Conclusions

Land tenure systems in the Muslim world are often a convergence of state designs, customary practices and, increasingly, international pressures which are modernist and secular, but there is generally a consciousness of Islamic land conceptions. The range of land tenures, classifications and categories in the postcolonial Middle East and many parts of the Muslim world is derived from Islamic principles developed and manipulated by successive regimes, particularly during the long period of Ottoman rule, and to varying degrees under the colonial and postcolonial governments. The current dominant forms of land tenure are also rooted in resilient customary practices and state interventions, which together form the basis through which individuals and groups in particular contexts think through their relationships with land and with one another. With the increasing calls for 'authenticity' through return or reinvigoration of Islamic and indigenous principles and practices, the strategy of legitimizing innovative land tenure arrangements through recourse to Islamic historical and spiritual principles could facilitate reforms capable of enhancing access to land for the vulnerable and landless. What is necessary, though, is the articulation of the potential of Islamic land systems to be the reverse of static, monolithic or exclusive formulae, emerging instead as responsive, flexible and capable of catering to a wide range of contexts and diverse constituencies of claimants.

Islamic law facilitates full ownership, conceives of 'state' lands which could be used in the public interest and even accommodates collectives and group land access and usufruct rights. It is striking that communal relations to land have endured both in practice and as a state of mind within the Muslim world. They have survived in the face of legal systems in which the concept of *miri* dominates and is manipulated by successive regimes to establish control over any land in which individual ownership claims cannot be maintained. In some areas these customary tenures have subsisted despite the attempts by tribal leaders to use land registration as a means to turn communal land into a large individual landholding. Communal land relationships exist often in areas where the people concerned are particularly vulnerable, amongst nomadic pastoralists, in areas of marginal rainfall, but also in the village, peri-urban or urban context. It is crucial in these contexts, where change is proposed or state policies are likely to impinge on the area, that the local populations are engaged in participatory development processes in order to find their own indigenous solutions.

More generally, Islamic land tenure regimes offer a range of options relating to the protection of rights of occupation, possession, use, usufruct and full ownership for a wide range of constituencies, including the urban poor, squatters and slum dwellers. There are several avenues for regularizing informal settlements. Land registration is widely touted as the way forward and can have advantages, but it is not always preferred or possible. It has a long history and is well embedded in many Muslim countries, including parts of the Middle East, with some sophisticated systems using modern technology. At first sight this would appear to lay solid foundations for land regularization processes focused upon securing ownership and access to land through formal titling. However, vast tracts of land in the Middle East, even where modern registration systems exist, remain unregistered, not least much of the *waqf* land and land falling under the control of government. Moreover, strategies at local, household and individual level to avoid registration of title are also entrenched and have a long history. Relatively large and wealthy landowners choose to remain outside the official land titling processes, even where this may preclude the use of credit mechanisms and full engagement in land markets. The motivations that underpin such strategies are multifarious. They include a desire to circumvent the strict application of Islamic inheritance rules – and the consequent fragmentation in ownership and landholdings – and to avoid the high costs of registration, including those associated with fragmented plots.

Fear of appropriation may also be a factor in the avoidance of registration, as is the fact that 'unofficial' markets and tenure formations may operate relatively efficiently and be responsive to local needs. Contemporary policies surrounding the encouragement of land titling may be too abstract in the above climate and strategies concerned with access to land, rather than titling, may better encompass the requirements of many communities in relation to secure tenure. Current policy making around land regularization in the Middle East that seeks to encourage the registration of individual land titles should not be the only approach to address this issue. Equally, strategies to enhance land rights for women or disadvantaged/vulnerable groups must be aware that Muslims, like others, may prefer to keep 'ownership' outside the influence of official attempts to avoid further land fragmentation, even where this preference appears to be counter-intuitive to the outsider. Land readjustment strategies that find their authority and social legitimacy in enduring Islamic principles of equity and egalitarianism – as in communal (*'musha*) villages, using plot exchanges and compensation – could in appropriate circumstances enhance access to land where there are often fragmented parcels and a web of tenures. Similarly, as will be argued in a later chapter, the institution of the *waqf* can facilitate land rights that are often preserved within a smaller circle of the landed class.

Registration may not be chosen because it is difficult to bring the prevailing local forms of land tenure within the officially recognized categories, or because the state refuses to register land ownership which challenges or impedes the state's own development plans. In practice, the seemingly complex web of Islamic tenures can be mapped against a continuum model, which is not hierarchical but promotes choice regarding a range of options. Islamic tenure webs potentially offer innovative tenures that could be part of a dynamic continuum of tenure model choices that are efficient, appropriate and authentic. The mesh of complex, sometimes seemingly *ad hoc*, tenure forms is not necessarily a barrier to economic development and the provision of secure access to land; they may be used beneficially and become a positive force. In reality, there exist few 'clean categories', but rather a web of tenure with a local distinctiveness which may be focused even at the level of particular communities. This fluidity and the often overlapping situations could augment innovation and offer a range of choices. Some tenure forms are recognized by the state and incorporated into legislation or recognized as social practice. However, whether they are formally part of policy or tolerated as customary arrangements, they work best because, unlike top-down approaches, they are close to the lived experiences of the people who use them. Strategies to enhance access to land must be based upon detailed research as to the particular tenure categories that are relevant in specific localities. However, attention should also be paid to the well-articulated system of Islamic human rights, which can also contribute to enhancing access to land, particularly for vulnerable groups such as women, minorities and children.

4

Islamic Human Rights and Land

> Human rights in Islam [are] not about how man asserts his rights against man but how man discharges his duties towards God. It is not preoccupied with the horizontal relationship of man with his fellow man but with the vertical relationship that subsists between each man and his maker. If the vertical relationship is properly tended, all human rights problems fall automatically into place. (Weeramantry 1988: 116–17)

Rights of access to land, property and housing, of ownership and use, and of security of tenure with a guarantee against arbitrary eviction comprise an identifiable body of tangible and enforceable rights. They are considered to be of classical origin but further developed in recent decades at international, regional, national and local levels. These rights arise now from a variety of constitutional and legal principles, international human rights treaties, political declarations, customary practice and international standards. Land, property and housing rights are cross-cultural, asserted within every socio-economic and political system although the practices regarding their regulation and protection may take different forms. Effective land tools and strategies for specific countries or contexts are predicated on the choice of appropriate frameworks and methodologies. This chapter considers Islamic dimensions in articulating and realizing land rights that have not received equal attention. It will explore the relationship between universal and Islamic human rights and their implications for land and property rights in Muslim societies.

At the international level there exist well-articulated rights and expectations relating to land, property and housing rights. These rights are generally considered by the community of nations to be universal, indivisible, interdependent and applicable to all societies. The main international human rights treaties create not only binding norms, but also, through treaty body mechanisms and other means, the apparatus to monitor compliance with those norms. The international effort towards enhanced, equitable and inclusive land rights is thus a convergence of the inputs of UN specialized and designated agencies towards a set of international expectations and standards within a 'soft law' creating various levels of recognition and obligation on the part of states. However, at least since the 1948 Universal Declaration of Human Rights (UDHR), there appears to have been an ideological challenge – diverse in strategy, scope and effect – to the ownership, substance and form of modernist human rights. One of the points of enquiry is whether the absence of a religious orientation in the UDHR and the other international instruments limits their legitimacy and currency in faith-based communities such as parts of the Muslim world.

Not only are we living in an 'age of rights' (Bobbio 1996) but the universal human rights movement has come to be a marker for 'the new standard of civilization' to which states are held accountable (Donnelly 1998). It is the source of power, authority and legitimacy. Yet, as Ignatieff puts it (1999), human rights face a 'midlife crisis', with the resurgence of perspectives demanding the incorporation of religious dimensions. Universalists who believe that human rights are the same everywhere generally discount cultural relativist claims that human rights to an extent depend on the context and subscribers, but the Islamic critique of universal human rights has not been easy to ignore. An Islamic ideological challenge, concerted although diverse in its strategies and its outlook, has emerged through the formulation of 'alternative' Islamic human rights approaches. These form the basis of enquiry of this chapter.

International Land and Property Rights Framework

A convenient starting point when interrogating modern human rights is the 1948 Declaration itself. Article 25 (1) of the UDHR states: 'Everyone has the right to a standard of living adequate for the health and well-being of himself and his family, including food, clothing, housing and medical care and necessary social services....' Further, Article 17 of the UDHR enshrines the right to own property alone as well as in association with others. This has to be read alongside the general principles such as non-discrimination (Article 2) and equal rights for men and women (Article 16). The central international instrument in relation to land is the 1966 International Covenant on Economic, Social and Cultural Rights (ICESCR), which calls for non-discrimination and progressive realization of the Covenant rights (Article 2), while stipulating equal rights of men and women in the enjoyment of all economic, social and cultural rights (Article 3). The key provision in relation to secure tenure and access to land is found in Article 11 (1), which states: 'The States Parties to the present Covenant recognize the right of everyone to an adequate standard of living for himself and his family, including adequate food, clothing and housing, and to the continuous improvement of living conditions.'

Land rights are also well established as civil and political rights. Article 17 (1) of the 1966 International Convention on Civil and Political Rights (ICCPR) states that: 'No one shall be subjected to arbitrary or unlawful interference with his privacy, family, home or correspondence, nor to unlawful attacks on his honour and reputation.' This is guaranteed through the process of non-discrimination (Article 2), gender equality (Article 3) during and at dissolution of marriage (Article 23), choice of residence (Article 12), equality before courts (Article 14) and protection before the law (Article 26). Thus, the ICCPR provides both international norms and procedural guarantees for the protection of property rights.

The human rights approach to access to land envisages enhanced protection for vulnerable categories, including women, children, minorities and migrants. The 1965 International Convention on the Elimination of All Forms of Racial Discrimination (ICERD), the 1979 Convention on the Elimination of All Forms of Discrimination against Women (CEDAW), the 1989 Convention on the Rights of the Child (CRC), the 1951 Convention relating to the Status of Refugees (CSR) and the 1990 International Convention on the Protection of the Rights of All Migrant Workers (CMW) all contain specific guarantees regarding property rights. To this list must be added the 1989 ILO Convention (No. 169) concerning Indigenous and Tribal Peoples in Independent Countries, the 1962 Convention (No. 117) concerning Social Policy and the 1973 International Convention on the Suppression and Punishment of the Crime of Apartheid.

However, the mere existence of human rights does not guarantee their implementation and it is well recognized that the enforcement of human rights is problematic. On one hand, the intrinsic nature and scope of particular rights may make it difficult to realize them in specific contexts. On the other, there may be contentious issues and a lack of political will in the drive towards their fulfilment. The promotion of land, property and housing rights has been propelled by global initiatives seeking to prioritize and mainstream these rights. Muslim countries have participated in global initiatives that include the 1976 UN Conference on Human Settlements and the 1988 Global Strategy for Shelter to the Year 2000, together with the Second United Nations Conference on Human Settlements (Habitat II) in 1996. The latter led to the Istanbul Declaration and the Habitat Agenda, which constitute the global framework for realizing land and housing rights. Apart from elaborating international norms, the Habitat Agenda (see paragraph 61) also clarifies the obligations of states in fulfilling those objectives. Over the past three decades the community of nations, through the UN General Assembly, has conceived and carried forward the global shelter strategy based on Resolutions 41/146 (1986), 42/146 (1987),

43/181 (1988) and, more recently, 59/484 (2004). These efforts have developed the general framework, as well as specifically targeting special groups such as women, indigenous people and internally displaced persons. The shelter strategy has been supported by the work of the Economic and Social Council, starting with Resolution 1987/62 on the Realization of the Right to Adequate Housing and the UN Commission on the Status of Women regarding Human Rights and Land Rights Discrimination (Resolution 42/1 (1998)).

The international regime for the promotion and protection of the rights to land and housing derives from the work of the UN Commission on Human Settlements (UNCHS which became UN-HABITAT in 2002): Resolution 14/6 (1993), for example, dealt with the human right to adequate housing, while Resolution 16/7 (1997) identified the collaborative role of UN-HABITAT and the UN Office of the High Commissioner on Human Rights (OHCHR) in realizing that right. UN-HABITAT, by Resolution 19/3 (2003), also implemented the Global Campaigns on Secure Tenure and Urban Governance. The UN Human Rights Commission, likewise, is active in the promotion of the right to adequate housing as a component of the right to an adequate standard of living (Resolutions 1986/36, 1987/22, 1988/24, 2001/28, 2002/21 and 2003/27). This right has been extended to ensure coverage of vulnerable categories and to incorporate guarantees against forced evictions (Resolution 1993/77). These standard-setting initiatives are also reflected in the work of the UN Sub-Commission on the Promotion and Protection of Human Rights, which developed principles on a range of issues relating to the realization of the right to adequate housing (Resolutions 1991/26, 1992/26, 1993/15, 1993/36, 1994/38, 1994/20, 1995/12, 1995/19 and 1995/27). The Sub-Commission has also focused on safeguards against forced evictions (Resolutions 1991/12, 1993/41, 1994/39, 1996/27 and 1998/9). The Governing Council of UN-HABITAT also has a number of resolutions against forced evictions and a 2003 resolution on women, housing, land and property. In September 2000, the member states of the United Nations unanimously adopted the Millennium Declaration and the Millennium Development Goals. States, stakeholders and international agencies, including the World Bank, the IMF, the OECD, and the specialized agencies of the United Nations such as the UNDP and UN-HABITAT all play roles as implementing agencies. UN-HABITAT, which is also concerned with urban land management (Agenda 21 of the Habitat Agenda) focuses its efforts on Millennium Development Goal 7, on slums (UN-HABITAT 2003).

A considerable and increasing number of member states of the 57-member Organization of Islamic Conference (OIC) have ratified the relevant international human rights treaties: ICCPR, ICESCR, ICERD, CRC, CEDAW and CSR. The ratification record of the 22-member League of Arab States is instructive: 13 states are party to the ICCPR; 13 states are party to the ICESCR;

18 states are party to the ICERD; and 13 states are party to CEDAW (International Commission of Jurists 2003). All 22 states are party to the CRC. Muslim states have also participated in the political process towards augmenting promotion and protection of housing and land rights. They subscribe to the United Nations Charter and are amenable to customary international human rights norms and developing general international standards relating to land and housing rights. Through these ratified treaties, Muslim states have also assumed specific human rights obligations with respect to housing and land rights (for a chart, see OHCHR 2004; Interights 1996). Mayer (1999a; see also Baderin 2001) argues that Muslim states are bound by these treaties either as a consequence of their formal acceptance through ratification or because customary international law has absorbed some of the key human rights principles and is binding on all states. She further argues that derogation from these obligations is only possible on very narrow grounds, which do not include any appeal to particular religious values or doctrine.

However, there may be a deep reluctance on the part of many Muslim countries to engage with and participate fully in the international human rights system, masked to a degree by their formal ratification record. Despite assertions to the contrary, Muslim societies are pluralist, exhibiting a range of religious and secular ideals, and the experience of Muslim countries cannot be generalized. Nevertheless, it is intended here to attempt an exploration of problematic aspects of the relationship between international human rights norms and Islamic critiques, as a way of understanding difficulties in implementing human rights principles with respect to access to land and security of tenure. Muslim and non-Muslim countries face similar kinds of human rights and development issues. There is, however, a heightened concern over human rights abuses in a number of Muslim countries due to socio-cultural practices perceived as hostile to human rights, some instances of repressive regimes, and resistance to the universal human rights movement emerging from vocal quarters within Muslim communities.

A number of Muslim countries ratifying international human rights treaties have entered reservations (exemptions) against some of the provisions of those treaties, usually in the name of religion. However, it is significant to note that none of the reservations relate directly to property rights, though there are some caveats regarding equality that have implications for land, property and housing rights. It is intended here to examine the relationship between international human rights and Islamic conceptions of human rights in theory and practice. The argument will be made that any differences between these two sets of rights, with respect to land rights, appear minimal; and that a sensitive and careful recognition of Islamic religious and political sensitivities can help deliver international human rights more effectively in Muslim societies, without offending Islamic principles. To recognize the dynamics of the human rights discourse in Muslim societies it is relevant to examine first the debate over the ownership, origins, nature and scope of international human rights.

Debating the Universal Declaration of Human Rights

The drafting of the 1948 UDHR is generally agreed to be the starting point of the modernist conception of human rights. The strength of the Declaration, though it is not binding and lacks an enforcement mechanism, is in its promulgation of a range of civil, political, economic, social, and cultural rights as 'a common standard of achievement for all peoples and nations'. Nickel (1987: 7) writes that 'the first twenty one articles of the Declaration present rights similar to those found in the US Constitution, while Articles 22 to 27 deal with 'innovative' socio-economic and welfare rights. He adds that contemporary human rights differ from earlier conceptions, particularly those in the eighteenth century, in three ways: 'Human rights are more egalitarian, less individualistic and have an international focus'. When the UDHR was adopted by the then members of the Assembly without dissent, 48 nations voted for the Declaration, eight countries abstained (the Soviet bloc countries, South Africa and Saudi Arabia) and two countries were absent (Humphrey 1984). In abstaining, Saudi Arabia complained that the UDHR did not reflect the Islamic human rights ethos and raised objections to the Declaration's conception of religious freedom and the extent of human choice. Attention has focused on the liberal Lebanese Christian statesman Charles Malik and the Pakistani foreign minister Zafarullah Khan (see Khan 1989), who played a persuasive role, but could not find Muslim support back home (Mawdudi 1980; Kelsay 1988: 49).

This debate over the ownership of the human rights movement has continued, as evidenced at the 1993 Vienna World Conference on Human Rights, which barely reasserted the universality, indivisibility and interdependence of all human rights, allowing the caveat that religious dimensions must be taken into consideration (Vienna Declaration 1993; Artz 1990; Pollis 1996). According to Article 5 of the Vienna Declaration and Programme of Action, adopted by the 1993 World Conference on Human Rights (a major UN conference attended by almost all members of the Arab League):

> While the significance of national and regional particularities and various historical, cultural and religious backgrounds must be borne in mind, it is the duty of states, regardless of their political, economic and cultural systems, to promote and protect all human rights and fundamental freedoms.

Several Muslim commentators find the UDHR compatible with Islamic conceptions of human rights, pointing out that the subsequent 1981 Universal Islamic Declaration of Human Rights (UIDHR) bears close resemblance to the UDHR (Al-Ghunaimi 1997; Koraytem 2001). Other comparative studies of the

UDHR and Islamic human rights, such as the one by Tabandeh (1970), have settled on a reading that finds a general convergence of the two sets of principles. In the view of the prominent modern theologian al-Ghannouchi (1993), Muslims with a secure understanding of their religion recognize the correlation between Islamic human rights and international treaties. In some ways, the presentation of the debate over the universality of rights as a clash between religion and a modern secularized dogma of human rights is unhelpful and does little to enhance the cross-cultural and inclusive promise of human rights. Furthermore, the characterization of Islamic critiques as either irrelevant or an incomprehensible threat to civilized norms has further entrenched divisions, not only between the Muslim and non-Muslim worlds, but also within Muslim communities, where there is considerable debate about the role of international human rights principles (OIC 1998).

Universalism and Cultural Relativism

Questions persist over where 'universal' human rights come from, why they are priorities, and how they should be implemented in societies – although from the perspective of universalism a study of the philosophical foundations of human rights is unnecessary because it would not affect the validity of the existing consensus (Donnelly 2003). Attempts to unravel the nature of human rights and their implications become entangled in the traditions of diverse constituencies and competing goals. There is no agreement on whether human rights are derived from divine authority, natural law, or considerations concerning human nature. No single theory of human rights emerges because political scientists, philosophers, historians, international relations experts, politicians, philosophers, lawyers, theologians and anthropologists dispute the foundations and rationale for rights. According to the formulation of human rights in international agreements, human rights are those rights that are inherent in our nature, without which we cannot live as human beings. Thus, 'universal' principles based on a constant human dignity, need and interests can be enforced across borders without distinction – covering a tribesman in Kenya, a slum dweller in Delhi, a gypsy in Slovakia, or a city dweller in Manhattan, New York. Thus, the right to housing and security of tenure are common aspirations that human rights must unequivocally address for all people. It is also a non-discriminatory approach, which extends rights to all people at all times. Human rights emerge as a global modernist secular ideology capable of resisting the deleterious effects of wasteful, injurious and discriminatory practices by setting out common goals.

International human rights are needed, but where they are manifested top-down, ahistorically and in isolation from their social, political, and economic milieus, they ignore the lived experience and expectations of those outside the

'Western' consciousness (Pollis and Schwaeb 1979: 17). A range of countries, particularly those in Latin America, the Muslim world and East Asia, proffer cultural relativist arguments against a variety of human rights hypotheses. The term 'cultural relativism' is derived mostly from debates amongst anthropologists (who consider human nature as biological as well as social) and moral philosophers (who often denounce hierarchies and essentialism). No international human rights convention recognizes cultural relativism as a defence for not implementing human rights. However cultural values, social institutions and moral attitudes – from 'Asian values' (as the critique is called) to the African collective rights approach – reflect significant challenges from many parts of the world to the simplified notion of human rights, demonstrating why universal rights are difficult to implement (Tilley 2000; Bell 1996). Affected persons rarely make cultural relativist arguments themselves. Instead, they are the work of governments, self-appointed spokespersons or theoreticians, some of whom may have hidden agendas. They may exaggerate differences or rely on a mythical, imagined and unchanging past. These include religious groupings who emphasize the primacy of God, community representatives who fear the erosion of their customary practices, and local NGOs who characterize human rights as Western imperialism or as part of an unfair world economic order. Other voices come from political authoritarians (or from the state) who think human rights will create anarchy and from group rights supporters who consider their collective rights to be inadequately addressed.

Although both universalist and cultural relativist approaches are highly developed and offered as mutually exclusive stances, effective human rights strategies work on the interplay of the two methodologies. Human rights need flexibility and dialogue to enhance cross-cultural validity. International human rights are premised on their universal cross-cultural appeal and the laying down of priorities and goals (Mayer 1994b). They incorporate a range of overlapping fundamental rights. Individual rights do seek to offer protection against powerful groups, dominant interests and state authorities (Ignatieff 2001). However, universalism as a crusade not only undermines the opportunity for equal participation of all peoples in the determination of human rights strategies but also retards the development of indigenous and workable responses to each society's human rights issues. At the same time, many cultural relativists assume that the sole determinant is culture, tradition or religion – conceived as static entities not amenable to rational arguments or needs – a stance which is open to manipulation (Donnelly 2003). A balanced human rights approach may be one based on an assumed consensus but willing to consider legitimate challenges. Some rights that are not injurious may be subject to reappraisal, but not others. It may be that the contest is not over the particular principle of human rights but over the form in which it is presented, or the procedure suggested for its implementation. The question arises as to who will evaluate practices that could be internally defensible but externally unjustifiable (Sloane 2001). In engaging with Islamic cultural relativist arguments, it is strategically important not to dismiss them outright but to consider the validity of the objection, the effect of the competing formulation and the potential for negotiation or reconciliation. Though human rights are constructed to 'trump' other arguments, they do not silence the variations in approach to human rights, as discussed here in the context of Islamic critiques.

Religion as a Source of Human Rights

Classical theorists in the West and the Muslim world have most often attributed human rights to a supernatural divine authority, but the modern human rights regime is secular. The absence of religion or God as one of the sources of the UDHR and later human rights treaties is implicitly a recognition of the equality of all religions or the deliberate steering away from all religious discourse. The problem for modern secular human rights theorists is that, like truth, the existence of God is neither verifiable nor 'interactive' to clarify divine intent. The Islamic conception of rights, however, conceives of rights and obligations as not merely between human beings in the temporal political sphere but in a vertical relationship with God. Weeramantry (1988: 116) argues that this dimension, in fact, makes Islamic human rights more effective because rendered in more absolute terms of 'how man discharges his duties towards God'. This notion is part of a more general relationship between religion and human rights for followers of other faiths, too (Witte 1996). That people of faith are no longer dismissed as acting merely out of compulsion or self-oppressive false consciousness is exemplified by the strong pro-faith Jewish and Christian feminist lobbies.

Most Muslim societies see religious and secular values competing or cohabiting. A dilemma for most human rights activists, whether atheist, agnostic or secular, has been how to deal with the body of classical/traditional ideas, which many view as a bundle of anachronistic religious patriarchal beliefs and practices. As Voll (1994: 289) notes, secularism has long been assumed to be an inherent part of the process of modernization – yet a human rights approach that denies religious values which are part of the everyday life of believers cannot be valid. The dominance of secularism, as the ideological embodiment of capitalism and modernism, precludes any liberal or nuanced understanding of Islam, let alone any constructive dialogue with it (Majid 2000). At the same time, Al-Braizat (2002) reminds us that we must beware of casting religion as the single explanatory variable, for Islam coexists with other cultures and systems. In contrast to this secular view of human rights, the 1981 UIDHR repeatedly limits rights by reference to 'the Law'. The UIDHR clarifies that the term 'Law' denotes the Shari'a: the totality of ordinances derived from the *Qur'an* and the

Sunna and any other laws that are deduced from these two sources by methods considered valid in Islamic jurisprudence. However, formulations of the Shari'a vary and may well be driven by top-down perspectives or unclear views (Ali 1999). The Cairo Declaration (Article 25) states that 'the Islamic Shari'a is the only source of reference for the explanation or clarification of any of the articles of this Declaration'. Linked to this is a movement, which has gathered momentum, for discovering authentic Islamic human rights principles.

The evaluation of Islam's relationship with universal human rights conceptions may be conveniently divided into four major premises or methodologies. The dominant Western approach of those such as Mayer (1999a) takes a universalist stance, favouring an international human rights approach and critique with politicized and conservative readings of Islamic human rights as undermining international human rights. The opposite standpoint is taken by Weeramantry (1988) and, with greater fervour, by the Islamists and revivalists. They argue that Islam not only invented human and gender rights more than fourteen hundred years ago but still provides a wholesome and superior human rights protection regime. From this perspective the difficulty lies with the West's unwillingness to recognize the different form of Islamic human rights.

Cultural relativists such as Strawson (1997), without endorsing the Islamist positions, are concerned about the 'superior location' of Western intellectual judgement and question the research methodology underpinning universalism, which leads to value judgements about an essentialized Western-constructed Islam. Modernists, among whom An-Naim (1990) is a striking and successful example, recognize the differences between Islam and universal human rights norms, but explore reconciliation strategies, in their belief that Islam is a potentially responsive system, or in any case one that cannot be disregarded. All of these approaches are evident in debates over land and housing rights, with universalists seeking compliance with international standards, cultural relativists pursuing distinctive customary, cultural or religious norms or standards, and postcolonialists primarily concerned about origins and methodologies. However, the final approach presented here is that of reconciliation, arguing that while land rights can be evaluated through international standards, authenticated and durable proposals or solutions may emerge out of an exploration of Islamic conceptions of land rights. However, rather than merely looking at the approaches, it will be useful to evaluate the nature and scope of property rights as seen through Islamic declarations on human rights.

Islamic Human Rights and Land Rights

Property, land and housing rights are, at one level, part of *mu'amalat* or social transactions, amenable to the Islamic concept of public interest or *maslaha* and development through *ijtihad*. However, as discussed in earlier chapters, they also form part of the religious domain since land, in Islamic theory, belongs to God. Land ownership and land rights, moreover, have to be exercised within the ethical and economic framework of Islamic law. The 1981 UIDHR reflects this when it states in its preface that: 'it is unfortunate that human rights are being trampled upon with impunity in many countries of the world, including some Muslim countries. Such violations are a matter of serious concern and are arousing the conscience of more and more people throughout the world.' It emphasizes that 'human rights in Islam are an integral part of the overall Islamic order and it is obligatory on all Muslim governments and organs of society to implement them in letter and in spirit within the framework of that order'. It further adds that 'human rights in Islam are firmly rooted in the belief that God, and God alone, is the Law Giver and the Source of all human rights. Due to their Divine origin, no ruler, government, assembly or authority can curtail or violate in any way the human rights conferred by God, nor can they be surrendered'. Land rights in Muslim countries cannot be fully secularized as the formulation of doctrines such as access to land or security of tenure are fashioned within the framework of obligations not only to fellow human beings but also to God. These approaches have enriched the Islamic property rights regimes but, equally, can restrict land rights.

The 1981 UIDHR adopted by the Islamic Council of Europe identifies property and other rights through Islamic religious sources. In Article 16 it states that 'No property may be expropriated except in the public interest and on payment of fair and adequate compensation.' It quotes the *Qur'an* (2: 188) as well as *hadith* from the classical compilers Bukhari, Muslim and Tirmidhi. The UIDHR is strong in casting the right to housing as a right to a social security creating obligation not only for the state but for the community. Article 18, deriving authority from the *Qur'an* (33: 6), states that:

> Every person has the right to food, shelter, clothing, education and medical care consistent with the resources of the community. This obligation of the community extends in particular to all individuals who cannot take care of themselves due to some temporary or permanent disability.

Offering further *Qur'anic* references, the UIDHR situates the right to property within an Islamic economic order on the basis that 'all persons are entitled to the full benefits of nature and all its resources. These are blessings bestowed by God for the benefit of mankind as a whole' (Article 15). In the same Article, it notes that 'every person is entitled to own property individually or in association with others' but adds that 'state ownership of certain economic resources in the public interest is legitimate'.

The 1990 Cairo Declaration on Human Rights in Islam adopted by the OIC (Rishmawi 1998) also proclaims the right to property, in Article 15:

> (a) Everyone shall have the right to own property acquired in a legitimate way, and shall be entitled to the rights of ownership without prejudice to oneself, others or the society in general. Expropriation is not permissible except for requirements of public interest and upon payment of prompt and fair compensation.
>
> (b) Confiscation and seizure of property is prohibited except for a necessity dictated by law.

Though this provision is general, it contains several important rights. It speaks not only of the right to own property and the rights of ownership, but of protection from arbitrary state action. It does not use the current terminology of access to land or secure tenure but stresses both the rule of law and the Islamic concept of public interest discussed in previous chapters, which clearly limit confiscation or expropriation. The right to live in security for one's self, dependants and property as well as privacy with regard to enjoying one's property is provided in Article 18. This provision further states:

> A private residence is inviolable in all cases. It will not be entered without permission from its inhabitants or in any unlawful manner, nor shall it be demolished or confiscated and its dwellers evicted.

Article 17 of the Cairo Declaration, echoing the UIDHR, notes: 'The state shall ensure the right of the individual to a decent living which will enable him to meet all his requirements and those of his dependants, including food, clothing, housing, education, medical care and all other basic needs.'

As alternative human rights frameworks, the problem is that neither the UIDHR nor the Cairo Declaration bind states, provide monitoring options, or offer adequate mechanisms for the vindication of even the modestly enumerated rights. Moreover, the authenticity and credibility of these documents have been challenged by sections of civil society over questionable drafting methodology and inadequate consultative processes in their preparation. It is argued that, for the most part, conservative and reactionary views are packaged as settled readings of sacred texts, as if oblivious to the vibrant internal Islamic discourses on human rights (Mayer 1994). However, property rights declared by these documents are less of a problem as compared to other rights, though it may well be possible to find, through a more dynamic or liberal methodology, fuller Islamic property, housing and land rights conceptions.

There appear to be several points of divergence in the classical Islamic conception of rights and modern human rights expectations. However, this is not surprising given the period in which classical Islamic law evolved and the recent acceleration of modern human rights approaches (Bielefeldt 1995). The fundamental question is one of compatibility. As discussed above, this is an ongoing debate over the ownership, authenticity and flexibility of the international rights regime. Some have commented that the role of religion must not be overstated, or that at any rate it must not be considered as static or unresponsive to modern-day challenges (An-Naim 2004). Comparative studies of Islamic and international human rights regimes often find less of a conflict with respect to land, housing and property rights (Baderin 2003; Berween 2001). Mayer (1999a: 45) notes 'in contrast to other Shari'a doctrines which remained idealistic without implementation mechanisms the single exception of the area of property rights, where Shari'a did provide remedies for the individuals wrongly deprived of property by official action'. This is not surprising because Islam has a strong socio-economic rights ethos and promotes equitable distribution of resources (Chapra 1970). Mayer points out that

> not a single Muslim country has entered any Islamic reservations to the International Convention on Economic, Social, and Cultural Rights. Indeed, in ratifying this convention Egypt asserted that these rights presented no conflicts with the Shari'a, Islamic law. That is, the assumption seems to be that Islam and economic, social, and cultural rights are complementary. (1999b: 177)

The right to basic necessities of life is an important feature of Islamic human rights principles. The state and the community have an enhanced welfare role in securing land rights. As outlined before, the notion that land belongs to God and that philanthropy is an act of piety towards God helps concretize these rights. A study of the UIDHR, the Cairo Declaration and, in the Arab states, the revised Arab Charter on Human Rights (2004), which is discussed in more detail below, substantiates the conclusion that land rights under Islamic principles broadly correspond to international standards, although there are differences in the pursuit of civil and political rights. The Islamic cultural relativist argument resurfaces in how these rights are to be realized, but it is not fundamental to the recognition of land, property and housing rights in Islamic societies.

Islamic human rights principles with relation to land rights are a manifestation of Islamic conceptions of property and land, its economic principles, its legal structures and processes, and the distinctive land tenure arrangements. Unfortunately, very little systematic study of Islamic land rights as part of an international human rights framework has been carried out. This is partly because international land rights are often neglected but equally because the debate over Islam and human rights has been dominated by other matters such as the treatment of women and minorities, its criminal laws, its compatibility with democracy, and the Islamic perspectives on 'holy war' (*jihad*) and terrorism. Assumptions about the general incompatibility of Islam and human rights have been extended to the conjecture that Islamic notions with respect to land rights must be deficient. There is no doubt, as argued in the preceding chapter, that Islamic land rights are distinctive and varied. However, there is also no doubt that there exists a sophisticated and alternative human rights framework for realizing property, land and housing rights. The Islamic human rights paradigm, as seen from the above declarations despite their traditionalist flavour, does prioritize land and property rights, mostly in ways corresponding to international formulations. There are some divergences and departures, but given the dynamic and evolving nature of Islamic human rights interpretation, further studies or *ijtihad* may yield further encouraging results.

Islamic Rights for Women, Children, Minorities and Migrants

Though extensive land rights are generally guaranteed under Islamic human rights principles, their extension to particular categories such as women, minorities, children and migrants have been matters of concern. An issue frequently brought to the attention of the UN-HABITAT governing council is that well-known position of Muslim states refusing to allow words in resolutions that give women equal land rights: what they allow is equal access to land. Women's rights to acquisition, management, administration, enjoyment and disposition of property have been an increasing component in efforts to mainstream gender rights. Non-discrimination against women in general, and particularly with respect to property, land and housing rights, is dealt with by the UDHR, ICESCR, ICCPR and other treaties. CEDAW (1979) calls for equal rights in owning and administering property without discrimination (Article 15) and 'equal treatment in land and agrarian reform' (Article 14 (2) (g)). Article 14.2 (h) forbids discrimination against women in their enjoyment of 'adequate living conditions, particularly in relation to housing'. CEDAW's approach to women's access to property is wide-ranging and includes non-discrimination in Article 1, as well as the proactive clauses in Article 13 pointing to women's equal rights to credit, and access to property for rural women. CEDAW provides that within the family both spouses have equal rights in the 'ownership, acquisition, management, administration, enjoyment and disposition of property' (Article 16).

The above property rights have been elaborated by various human rights bodies and specialist agencies such as the CEDAW committee and the UNCHS. The latter, through its Resolution 19/16 on Women's Role and Rights in Human Settlements Development and Slum Upgrading (9 May 2003) is also reflected in UN-HABITAT's gender-mainstreaming approach to land and housing rights. These efforts at standard setting emerge from other sources such as the UN General Assembly on rural women (Resolutions 48/109 (1994), 50/165 (1996), 52/93 (1998)), the UN Commission on Human Rights (Resolutions 2000/13, 2001/34, 2002/49 and 2003/22 on Women's Equal Ownership of, Access to and Control Over Land and the Equal Rights to Own Property and to Adequate Housing); the UN Sub-Commission on the Promotion and Protection of Human Rights (Resolutions 1997/19 and 1998/15 on 'Women and the Right to Land, Property and Adequate Housing') and the UN

Commission on the Status of Women (Resolution 42/1 on 'Human Rights and Land Rights Discrimination' (1998)). International conferences have also highlighted the need to address women's property rights. The 1995 Beijing Platform for Action pointed to legislative and administrative reforms to ensure gender equality in access to land, including inheritance and ownership rights (paragraph 61 (b)). Principle 20 of the 1992 Rio Declaration emphasizes women's 'vital role in environmental management and development', and towards 'sustainable development'. The right to participation in land management is implicit in the Convention on Biological Diversity (paragraph 13) signed by 150 government leaders at the 1992 Rio Earth Summit, as it is in the 1994 Convention to Combat Desertification (Articles 5, 10 and 19). Similarly, the 1996 Rome World Food Summit Plan of Action affirms the objective of ensuring gender equality and women's empowerment (Objective 1.3) and 'equal access to and control over productive resources including credit, land and water'.

A widely discussed problem regarding the implementation of CEDAW has been the extensive reservations (allowing them to opt out of specific provisions) entered by Muslim states (Artz 1990: 218–21). Of the thirty-odd OIC states which have ratified the convention (just over half the OIC members), the treaty reservations entered by a dozen states in the name of Islamic principles have severely restricted the application of CEDAW provisions. In particular, caveats have been directed against Article 16 which stipulates equality of the sexes in marriage and family matters (Khaliq 1995). Mayer (1999b: 106), like others, rightly concludes that evolving political contingencies and not Islamic beliefs determine most Muslim states' CEDAW reservations. Several NGOs in the Muslim world have called for the reservations to be lifted (CIHRS 1996). Muslim women – unmarried, married, divorced or widowed – have extensive rights to property under Islamic law and human rights. They possess independent legal, economic and spiritual identity, supported by Qur'anic injunctions which facilitate access to land. The UIDHR's provisions on property and land rights generally support the rights of women. For example, Article 6 refers to 'everyone', clarified to include 'both the male and female sexes', but equal rights are not explicit and the UIDHR speaks only of 'impermissible discrimination' (Article 3) and refers to 'rights of married women' (Article 20), seemingly excluding others (Halim 1994: 416). As will be argued in detail in the following chapters, there are particular difficulties in terms of both fixed Islamic inheritance rules and the prevalence of patriarchal or gender-deprecating practices in the name of Islam, but it is clearly possible to develop a far more gender-egalitarian Islamic approach to women's property rights through *ijtihad*.

Children's access to land and housing is often ignored on the assumption that the family will provide housing security and that property rights are almost exclusively an adult concern. The gap in the study of children's rights to land is particularly true in the context of Muslim countries. However, conflict, displacement and epidemics such as HIV/AIDS (Lim 2003), not just orphanhood and broken families, are some of the situations where the assumed protective layer of family support and housing evaporates. This is equally true of conditions for children in Muslim countries. The UN Sub-Commission on the Promotion and Protection of Human Rights in its Resolution 1994/8 on 'Children and the Right to Adequate Housing', identified the serious nature and extent of the problem, with ever-growing numbers of children living on the streets and in slums.

The 1989 Convention on the Rights of the Child is the most widely ratified human rights treaty (only the United States of America and Somalia have not ratified it). For several Muslim governments which participated in the drafting of the CRC it was to be an entry point into the international human rights system (Johnson 1992: 133; LeBlanc 1995: 34). In signing up to the CRC, the Muslim states were in fact recognizing civil and political rights alongside socio-economic and cultural rights rejected in other treaties. At least twenty Muslim countries who had signed neither the ICCPR nor the ICESCR became parties to the CRC. With the endorsement of several child-centred guarantees the child was privileged over the adult, since the formal acknowledgement of corresponding rights for adults had often been withheld. Muslim countries also registered a number of reservations or declarations, generally in the name of Islam, while signing up to the CRC (Schabas 1997: 79–112). However, a majority among them entered no reservations at all. Muslim responses have been neither unified nor consistent with regard to specific provisions.

The CRC calls for non-interference with the child's 'privacy, family, home or correspondence' in Article 16 (1), alongside support in the provision of nutrition, clothing and housing' in Article 27 (3). This has to been seen in the context of the guiding CRC principles: the right to non-discrimination (Article 2); the right of the child to have his/her best interests as a primary consideration (Article 3); the right to life; the right to survival and development (Article 6); and the right to have his/her views respected (Article 12) (see Sait 2003: 57–8). Van Bueren argues that the strength of the Convention lies in 'promoting an ethos of both cultural plurality and universalism.... It does not want to promote a single fixed universal image of childhood. Yet it does want to promote universal opportunities for children' (van Bueren 1995: 19; Sait 2004). The pragmatic way to achieve normative consensus, An-Naim (1994: 62–81) argues, is through procedural universality where the dynamic interplay between changing Islamic folk models and international standards is heard through internal discourse and cross-cultural dialogue. Minimum safeguards, he argues further, protect the best interest of the child from the abuse of the cultural trump card.

The Cairo Declaration (in Article 7) deals with the rights of the child thus:

> As from the moment of birth, every child has rights due from the parents, society and the state to be accorded proper nursing, education and material, hygienic and moral care. Both the foetus and the mother must be protected and accorded special care.

The UIDHR, too, contains several references to child rights and responsibilities, including inheritance, but does not specifically deal with access to land. However, there are extensive Islamic property rights of orphans and to a lesser degree grandchildren, which will be discussed in the next chapter. The *Qur'an* is replete with references such as 'Do not tamper with the property of orphans, but strive to improve their lot until they reach maturity' (*Qur'an* 6: 152). As Sait (2000) argues, after pointing out the substantial potential in Islamic sources for enhancing child rights: 'Without an endeavour to engage with internal Islamic discourses, the battle for international child rights standards under the CRC for Muslim children, or those living under Muslim laws, stands seriously compromised.'

Generally, the international community has struggled to define the concept of minorities, but it is agreed that they include national, ethnic, religious and linguistic minorities (Thornberry 1993). The international human rights standards relating to the land rights of minorities are extensive, following from the general principle of non-discrimination which is a feature of all instruments. This is elaborated by the 1965 International Convention on the Elimination of all Forms of Racial Discrimination (CERD), which in Article 5 enshrines the rights of minorities to inherit and own property as well as the right to housing. In particular, the Economic and Social Council (ECOSOC) (Resolution 2000/22) and the UN Commission on Human Rights (Resolutions 1998/21, 1999/21, 2000/14, 2001/10, 2002/15 and 2002/1, 2002/15) have laid considerable emphasis on the land rights of indigenous people. These emerge more fully as binding obligations in the Convention (No. 169) concerning Indigenous and Tribal Peoples in Independent Countries.

One of the general concerns about a faith-based ideology such as Islam is the rights of minorities, whether they are non-Muslims or minority Muslim groups within dominant Islamic areas (Bielefeldt 1995; An-Naim 1990; Mayer 1999a). This is particularly relevant because minority status not only creates marginality but can add further risks to the status of women, children, displaced or disabled people, or individuals of particular sexual orientation. Forced evictions are more likely to target the minority, particularly the poor who are often voiceless. Yet many Muslim writers such as Doi (1997: 246) refer to non-Muslim minorities or *dhimmis* (the 'protected' or 'covenanted' people) who live in an Islamic state as 'guaranteed irrevocable protection of their life, property and honour exactly like that of a Muslim'. The UIDHR and the Cairo Declaration point to Islam as the sole validating source, trumping other human rights authorities. At the same time, the UIDHR relies on several Qur'anic principles such as verses 2: 256; 5: 42–3 and 5: 47, to declare in Article 10, in relation to minority rights:

> a) The Qur'anic principle 'There is no compulsion in religion' shall govern the religious rights of non-Muslim minorities.
>
> b) In a Muslim country religious minorities shall have the choice to be governed in respect of their civil and personal matters by Islamic Law, or by their own laws.

The recognition of religious pluralism within Islam is traced back to the Prophet when he established the first Islamic state in Medina on the basis of the Covenant of Medina, a Jewish–Muslim agreement, which extended to religious minorities the rights that are guaranteed to them in the *Qur'an*. Non-Muslims are entitled to acquire, enjoy, manage and alienate land just as Muslims, but in classical times they had a higher tax to pay, *jizya,* in lieu of both their exemption from military duty and *zakat* (Hamidullah 1997: paragraph 210). However, while the tolerance and rights of non-Muslim minorities under Muslim rule is widely acknowledged by most historians, the religious zeal of particular individuals and communities has had an adverse impact on access to full land rights of non-Muslims and Muslim minorities in some contexts. But, from Palestine, where Christians possess equal property rights, to Malaysia, where Christians, Buddhists and Hindus are all equal citizens of the country, there are sterling examples of equal rights in Muslim societies. Nevertheless, a clearer reading of Islamic law could pave the way for enhanced minority rights to land, property and housing.

Migrants and the displaced are among those most defenceless against arbitrary deprivation of property, forced evictions or exclusion from access to housing. Refugees are those fleeing persecution on the grounds of race, religion, nationality, political opinion or social group (Goodwin-Gill 1996). In some countries, they are 'warehoused' with limited rights in camps that turn out to be almost permanent. Their situation is particularly precarious in countries where they are defined as 'illegal immigrants' and perceived as threats to the security, stability, culture or economic well-being of the host country, leading to their destitution (Nicholson and Twomey 1999). Article 21 of the 1951 Convention relating to the Status of Refugees posits treatment regarding access to housing which is as favourable as possible. Article 13 calls for rights 'as regards the acquisition of movable and immovable property and other rights pertaining thereto, and to leases and other contracts relating to movable and immovable property'. Equitable housing, land and property rights, although not dealt with in the CSR, are a crucial component of the search for 'durable solutions' such as voluntary return, integration within the host state or relocation in a third country. Indeed, land, housing and property rights in post-conflict situations are an integral part of reconstruction and reconciliation.

The CSR, which has about 140 state ratifications, has been controversial for Muslim states. This is because – as with United Nations High Commissioner for Refugees (UNHCR) operations – it excludes the Palestinian refugees on the premise that they are being afforded protection by another agency, although this is no longer the case (Takkenberg 1998). The United Nations Relief and Works Agency for Palestinian Refugees in the Near East (UNRWA) provides some humanitarian assistance but not protection (Sait 2002). As a consequence several Arab states such as Jordan, Syria, Lebanon, Iraq, Kuwait, Libya, Qatar, Saudi Arabia and the United Arab Emirates have not signed the Convention. The Casablanca Protocol on the Treatment of Palestinians in the Arab states of 11 September 1965 and the 1992 Cairo Declaration on the Protection of Refugees and Displaced Persons in the Arab World are often cited by states, but these do not give rise to binding obligations.

The UNHCR has devoted considerable efforts towards housing and property restitution (UNHCR 2000) and the UN Sub-Commission on the Promotion and Protection of Human Rights has adopted several resolutions in the context of refugees and other displaced persons (1998/26, 2002/7, 2002/30). The UIDHR, the Cairo Declaration and the 2004 revised Arab Charter on Human Rights (see below) recognize asylum rights. The OIC and the UNHCR have, through a joint enterprise, sought recently to address the problems of refugees. A working paper for the OIC Ministerial Conference on Enhancing Refugee Protection in the Muslim World states that 'Islam laid the foundations for the institution of asylum in its public law through the holy Koran and the Tradition (*Sunna*)' and that 'respect for migrants and those seeking refuge has been a permanent feature of the Islamic faith' (OIC 2005).

The internally displaced persons (IDPs), not addressed in the 1951 Refugee Convention, are most at risk of losing their land rights (Leckie 2000). It is left to the UN Guiding Principles on Internal Displacement (1998) to offer rights and protection and Principle 21 recognizes the risks to the property of IDPs. However, the principles are influential but not binding. Article 23 of the 1981 UIDHR guarantees: 'No one shall be forced to leave the country of his residence, or be arbitrarily deported therefrom without recourse to due process of law'. This is also the approach of the 1990 Cairo Declaration of Human Rights in Article 12. Analogous to the problems faced by minorities, migrants generally face obstacles in accessing their rights, including land. Article 43 (1) of the 1990 International Convention on the Protection of the Rights of All Migrant Workers speaks of access to housing and protection against rent exploitation, of non-discrimination (Article 7) and of a generic right to property (Article 15). As with refugees and internally displaced persons, Islamic conceptions of justice and universal respect for all may well provide, as the OIC is suggesting, greater impetus towards land rights for migrants and other vulnerable sections of society.

Implementing Land, Property and Housing Rights

Muslim states are bound by human rights treaties, when and to the extent that they have been ratified. They also subscribe to international human rights standards simply by virtue of being members of the United Nations. In the preceding sections, reference has been made to the role of the UN organs as well as its specialist human rights agencies in promoting and protecting land, property and housing rights. These are 'soft law' principles adopted by the human rights bodies of the UN, including the UN Human Rights Commission. These range from the 1986 UN Declaration on Development to the 2000 UN Millennium Declaration leading to the Millennium Development Goals. An example is the 1996 Istanbul Declaration and the Habitat Agenda, which constitute the framework for realizing land and housing rights. Apart from providing international norms, the Habitat Agenda (see paragraph 61) also clarifies the obligations of states and stakeholders in achieving those objectives. For example, it creates obligations for governments to generate conditions in terms of which these objectives can realistically be reached.

Land, housing and property rights straddle civil and political rights (referred to as first generation rights because they are well developed), socio-economic rights (referred to as second generation rights), as well as collective rights (the emerging third generation of rights). Civil and political rights are predicated on principles such as fair and equal treatment, justice and political freedom, and protection from abuses of power. Both the right to property and non-interference (negated where there are expropriations or forced evictions) are civil and political property rights. Rights to property, housing and land are also subsumed within the socio-economic and cultural rights to an adequate standard of living and have to be read alongside the right to development, freedom from hunger and the rights to health and education. As such, land rights cannot be seen in isolation or in the abstract, but are part of the interdependent and indivisible human rights regime, where the fulfilment of land rights is dependent on the existence of a broad range of other rights.

The state has two types of obligations with respect to land rights. First, there are negative obligations: it is to abstain from interfering in the enjoyment of rights while at the same time recognizing and protecting them. Second, there are positive obligations: the duty to provide and protect land rights, which require state intervention. Some commentators take the view that socio-economic rights are not really 'rights' but merely aspirations, due to the lack of enforceable remedies, which can be found in relation to civil and political rights. However, as Higgins (1994: 100) points out, 'a right is just as much a right if its implementation requires positive steps rather than negative abstinence. Moreover, the concept of positive duties is increasingly becoming part and parcel of the normative requirement of civil and political rights.' The other popular differentiation to the effect that civil and political rights are cost-free while social rights necessitate spending is also disputed (Tomasevski 1994: 90). There is convergence between both negative and positive obligations with respect to various types of rights. Article 2 (1) of the ICESCR explains the nature and scope of obligations:

> Each State Party to the present Covenant undertakes to take steps, individually and through international assistance and cooperation, especially economic and technical, to the maximum of its available resources, with a view to achieving progressively the full realization of the rights recognized in the present Covenant by all appropriate means, including particularly the adoption of legislative measures.

This is similar to the UN Habitat Agenda (paragraph 61) which refers to the 'progressive realization of the right to adequate housing'. While, at first glance, land rights as socio-economic principles appear to be merely persuasive, to be achieved within limitations of resources and capacity, there are basic minimum thresholds and obligations of conduct. These flow from the 1987 Limburg Principles on the rights and obligations under the ICESCR and the 1998 Maastricht Guidelines on Violations of Economic, Social and Cultural Rights. The latter document points out that: 'Like civil and political rights, economic, social and cultural rights impose three different types of obligations on states: the obligations to respect, protect and fulfil. Failure to perform any one of these three obligations constitutes a violation of such rights.'

Human rights treaties relevant to land rights have created monitoring committees to supervise their compliance by states. Some, like the ICCPR, have an individual complaints system with respect to states that have agreed to it, but the international supervision of land, property and housing rights as part of the economic, social and cultural rights paradigm is based entirely on the reporting system. Under the ICESCR, the only compulsory obligation for states is to submit periodic reports indicating the extent of their compliance with the treaty provisions they have signed. Reporting is now an established feature of treaty-based human rights instruments: it goes far beyond the mere requirement for states to file reports and provides the basis of 'constructive dialogue' – discussion between states and the monitoring committee set up by the treaty – in the realization of those rights. As Alston (1992) puts it, state reporting is but a 'modest part of a far grander enterprise' – a continuing process that assists in bringing about domestic changes in human rights protection. The participation of Muslim states, who are members of the treaty, has produced a rich record of their progress in securing international land rights.

Despite the lack of direct enforcement capacity, the ICESCR Committee has developed a new range of its own monitoring procedures and practices. A most direct example of its innovations are days of 'General Discussions' involving NGOs and experts to deal with the obfuscated and imprecise nature of most of the rights it is to monitor (Alston 1991). The Committee has been able to come up with 'General Comments' such as the influential statements on housing rights and forced eviction (see for example ICESCR, General Comments 4 and 7). It has clarified the nature of States Parties' obligations under the Covenant, pointing out various obligations which are of immediate effect. It has also highlighted a minimum core of obligations incumbent on States Parties and the absence of satisfaction which would lead to a *prima facie* assumption that the state concerned is failing to discharge its obligations under the Covenant (Eide 1989: 68). The ICESCR has gone beyond looking for the existence of legislative, judicial, administrative or other measures and is seeking realistic results. Another feature of the work of the ICESCR Committee is its receptivity to NGO reports, which has led to its taking action on housing rights, for example with respect to mass evictions of squatters (Craven 1995: 72–3).

Implementation of human rights norms takes places at the international, regional and domestic levels. Given the spread of Muslim communities across the world, several regional human rights frameworks are implicated. As the Vienna Declaration and Programme of Action adopted by the World Conference on Human Rights (1993; paragraph 37) notes, such regional 'arrangements play a fundamental role in promoting and protecting human rights, although several Muslim countries, particularly in Asia, are located in parts of the globe without such standards and monitoring mechanisms' (Ghai 1998). The Inter-American Convention on Human Rights, ratified by over 25 countries, has extensive rights to property enumerated in Article 21, which since 1979 have been enforced by an Inter-American Human Rights Court. Similarly, the European Convention on Human Rights has a relatively well-developed property rights jurisprudence (Coban 2004), with the European Court of Human Rights enforcing Article 1 of Protocol 1 specifying the right to property. While the Inter-American and European Conventions are relevant for Muslim minorities living in their regions, Turkey is the only Muslim country to have signed the European Convention, making it subject to the jurisdiction of the European Court on Human Rights.

The 1981 African Charter on Human and Peoples' Rights deserves closer examination, since 10 of the 22 member states of the League of Arab States are also African, of which Algeria, the Comoros Islands, Djibouti, Egypt, Libya, Mauritania, Somalia, Sudan and Tunisia are party to the African Charter and bound by its provisions. The African Charter (which entered into force in 1986) represents a convergence of international standards and distinctive African experience and values (Welch and Meltzer 1984). In fact, the addition of 'People' in its title reflects an emphasis on socio-economic and cultural rights – collective rights as well as individual duties – arising out of cross-cultural perspectives and the diversity of the continent. Land is a highly significant matter in most parts of Africa, where there is still great dependence on agriculture. The legacy of colonialism and its impact on landholding patterns, erosion of the land rights of indigenous people, displacement due to civil war and conflict, rapid urbanization and environmental and health challenges are some of the land issues. Article 14 of the African Charter spells out a guaranteed right to property, which 'may only be encroached upon in the interest of public need or in the general interest of the community and in accordance with the provisions of appropriate laws'. The Charter also asserts the right to dispose of wealth freely and offers protection to the property of the dispossessed (Article 21). However, it makes no specific mention of the right to adequate housing.

While the distinctive approach of the African Charter to human rights has been debated, the biggest concern was an inadequate monitoring mechanism for implementation of Charter rights. The impact of the Charter on African human rights records, considered minimal until recently, was ascribed to limited political will and resources (Evans and Murray 2002) and a relatively weak compliance mechanism in the African Commission on Human and People's Rights, created under the Charter to supervise State Parties' compliance. However, the Constitutive Act of the African Union (AU), replacing the Organization of African Unity (OAU) in July 2002, specifically upgraded human rights, the promotion of the rule of law and good governance as priorities. This has received impetus from the African Court of Human and Peoples' Rights, created by a protocol to the African Charter, which came into force on 24 January 2004. This paves the way for greater enforcement of human rights at the regional level, and will have an impact on Muslim countries and communities in Africa, supplementing international human rights standards.

The League of Arab States have found consensus on a regional human rights treaty difficult to achieve. In the past, its language of human rights has been almost exclusively directed externally at the Israeli human rights violations against the Palestinians. The 1971 draft human rights treaty by a committee of experts was not well received and was reworked in 1983, but many states felt that the Cairo Declaration on Human Rights achieved the purpose, even though the Declaration was neither specific to Arab states nor binding. In 1994, the Arab League did adopt the Arab Charter on Human Rights amidst objections from seven states but ultimately only one country – Iraq – signed it. Since 2002, however, in coordination with the United Nations Office of the High Commissioner for Human Rights, the League has moved to modernize the Arab Charter on Human Rights. Comments and suggestions received from Arab states, with the participation of legal and human rights experts, have informed this process 'in line with international standards of human rights and remove any inconsistency therewith' (Amnesty 2004).

After several drafting sessions, the Standing Committee for Human Rights prepared a new draft Charter on Human Rights. The sixteenth meeting of the League of Arab States at Tunis on 22–23 May 2004 recognized the significance of human rights in politically imperative terms and adopted the revised Charter. The League did this in the context of highlighting the plight of Palestinians and the territorial integrity of Iraq, Syria, Sudan and Somalia. It initiated 'the process of reform and modernization in the Arab world, to keep pace with the rapid world changes, by consolidating the democratic practice'. In particular, it announced the adoption of the Revised Arab Human Rights Charter thus:

> [We] reaffirm our states' commitment to the humanitarian principles and the noble values of human rights in their comprehensive and interdependent dimensions, to the provisions of the various international conventions and charters, and to the Arab Human Rights Charter adopted by the Tunis Summit, as well as to the reinforcement of the freedom of expression, thought and belief and to the guarantee of the independence of the judiciary.

The Arab Charter on Human Rights has been ratified by a number of countries in the Arab world, including Tunisia, Morocco, Saudi Arabia and Palestine. The Charter in its preamble reaffirms

> the principles of the Charter of the United Nations, the Universal Declaration of Human Rights and the provisions of the two International Covenants on civil and political rights and on economic, social and cultural rights, and the Cairo Declaration on Human Rights in Islam.

Land and housing rights in the Arab Charter bear a striking resemblance to those in international human rights treaties and, despite criticisms of the scope of several provisions (Amnesty 2004; Human Rights First 2004; International Commission of Jurists 2003), the Charter's stipulations on land rights are not controversial. For example, in Article 38 the Charter emphasizes that

> Every person has the right to an adequate standard of living for himself and his family, that ensures their well-being and a decent life, including food, clothing, housing, services and the right to a healthy environment. The States' Parties shall take the necessary measures commensurate with their resources to guarantee these rights.

Article 21 establishes a person's right to be protected from 'unlawful interference with his privacy, family, home or correspondence'.

The mere elaboration of these rights is not sufficient, unless it is backed up by enhanced space for civil society, as well as greater judicial autonomy in protecting these rights. The NGOs in the region have played a significant role in promoting human rights and standard setting, for example through the Casablanca Declaration of the Arab Human Rights Movement (1999) and the Beirut Declaration on the Protection of Human Rights in the Arab World (2003). There is an opportunity for organizations such as the Economic and

Social Commission for Western Asia (ESCWA), established originally in 1973 but working with its expanded mandate in accordance with Economic and Social Council resolution 1985/69 of 26 July 1985, to stimulate further development and rights protection in the region. However, the legitimacy of human rights as a movement will be judged through their capacity to address the issues which people feel are priorities – from the Arab–Israeli dispute to the need for greater democratization and freedoms.

Conclusions

The relationship between Islamic and international human rights conceptions has often been cast as dichotomous and incompatible. Universalists fear that yielding to Islamic discourses could unravel the tentative and hard-fought consensus over human rights. Islamic cultural relativists debunk the notion of international human rights standards trumping faith-based human rights perspectives, and query both the legitimacy and agenda of the modern human rights movement. However, there is a vibrant internal debate in Muslim societies regarding the role of human rights and several efforts at reconciling the differences are evident. While international human rights may be taken to reflect the general aspirations of all people, it would be beneficial to engage with the range of Islamic voices in order to generate authentic and durable human rights implementation strategies. This is important since some of the Islamic dissent is largely rhetorical, and develops in response to the perception that the West seeks to impose its values on Muslim societies and produces negative stereotypes of Islam. In the long run, a cross-cultural dialogue over how to secure rights could help render the human rights movement more inclusive and effective. Secular human rights and religion should not be presented as mutually exclusive choices for people of faith. Instead, religious practice can provide a momentum towards human rights activism as people move from structures of oppression to strategies of liberation.

Given the classical period of the formulation of Islamic law, it is not surprising that there is some divergence from international human rights formulations on civil and political rights standards, but Islam has strong foundations in socio-economic rights. It is therefore not surprising, either, that all the major human rights documents – UIDHR, the Cairo Declaration and the Arab Charter – support extensive property rights, and that Islamic human rights with respect to land have the potential to enrich universal human rights implementation. However, there is, as yet, no broad consensus, and norms relating to land, property and housing rights are easier to establish than to implement or enforce. Islamic human rights documents such as the UIDHR and Cairo Declaration do not bind Muslim states, nor do they provide enforcement mechanisms. On the other hand, a number of Muslim countries have signed international human rights treaties providing clear principles relating to land, property and housing rights, and should be held to account, just like other states, over their obligations. These includes participation in the treaty-monitoring process, particularly through the timely submission of periodic reports. While some states have entered reservations with regard to provisions in several treaties, there are none specifically relating to land, property or housing rights.

States, while agreeing with land rights principles in general, appear to take a view that their obligations with respect to security of tenure and access to land are limited and incremental, and can be justified on the basis of limited resources. However, there are clearly basic principles such as non-discrimination, as well as equal access, which are part of minimum core obligations, some of which are immediate and evaluated on the basis of results rather than conduct. Muslim states, just like other states, need to work towards prioritizing and realizing these rights through legislative, administrative, judicial, policy and other measures. Islamic human rights conceive a proactive role for the state in realizing adequate standards of living, of which land rights are an important component. While the state bears primary responsibility with respect to realization of land rights, it is equally important to involve all stakeholders in the process. One of the reasons why land rights have faltered, in Muslim as in other countries, has been the lack of space for civil society to articulate its concerns or input into policy responses. A top-down, state-driven approach will not work as satisfactorily as a broader consultative and participatory initiative involving all sections and interests, especially in the face of problems such as forced evictions and discrimination against various vulnerable sections of society. There is also scope for improved facilitation of land rights through participation in regional development and human rights frameworks, particularly in sharing best practice. Regional bodies such as ESCWA have a significant role in the promotion, standard setting and protection of land rights in the Muslim world.

The one exceptional departure by Islamic human rights from international standards with respect to land, property and housing rights is with respect to women's equal rights to land, with equal access to land being the preferred language. However, as has been pointed out, Islamic land rights are extended to specific categories, including women as well as children, migrants and minorities. In the following two chapters the rights of women with respect to property within the Islamic framework are the focus of exploration, with attention to their apparently unequal position regarding inheritance. It will be argued that women's property rights should be addressed holistically, as part of a compensatory framework. It will also be argued that there is considerable scope for using *ijtihad* to elaborate on Islamic principles regarding women's access to land and security of tenure. For women and more generally, the Islamization of the human rights initiative could be seized upon as an opportunity to reopen and rework the human rights formulations through informed *ijtihad*, authenticated by Islamic jurisprudence. It may well turn out that human rights aspects of Islamic land rights principles offer a broader net of protection since these are not merely temporal rights but obligations owed to God. Likewise the Muslim welfare state, acting in the public interest and carrying out faith-based principles, is mandated to work towards achieving equitable distribution of wealth and rights for all.

5

Inheritance Laws and Systems

> Any person contemplating death and considering the future distribution of his or her property will place in the balance a whole range of factors, which will be specific to his or her personal, family and social circumstances. . . . In Muslim societies, a person's ability to make such calculations is frustrated, in theory, by the compulsory Islamic inheritance rules that impose substantial constraints upon the freedom of a person ... to determine the devolution of his property. (Powers 1999: 1167)

Inheritance is often treated as marginal to general debates and policy formation concerning land rights, security of tenure and land reform. However, inheritance is one of the commonest ways of acquiring land or access to land, particularly in the Muslim world. In Muslim societies generally, irrespective of the specific faith of the Muslims concerned, inheritance rules are derived from religious sources for the division of an individual's property upon death. Islamic inheritance rules are deeply embedded in popular consciousness and a source of pride because of their particularly close association with the *Qur'an*, surpassing in this perhaps any other area of law. The divinely revealed guidance (*Qur'an* 2: 180, 2: 240, 4: 7-9, 4: 11, 4: 12, 4: 19–33, 4: 176 and 5: 105–8) on inheritance is amongst the most detailed areas of Islamic law. This field of law has developed through interpretation by the various schools of Islamic jurisprudence over centuries, both Sunni and Shi'a. While modern reforms and changes have influenced several fields of Islamic law, the structure determining inheritance has been one of the enduring legacies of classical Islamic law or the Shari'a.

Under Islamic law, specific fractional shares of the estate are distributed – after payment of debts and legacies – to certain defined heirs, 'sharers', sons, daughters, a father, a mother or spouse and, in the absence of children, siblings, according to compulsory rules derived from Qur'anic verses. This framework is remarkably inclusive in that a large number of family members may inherit property. The rules are in the main rigorously implemented by the family and community, and upheld by the state. A further well-known feature of the rules concerning fixed shares is that women have specific rights, but a woman will always receive a half share of that which a man would receive in a similar situation. Inheritance law often lies at the heart of discussions about gender equality and women's property rights. The focus on inheritance is perhaps understandable since women's inheritance rights appear deficient, at first sight at least and from the Western perspective. The association between women and inheritance law may also derive in part from its modern discursive location in the wider field of personal status and family law.

Beyond the simple differentiation between men and women, there are both benefits and disadvantages of the fixed share system, which are a matter of contemporary debate and in some instances proposals for legal reform. In practice, however, inheritance systems, although guided by religious norms, are shaped by the interplay of competing, alternative and overlapping legal and cultural norms. The application of these formal inheritance rules must be understood from a broader socio-cultural and economic perspective and within wider inheritance systems of practice. These include post-inheritance adjustment practices, such as consolidation and renunciation of inheritance rights, which have particular pertinence to the power and status of women. Demystifying the complex dynamics of Islamic inheritance rules and practice may reveal important information for the implementation of strategies designed to enhance security of tenure. Certainly the interplay between competing legal and cultural norms is evident when women's rights are concerned.

Nature of Islamic Inheritance Laws

Islamic inheritance rules are not merely a set of abstract rules. These inheritance principles are intended to facilitate distinctive Islamic conceptions of property, family, community, empowerment and justice. It is in this context that Islamic inheritance systems have to be appreciated and implemented to meet their divine objectives in faith-based societies. The formal inheritance rules have several distinctive features. First, they are fairly rigid in terms of predetermined shares, but at the same time the system has some flexibility through bequests and legitimate estate planning. Second, Muslims, like their non-Muslim counterparts, can choose to make gifts that will take effect when they die by means of a will (*wasaya*). However, all such gifts are restricted to a total of one-third of an individual's estate, with the remaining two-thirds devolving according to the compulsory inheritance rules. Third, the scheme of mandatory fixed shares is remarkably inclusive, since estates are distributed across a wide range of immediate, near and distant relatives – depending on the closeness of kinship in relation to the deceased. Finally, legitimate claimants cannot be disinherited, or their shares altered, by means of a will or other methods.

Far from invoking a set of arbitrary proportions for property division, the Islamic inheritance rules seek to support a conscious socio-economic religious ideology. They ensure that a range of family members are able to access property, thereby reflecting the need to maintain cohesiveness of the extended as opposed to the immediate family. Moreover, it ensures that legal entitlements to property are not conditional on the vagaries of relationships but rather can be asserted as rights which cannot be withdrawn. Despite the apparent fixity of rules, there are also a set of pragmatic principles which ensure that the rules function within the wider practical context of social welfare and effective use of property – which we refer to as Islamic inheritance 'systems'. Finally, the inheritance rules have to be read alongside the bequest provision in the *Qur'an* and the institution of the *waqf* which encourage Muslims, as an act of piety, to provide for needy and poor relatives.

A closer reading of the Islamic inheritance scheme, when considered beside other Islamic institutions such as *waqf* and *zakat*, shows that 'the institution of inheritance plays a major role in providing distributive justice' (Sahibzada 1997). Ferchiou (1985, quoted in Cotula 2002) found in a study of Tunisian villages that inheritance accounted for over 70 per cent of land acquisitions. Such is the impact of the Islamic inheritance principles on social structures that Issawi notes this was one of the major factors frustrating 'the development of a strong bourgeoisie which could generate the equivalent of European capitalism' (Issawi 1984: 32). Feudalism, which prevailed in many Islamic societies, was customary and not religious in its origins. Although there is no ceiling on the quantum of property an individual could acquire through legitimate means, the distributive aspect of the rules also supports another facet of Islamic property law, namely the injunction against hoarding and excessive accumulation of wealth in the hands of one individual.

Adherence to inheritance rules is not only symbolically important but also a serious matter of religious ethics and consequences, as exemplified by the Qur'anic verses which stipulate that those who appropriate the property of orphans face hellfire (*Qur'an* 4: 10). The Islamic inheritance principles emerge from the dualism of the concept of Islamic property. Property ownership is both a legitimate individual right and at the same time accountable to God and to be used and transferred on the basis of Islamic principles. Thus property is a part of personal law but it also serves several purposes which are public or communitarian in nature. A whole range of actors, from politicians to legal officials to ordinary men and women on the street, are implicated in ensuring the integrity and dynamism of the Islamic inheritance system.

Key Features of Islamic Legal Rules of Inheritance

Unlike many other legal systems, *mirath* (the Islamic law of succession) makes no distinction between different kinds of property. It is immaterial whether property is real (land) or personal, movable or immovable; *mirath* covers all assets. However, as with every other aspect of Islamic property law, this legal stance must be read against the fundamental principle that ultimate ownership of property lies with God. Individual property rights are always limited and this is particularly the case with respect to land, which is the most readily apparent gift from God. This fundamental principle gave rise to the distinction between two classifications of landholding: *mulk/milk* and *miri*. Land held in full ownership (*mulk/milk*) is inherited through the Islamic law of succession. The right of possession (*miri*) in state land can also be inherited but, as discussed in the previous chapter, it is regarded traditionally as outside the domain of the compulsory succession rules of Islamic law (Shari'a). It is a distinction that has helped to shape social practices regarding inheritance in some Muslim societies.

Within the Islamic framework, the fixed shares serve as a reminder that all property is ultimately owned by God and must, therefore, be divided according to the divine formula. Given the wide range of beneficiaries that the Islamic inheritance system seeks to cater for through a sophisticated balancing process, the results can turn out to be hairsplitting permutations and combinations varying according to a given scenario. Yet, as Rosen indicates, writing in the context of rural village life in Morocco, the general principles are widely known:

> Everyone knows the Tradition that has the Prophet saying that knowledge of the laws of inheritance constitutes half of all useful knowledge in the world. And everyone in Morocco, however well or poorly educated, has a firm grasp of the essentials of inheritance law .... (Rosen 2000: 89–90)

In relatively simple cases, relating to Sunni Muslims, the estate will be shared according to the compulsory rules between the deceased's parents or parent, husband or wife, and children. A surviving parent will receive one-sixth of the estate, the surviving spouse either one-eighth (a wife) or one quarter (a husband), with the balance shared between the surviving children and the sons receiving twice the share of the daughters. Where the deceased has no sons and only one daughter, she will receive one-half of the estate. If there are no sons but two or more daughters, they will share two-thirds of the estate. The residue of the estate in this case will pass to the closest surviving male agnate (*asaba*), the deceased's father, brothers, uncles, cousins or more distant male relative (Nasir 2002: 207–17). If the deceased has no children, a wife will receive one-quarter of her husband's estate, while a husband will receive one-half of his wife's estate.

Where the deceased dies with no descendants or siblings and the parents are the only heirs, the mother will receive one-third of the estate. The father will receive the remainder of the estate as the nearest male relative. However, the mother's share is reduced to one-sixth where the deceased has no children, but has siblings.

There are many combinations of surviving relations of the deceased that can arise. Every case is not dealt with directly in the Qur'anic verses. It is on matters where the *Qur'an* gives no direct instruction that Sunni and Shi'a have established different methods for the allocation of shares. While it is not intended here to discuss the minor variations that exist between the various schools of jurisprudence within the Sunni or Shi'a sects, there are some basic differences. If, for instance, a man dies leaving a wife and both his parents, the Sunni scheme of shares will give one-quarter of the estate to the wife, one-third to the mother and the remainder (five-twelfths) to the father as the nearest male relative. Under the Shi'a system of allocation, the wife would receive one-quarter of the estate, but the remainder would be divided between the mother (one-third) and the father (two-thirds). In other words, the mother will receive one-quarter of the original estate and the father will receive half of the original estate.

Defining the precise rights of siblings has also proved to be difficult, for the *Qur'an* only directly mentions siblings as heirs where no children exist. Again, Sunni and Shi'a have approached the matter differently, particularly where the deceased leaves a daughter but not a son. For example, if a man dies leaving a wife, one daughter and a brother, according to the Qur'anic verses the daughter should receive one-half and the wife one-eighth. However, there is no clear instruction as to the destination of the surplus. Under Sunni principles the remaining three-eighths of the estate will go the nearest male agnate, namely the brother. However, Shi'as would allocate the surplus to the daughter.

There are instances where an application of the compulsory rules gives rise not to a surplus that needs to be allocated, but a deficit. In other words, the estate will be insufficient to provide the prescribed shares. Such a problem would arise if a man died leaving both his parents alive, as well as a wife and two daughters. Each of his parents would be entitled to one-sixth of his estate (one-third in total), his daughters would be entitled to two-thirds of the estate to share between them, but his wife would also be entitled to one-eighth of the estate. Within the Shi'a legal code, the wife would be paid first and the remainder of the estate divided in the appropriate shares between the parents and the daughters. The Sunni schools of jurisprudence, on the other hand, solve the difficulty by reducing all the shares proportionately. (Given these complexities, it is interesting to note the not altogether surprising development of several software packages and online calculators in order to facilitate a quick assessment of the precise shares in specific cases.)

There are some easily perceived potential benefits to a scheme of specified shares, as compared with systems of inheritance giving greater apparent legal freedom to the testator. The inheritance rules are an integral part of the property system within Islamic law, which accords men and women separate property rights. Inheritance rules which provide women within the family of the deceased with their own specific shares, support women's more general rights in Islamic law to gain, retain and manage their own land and wealth. Women's rights in relation to inheritance under the Shari'a signified an improvement upon their pre-Islamic position and historically stood in marked contrast to the less privileged position of women in the West, until a few decades ago. Despite barriers and constraints on women's access to inherited land and their lesser shares in comparison with men, inheritance remains an important source of access to land for women. For example, Stauth, who was considering the position of women from all social strata of rural village communities in Egypt, stated: 'Bought land is men's land, women's land is inherited' (1990: 40).

Compulsory shares may offer the possibility of reducing familial strife, since an individual's behaviour will not affect, except in an extreme circumstance such as causing the death of the deceased, his or her competence to inherit. However, in practice, where a person feels entitled to a specific share and for whatever reason does not receive the expected share, or does not receive it sufficiently quickly, there remain possibilities for the fuelling of resentments and breakdown in family relationships. This may be the case, as mentioned earlier, where the application of the rules leads to fractional shares adding up to more than 100 per cent, and there is some readjustment of shares to accommodate the apparent deficit.

Issawi (1984: 31) argues that the notion of a contract, transferring property between parties, 'is so central to Islamic law that many other social relations are assimilated into it', as for instance in the payment of money from the husband to the wife at the time of marriage, known as *mehr* or *mahr.* Beyond family relations and monetary payments for failure to perform certain rituals or acts of faith, the extended family is preserved through some distribution of resources. Yet, the same inheritance share rules – which apply to big or small estates, residential or commercial property, liquid assets or investments – can lead to minute divisions.

This fragmentation of property is particularly, although not exclusively, of importance in relation to agricultural land. The system may give rise to a land parcel involving many partners in unequal or equal shares. Wahlin (1994), for instance, analysed 126 fairly recent inheritance records within Muslim families in villages of the hill country in Jordan. The number of inheritors varied widely, from a single person up to 40, with an average of 7.5. In addition, taken as a whole Shari'a law with respect to inheritance legally institutes and reinforces the extended family, as opposed to the conjugal family. In the more modern context, some commentators and campaigners for reform have identified a tension or contradiction between the shift towards the social primacy of the nuclear family in many communities and the emphasis on relations with extended family within Islamic law.

Inheritance Rules as Part of Wider Islamic Inheritance Systems

Inheritance systems are shaped by the interplay of competing, alternative and overlapping legal and cultural norms. Devolution of land in a number of Muslim communities takes place exclusively through the compulsory formula. Stauth (1990: 38) gives an example of a village in rural Egypt where rights to land devolved only in fixed shares. However, these rules are mostly not implemented in a mechanical or abstract manner. A variety of legal tools have developed in different contexts to permit individuals to make arrangements for the transmission of property, according to their own determination. One obvious tool is the *wasaya* or will, but we have seen that only up to one-third of an individual's estate can be bequeathed in this manner, with the remaining two-thirds devolving according to the compulsory rules. Such bequests are optional and for a Sunni cannot be made to anyone who is entitled to a share under the compulsory inheritance rules (Zaid 1986: 12). It should be noted, however, that Shi'a do permit bequests to those entitled to fixed shares in certain circumstances. If an individual wishes to provide for a non-Muslim relative, it must be by means of a bequest and the will also enables gifts to charity.

Looking at the chronology of divine revelation through the Qur'anic verses over a period of years, the Islamic system moved from complete freedom to make bequests (wills) to a restricted and calibrated scheme. The first relevant Qur'anic revelation was in fact a stipulation: 'it is prescribed when death approaches any of you, if he leaves any goods, that he make a bequest to his parents and near relatives, as per reasonable usage' (*Qur'an* 2: 10). This was the pre-Islamic practice of free wills but one which excluded women and children under prevailing social practice. Then came verse 4:7 which abrogated (annulled) this earlier verse: 'From what is left by parents and those near related, whether the estate is small or large, a determinate share shall be for both men and women'. The *Qur'an* then went on to specify the shares (see, for example, *Qur'an* 2: 11).

The relationship between bequests in wills and inheritance has been widely envisaged as forming part of an integrated system. Legacies provide an opportunity for estate planning by the individual who is able to foresee any anomalies arising out of the operation of the Islamic inheritance rules in his or her specific case. A debate continues as to whether a Muslim has a duty (*fard*) to make a bequest or whether it is a highly recommended (*wajib*) or merely a praiseworthy (*mustahab*) act (Zaid 1986: 13). Some modern legislation has viewed the bequest as a correctional tool. The Egyptian law, for example, states:

> It is necessary for every person to make a bequest to those near relatives excluded from succession, such as the two main lines ascendant or descendent, whether grandparents or grandchildren, who have super agnatic male line, without including the daughter's children. (Zaid 1986: 13)

Islamic wills have developed an important role with respect to provision for particularly vulnerable children. Since a child is deemed to be in existence from the point of conception, a child in the womb is competent to inherit within Islamic law. However, an illegitimate child whose paternity was contested may not inherit from the wife's husband, although that child may inherit from its mother and its mother's family (Nasir 2002: 216–17). Adoption is not recognized under the Shari'a, so inheritance through legal adoption into a family is not feasible. However, children are raised within Muslim families, as part of the family, without having a blood relationship to the other members. It is not uncommon for the 'parent' contemplating the devolution of their property after death to seek to provide for such a child. It is possible to use a will in order to benefit such an informally 'adopted' child, subject to the legal constraints upon an individual's freedom to adjust the distribution of property by this method, such as the injunction to confine bequests to one-third of the estate. An individual seeking to provide for an 'adopted' child may, therefore, experience difficulties in finding a suitable legal means to fulfil all his or her personal wishes or obligations with respect to the child.

A grandparent may also face barriers in seeking to provide for an orphaned grandchild. An orphaned child may be maintained by a grandparent during his or her lifetime, but as a rule will not inherit from that grandparent. Under Islamic law an orphaned grandchild cannot step into the shoes of the deceased parent and succeed to a parent's share (Khan 1989: 189–201). Layish (1994) points out in the context of his study of modern Jerusalem that wills are quite frequently used to provide for the orphaned grandchild, who cannot succeed to a parent's share because there is no doctrine of representation. Such bequests are relatively common and are often explained in terms of the 'verse of bequest' in the *Qur'an,* which encourages provision for relatives in need.

While female relatives and spouses are accorded shares, it is the case that male relatives are more likely to inherit and to enjoy a greater share of the estate. Women may also be regarded, therefore, as inhabiting a vulnerable position under the inheritance rules. The limits on the scope of the Islamic will mean that it is not necessarily a useful tool in this context. However, this apparent legal inequality must also be considered within a wider framework. The difference in treatment between men and women is usually explained by reference to the fact that it is also a feature of Islamic law that a wife is entitled to maintenance from her husband, in terms of shelter, clothing, food and medical care (*Qur'an* 4: 34). Islamic law places no such corresponding obligation on a wife in relation to her husband. A wife is also entitled to receive from her husband *mehr/mahr* in consequence of a marriage. Despite the argument that women are compensated for their unequal inheritance shares through such material obligations on the part of husbands to their wives, problems in realizing this compensatory regime and the apparent formal paper inequality remain a matter of contemporary discussion. It will be argued later that the compensatory framework is central to considerations for the development of authentic strategies to enhance women's property rights and access to land. It is a matter, therefore, for especially detailed exploration in the following chapter which focuses in greater depth on women's rights to property.

Estate Planning

There are a variety of other legal techniques that a person contemplating death may deploy as a form of 'estate planning', in order to avoid the strictures of the compulsory inheritance rules. In some contexts there is a strong determination to ensure that the management of farmland, or indeed a business, remains under the control of the male members of the family. This may be because of a tendency to view women as outsiders to their families and villages following marriage, or simply because men are regarded, both culturally and legally, as the providers within the family. The compulsory legal norms derived from the *Qur'an* may be readily declared as legitimate by everyone concerned, but to many social actors the fragmentation of land, in order to comply with the formula for fractional division of an estate, makes neither economic nor social sense. From this standpoint it is appropriate to seek methods to avoid leaving the division of family wealth to the compulsory fractional shares, while at the same time being able to uphold the religious quality and validity of the rules themselves.

The most obvious tool for estate planning is the *hiba* (lifetime transfer or gift) and more rarely the establishment of a *waqf ahli* (family endowment). Islamic law recognizes transactions which transfer property from one individual to another, without any payment or exchange of property flowing in the other direction. This simple *hiba* is called a contract in Shari'a law, although it is a contract without consideration, without any exchange in money or money's worth. The donor may make such a gift during his or her lifetime even to someone who will be amongst the donor's heirs under the Islamic principles of fixed shares. It is also possible to make a lifetime gift to someone who does not appear amongst the donor's heirs. These gifts provide, therefore, some opportunities for estate planning for those persons who are concerned about the distribution of their property after death.

Such mechanisms do not always enjoy full social legitimacy, yet modern Islamic societies have given rise to a propensity towards several kinds of estate planning. The fragmentation of land in an agricultural context, particularly land that is cultivated as opposed to grazed, may be a matter of great concern to individuals. Wahlin (1994) explored patterns of land ownership from 1867 to 1980 using extensive land records in the province of al-Balqa in the Jordan hill country where the population is both Muslim and Christian. His evidence revealed a practice whereby the most active farming sons in a family acquire or gain access to more of their father's land. This practice was carried forward in a number of ways. The simplest method was the lifetime transfer of rights to land by a father to his chosen son or sons (Wahlin 1994: 74). However, a lifetime gift leads to the immediate and complete loss of control over the property on the part of the donor, which may make this unattractive. Some schools of law do permit the donor of a gift to retain use of the property, as opposed to ownership of the property itself, for life (Maliki), or stipulate that the recipient should maintain the donor during his or her lifetime (Hanafi). Carroll (2001) discusses a whole range of different kinds of lifetime legal transfers involving limited interests, making use of the distinction in Muslim law between usufruct (profits, benefits or use of a thing) and the corpus (the thing itself). As she points out, however, these tools present practical difficulties and tend to be expensive to implement, which may deter many small landowners and the poor.

The classification of land also affects access. Land categorized as state or *miri* is regarded as lying outside the compulsory rules, and its usufruct rights are often subject to lifetime transfer. Studies (Mundy 1979; Maher 1974, cited in Badran 1985: 15) point to rural women under greater pressure as a consequence, owing to the landholding patterns and the customary transfer of usufruct rights in *miri* land from father to son. There is evidence, for example in Yemen and Morocco, that peasant women are 'compensated' for such losses in terms of access to land. This 'compensation' takes the form of periodic gifts of property other than land that a woman receives and/or the fallback security that may be provided by her own family (Badran 1985). Whether such support fully compensates for exclusion from rights in land will depend very much on the particular position of the woman in question.

The tools deployed for estate planning are subject to debate and there may be tensions surrounding their use. Social attitudes to such practices as lifetime gifts vary and are often determined by women's status in particular communities, both generally and at the individual level. Rosen (2000) observed an elderly man who entered into a fairly complex arrangement whereby he signed over his properties to his sons in return for an unofficial legal agreement that he would have a limited life interest. Rosen recounts that other residents of the village in which this took place were ambivalent about the Islamic quality and nature of this arrangement, although it was regarded as legal. Some commentators regard such mechanisms as merely 'tricks' which 'keep the land from being inherited by women' (Amawi 1996: 151). In many contexts there is a strong social convention that land ownership is a male preserve and the compulsory inheritance of women is viewed in terms of channelling land away from her paternal family into that of her husband.

There are many examples, as in the story recounted by Rosen, of fathers using a lifetime gift, or an adaptation of *hiba*, to ensure that land ownership remains within their family. However, estate-planning techniques may be seen as a socially acceptable means of mitigating the effects of the unequal legal status of women with respect to inheritance in some Muslim societies. Such techniques will be deployed by those who would never deny the inherent perfection of the rules determining fixed heirs and their shares. These estate-planning methods are aimed at leaving the rules themselves untouched and Feillard (1997: 96) quotes a preacher from an influential *ulama* family in Indonesia explaining such processes as legally legitimate: 'Islam has ruled the question of inheritance in a complete way … [but] there is the possibility of sharing the inheritance while the parents are still alive. Let people do it. But after death, God proposes the best solution'. This allows acceptance of the rules in principle while adapting the results to perceived realities. Feillard's research demonstrated that most of the families of her respondents, across a range of different social groupings and classes, adopted some 'estate planning' tools. They were not dominated by the compulsory inheritance rules in considering the devolution of their property.

Moreover, in the Indonesian context estate planning was regarded widely as not only socially legitimate, but also wholly appropriate. Feillard (1997) records that *hiba* is used in Indonesia as a means of giving girls 'compensation' for what is customarily regarded as their disadvantaged position under the compulsory Islamic inheritance rules. Doumani (1998: 7) argues:

> While it is true that the Islamic inheritance rules governing the transmission of property after death are quite detailed and rigidly set, the application of these rules, in reality, was often the last resort for families and individuals, that is, property transmission was often a conscious and strategic social act, not an automatic, passive, or formulaic process. Thus property was devolved during the lifetime of property holders through a variety of strategies such as marriage, gifts, dowries and, most important for our purposes, the endowment of family (*dhurri* or *ahli*) *waqfs* … for the benefit of the endower's descendants and relatives.

Legal principles may be manipulated, therefore, both to the benefit and detriment of women in terms of their property rights and/or in order to concentrate ownership within the hands one person, or a small select group, within a family.

As indicated by Doumani (1998), another legal strategy for an individual seeking to control the devolution of his or her property, in particular to guard against fragmentation of ownership through inheritance rules, is to establish a *waqf ahli*. It is a legal mechanism which permits the owner/founder to settle the usufruct or income of property for the use of family members as beneficiaries, until the extinction of the founder's descendants, whereupon it is diverted to charitable purposes. It has considerable advantages over a gift, not least that the predominant Hanafi school permits the founder to reserve the benefits of the property for the remainder of his or her lifetime. Furthermore, when created to take effect upon the death of the founder, the *waqf ahli* can be revoked or changed at any stage until death.

The *waqf ahli* remains subject to the established limits on Muslim wills, in that the endowment may not exceed one-third of a person's assets and cannot benefit a legal heir without the consent of the other heirs. In many countries across the Middle East and beyond, the *waqf ahli* has either been abolished or subjected to severe limitations and its use is largely of historical interest. However, in circumstances where such legal restrictions are not in place, it is noteworthy that the *waqf ahli* continues to be deployed and appears to be regarded as a useful tool for estate planning (Layish 1994).

A major source of women's historic wealth appears to have arisen from beneficial interests in *waqf* (plural: *awqaf*) properties. Also, women have been active founders of *awqaf*. However, some commentators point to the use of the *waqf ahli* as a further strategy by which women are disinherited (Amawi: 1996). Layish (1994) analysed the creation of *awqaf* in East Jerusalem between 1967 and 1990, a period during which 90 new settlements were made, of which five-sixths were family endowments. He states that:

> [The founders were] in an advanced age-bracket, when people are troubled by questions concerning the disposition of their property and their loved ones, and if they are believers, by questions about their place in the next world. Some 30 per cent of the founders are women ....

With regard to the establishment of *awqaf*, Layish found a general trend towards favouring direct descendants, in contrast to the Islamic inheritance rules. He found evidence also of discrimination against daughters in the transmission of entitlement to descendants, even where the founder was a woman. However, Layish also found instances of founders giving preference to a wife over children. An additional feature of the *awqaf* in Layish's (1994) study was the quite frequent provision for orphaned grandsons and sometimes granddaughters, within the male line.

Bahaa-Eldin (1999) records that, when working for the legal department of a bank in Egypt, he encountered many customers with significant wealth who could not provide sufficient collateral for a loan – not because they lacked assets, but simply because they lacked documentary evidence of their ownership of those assets, particularly land. Bahaa-Eldin (1999) notes that Egypt has a fairly efficient and mature institutional framework for dealing with land transfers and land registration, but many assets remain outside the formal registration system. He cites two reasons for this lack of engagement with the registration process. First, high rates of taxes and fees associated with registration act as a barrier to many individuals. Second, and far more importantly for the purposes of the argument presented here, he states that 'in view of the strict rules governing the distribution of a deceased person's estate in Egyptian law – with its origin in Shari'a – the distribution is often conducted informally and remains unregistered in order to avoid those strict rules' (Bahaa-Eldin 1999: 212–13). He goes on to suggest that there is a clear gender dimension to this failure to register, since even women's lesser shares under the inheritance rules are 'resented and avoided'. He indicates that in many cases neither the death of an original title holder to land or the redistribution of his estate will be notified to the relevant authorities. Land and the distribution of ownership of land, therefore, will move out of the official sphere, in order to prevent its fragmentation, but with the detrimental effect that it cannot be used as collateral for obtaining formal credit.

Post-inheritance Adjustments

In addition to the legal strategies deployed during an individual's lifetime to control devolution of his or her property, there are other means by which the effects of applying the compulsory inheritance rules may be circumvented, after the inheritance shares are determined. In a process known as consolidation, the division of an estate into fractional shares may be followed by a series of sales and exchanges designed to reduce the number of co-owners. For instance, a daughter of the deceased may exchange her share in land for cash from her brother. The compensatory payment may be paid, thereby giving the transaction clear legal authority, or it may be 'a payment on paper'. This latter kind of 'symbolic' exchange is linked closely to a further method by which the results of applying the compulsory Islamic inheritance decrees are avoided: that is, through a person's voluntary renunciation of inheritance rights.

It is women who usually exchange their rights in land for movable property, cash or gold, and it is women in the main who decide to give up their fractional shares, particularly in land. Amawi (1996: 157) suggests that: 'One must always keep in mind the difference between law and custom when dealing with women in Islam, for often Islam grants them rights which social custom strips away.' Mundy (1979: 161) has argued that the 'local customs alluded to ... are often described only by a remark to the effect that "women are disinherited"'. It is definitely the case that commentators make similar statements quite frequently in a range of different contexts, although perhaps with some brief indication of the factors involved. For instance, in the recent collection *Islamic Family Law in a Changing World*, the following relatively bare sentences are included:

> In Kuwait, inheritance often follows tradition over Islamic decrees, particularly for women who married young. Often fathers leave their property ... exclusively to sons .... Among Palestinians, women in situations with no or few contending heirs fare much better than other women. Daughters without brothers and widows without sons stand the best chance of inheriting their due shares .... Saudi women inherit exactly according to Qur'anic rules, but only a few women actually manage their own property. (An-Naim 2002: 103)

There is little doubt that the application of the legal decrees on Islamic inheritance can spread the ownership of any property amongst a large number of people. When the holder of a share in jointly owned property dies, that share will in turn be subdivided. Progressively, ownership will become more fragmented and the property itself will be difficult to manage in a manner which suits all the sharers. Fragmentation will pose a particular problem with respect to land. In addition, when the property in question is rural agricultural land, a concern is often raised that shares will fall under the control of strangers or outsiders, especially where a woman who has married out of her village is persuaded to claim her share. The social convention in these circumstances may be for some of those entitled to shares in land to enter into agreements whereby they are compensated, or at least appear to be compensated, in money or money's worth for transferring their share to another family member (Charrad 2001: 44–5).

For instance, Wahlin (1994: 69) pointed out, on the basis of his Jordanian study, that in a rural agricultural context 'the distribution of inheritance is generally followed by operations of sale and exchange to consolidate ownership, that is to reduce the number of joint owners'. He suggests that a woman may receive other property or enter into a contract to sell her rights to land for a small sum of cash. In some cases the consideration may be paid; in others it may be a formality to provide legal authority for the transaction, which amounts in reality to a merely symbolic exchange with her male kin, particularly her brothers. Wahlin found also that the tendency for brothers to buy their sisters' shares was as prevalent amongst Christians in the area of his study as it was amongst Muslims. This is no doubt an indication that in agricultural areas, where decisions have to be made about farming and there is a need for heavy labour, there is a general dislike of fragmentation in ownership or possession. He suggests that while women appear in the official records of land ownership, they own less than 5 per cent of the land.

Moors (1995) found that women in the wealthier families of Nablus, Palestine, whose male kin were traders, ran flour mills, manufactured soap or rented out houses and shops, were more likely to be bought out of their shares in their fathers' estates in a process of consolidation. The consolidation process ensured that management of production and trade, and productive property, remained firmly in male hands, but some women did receive shares in the income, or capital sums, even if they had to wait for these payments and often did not receive full compensation. According to Moors (1995: 66), 'In such households giving daughters, even those who are married, a share in their father's estate was seen as enhancing the status of the family as a whole.'

In addition to the processes of consolidation, there is a widespread practice called *tanazul* whereby a person, typically a woman, may renounce her inheritance rights, after legal confirmation that she is competent and fully aware of her actions (Al-Mahmassani 2003). Though the Islamic inheritance process does not conceive of rejection by the beneficiaries of their share, over time this has been incorporated into the legal process under the Shari'a. It is an interesting example of 'God proposes, Man disposes' where pragmatic or socio-cultural considerations alter the impact of Shar'ia rules, even though they take effect after the Shari'a formula is implemented.

While gender rights advocates are justifiably concerned over women being forced to renounce their limited property rights, the reality may be far more complex. It may be a choice over empowerment through property or through enhanced family support. The voluntary renunciation of an inheritance will take place for a range of intricately woven reasons, relating largely to familial politics or custom. When women renounce their inheritance rights, either partially or totally, it may be because of their dependence upon a more powerful family member, particularly a brother, or perhaps as part of a bargain or negotiation within the family in question. For instance, Agarwal (1994: 260–2) emphasizes that women in much of South Asia, both Muslim and Hindu, will place great emphasis on their need for strong ties with their brothers: 'If I take my inheritance, my brothers will forget they have a sister. If I give it to them, they will remember me and take care of me if I need them' (Hartmann and Boyce 1983: 92–3, quoted in Agarwal 1994: 249).

The woman's need of this family tie of support and protection in these contexts may be strong, particularly when a woman is widowed. For instance, she may try to access her legal rights and make a claim upon her deceased husband's relatives, for her share of her husband's land or other wealth. A brother may be an all-important ally and a representative in any formal or informal dispute forum, which a woman may not be able to enter. In South Asia these needs and ties are connected also with access to their family (brother's) home. His home may be a safety net at times of economic, social and physical insecurity, with the family home being the only place where a woman is likely to have any respite from the monotonous toil of her day-to-day life. This is particularly the case where she has married out of her village. Agarwal (1994) further argues that in the context of Bangladesh, where access to the family home is widely regarded as a right, some scholars regard the renunciation of a woman's right to inheritance of land as the informal 'price' of retaining that right.

Renunciation will preserve a woman's kin relationships, where accepting compensation for relinquishing a share in land will not. Moors (1995: 55) recounts the story of a Palestinian woman forced by her husband to claim her share of her father's land, who was given cash for the land by her brothers. Her sister, who renounced her own share, retained good relations with her brothers, receiving presents on feast days. The woman who received money as compensation was cut off by her brothers and lost their affection; this loss led to an illness from which she did not recover. Moors (1995: 55) concluded on the basis of discussions with Palestinian women on matters of property that 'renouncing her inheritance rights is central to the brother–sister relation'. Cultural norms may permit a woman to make a claim upon her brother for support, protection or shelter at a difficult point in her life. However, as Kabeer (1985: 88, 90) observed, the reality is that this claim is more likely to be readily realized if a woman has renounced her share of inheritance. Within Palestinian society Moors (1995) suggests a disruption of kinship ties, specifically between a woman and her brother/s, is almost inevitable should she fail to renounce her rights. Johnson's own analysis of contemporary Palestine (2004: 150) also indicates a 'widespread phenomenon of women renouncing their share of inheritance in order to gain their brothers', sons', or other male relatives' putative social support'. Layish (1997: 355), again with respect to Palestine, explains that *tanazul* may take place 'upon or after the succession order by the court, sometimes even after the property has been registered in their name in the Land Register'.

Into the explicit and implicit bargaining and negotiation must also be placed cultural notions of whether an action or inaction is 'shameful' (Moors 1995). To make a claim upon a brother will detract from the vision of what it is to be a 'good sister' and may give rise to social censure. In some contexts, the ideology of *purdah* may demand also that male kin mediate a woman's social relations outside the family, highlighting the need for nurturing emotional ties with a brother or another close male relative. To those social pressures that a woman may internalize can be added pressure of a different and more direct nature, including threats of violence, which may be brought to bear by some brothers and other male relatives upon their female kin to forgo their inheritance shares. At its most extreme this pressure may amount to physical violence and even murder. Sonbol (2003: 190) has argued that there is a widespread belief amongst Jordanians that 'property and inheritance are at the heart of many honor crimes', 'getting rid of a sister (as is the case in many of these crimes) becomes a means of eliminating an obstacle to a brother's inheritance'.

Moors (1995) suggests that, in the Palestinian context, a woman is less likely to renounce her share in her mother's estate than her father's estate. In the

Nablus region this also means that a woman's property is more likely to be in gold than land. A woman will renounce her share in her father's land, for the sake of her brothers, but is more likely to succeed in any claim upon her mother's wealth, which is largely held in gold jewellery, such as bracelets. Furthermore, where a woman has no brothers, she is more likely to make and sustain a claim upon her father's estate, including a claim upon land, than where she has one or more brothers. It appears that the sister/brother tie is a central kinship relation which women will seek to preserve through renunciation, while the cultural and social pressures against making a claim are not so great outside that key relationship. Moors (1995) does indicate that widows, within the Palestinian context, often renounce their shares in their husband's estate in favour of their sons. If her children are young, renunciation on the part of a widow is likely to ensure that the estate remains undivided for a considerable period of time and may give her day-to-day control over her husband's house and land. Renunciation should also strengthen moral and emotional claims upon her sons when they grow up. However, there are few, if any, similar benefits in terms of the adjustment of power relations in the family for the childless widow or the widow with daughters to justify the voluntary renunciation of her share in the inheritance.

Legal Reforms to Inheritance Systems

Legal reforms have led to secularization of the legal systems of the majority of Islamic countries. Personal status/family law, which includes inheritance and *waqf*, remains within the domain of Shari'a, but there has been extensive codification of these Shari'a principles, including inheritance rules. These Personal Status and Family Codes were drafted at different times and in varied political contexts. While aspects of one Code may be modelled upon that of another, there are differences and it is important not to focus a universalizing perspective upon them. However, the legal reforms that have taken place with respect to inheritance, within the wider process of codification of Shari'a principles in some Islamic countries, limit the main focus of concern to the position of adopted children and grandchildren. Nevertheless, the possibilities for further changes to inheritance systems are subject to intense debate in some countries about modifications to family law and inheritance. A common dispute is between, on one hand, those arguing from a woman's rights perspective and, on the other hand, those who present their arguments in terms of absolute adherence to sacred law.

Some of this state legislation has made fairly radical changes to family law and the status of women, in terms of departing from strict Shari'a principles, notably the Tunisian Personal Status Code, which dates from the 1950s, and the new

Moudawana in Morocco, which was introduced early in 2004. However, the reforms in relation to inheritance are relatively modest. There has been little interference with the compulsory rules and daughters continue to enjoy only half as much as their brothers from the estate of a parent – a cause for concern for some women's organizations. Even in Tunisia, women still receive lesser shares than their brothers, despite the strengthening of women's rights and position as against more distant male relatives (Charrad 2001).

One example of a change in inheritance law, though subject to juristic debate, which has been widely justified on the basis of the Qu'ranic 'verse of bequest' and social practice is the obligatory bequest for orphaned grandchildren. The pattern of legal reforms in different countries derives from the Egyptian Will Act of 1946, which provides for a mandatory will applied to the estate of a grandparent. The mandatory will is to benefit the grandchildren of a predeceased father or mother in an amount equivalent to the deceased parent's share, up to a maximum of one-third of the estate. It is an adaptation to the structure of the nuclear or conjugal family, which reduces the need for the use of lifetime gifts or a will to circumvent the fact that in Shari'a law an orphaned grandchild cannot step into the shoes of a deceased parent and succeed to the parent's share of an estate. The obligatory bequest is an innovation adopted by several countries, including Tunisia, Morocco, Syria (1953), Kuwait (1971), Jordan (1976), Iraq (1979), Algeria (1984) and Indonesia (1991).

In Tunisia, the rights of spouses were enhanced to enable them to receive, along with the deceased's other close relatives, part of the surplus after distribution according to the rules for fractional shares (Charrad 2001: 228–9). The reform was also adopted by the more conservative Algerian Family Code. More radically and distinctively, under the Tunisian Personal Status Code the inheritance rights of collateral, distant male kin were limited, thereby increasing the benefits and shares that would go to the deceased's children. For instance, when the deceased has no son, no surviving spouse or parent, and only one daughter, one half of the estate will devolve to her, with the remainder being shared amongst the *asaba* (closest male agnates), the deceased's brothers, uncles, cousins, or more distant male relatives. The rules in Tunisia were adjusted to restrict severely the rights of the extended family, while increasing the rights of the nuclear family. This Tunisian Code also recognizes the practice of adoption and adopted children. The Indonesian Compilation of Islamic Law, while not taking such a direct approach with respect to adoption, does extend the obligatory bequest to 'adopted' children. Both changes are significant because Islamic law does not recognize the institution of 'adoption' as generally understood in many other countries.

Most Muslim countries have ratified the UN Convention on Elimination of Discrimination against Women 1979, notwithstanding the reservations. The differential treatment on the basis of gender regarding inheritance shares, on the face of it, violates international human rights. A number of NGOs and liberal personalities in Muslim countries have called for equal inheritance rights. The celebrated Egyptian feminist Nawal El Saadawi (2001) in a widely reported interview argued that

> we have to rethink about the inheritance law because we have 30 per cent of families in Egypt where the mother is working and paying for the family and the husband is not working. It is the mother who is the provider for the family, so why women inherit only half?

Sadaawi, however, became the first woman in Egyptian history to be threatened with a forced divorce on the charge of apostacy for expressing such views. Shortly after the interview, the Mufti of Egypt, Sheikh Nassr Farid Wassel, wrote to *Al-Midan* denouncing El Saadawi's comments as heretical and rendering her a non-Muslim.

Islamic inheritance rules are a complex and sensitive issue. In 2000 Kenyan Muslim women protested against a proposed civil rights bill to give equal shares in inheritance to sons and daughters, on the basis that such a change would amount to a breach of Shari'a law (An-Naim 2002: 50). A recent study on Morocco shows that while women generally assert their rights 'to independently own and manage property and businesses', when it comes to inheritance participants in the study stated that 'equal' is not the main concern, but should be subordinate to what the religion of Islam says (Katulis 2004: 17). In the words of one respondent who saw the choice as property versus religion: 'We shouldn't change inheritance laws just so women could get an equal share. If we want to change that, we are going to change religion and doctrine; I think this should not happen' (Katulis 2004: 18). A general refrain is that what God has ordained for shares cannot be changed. Many Muslim feminists such as Wadud (1999), Hassan (1982) and Barlas (2002) argue that the woman is adequately compensated by other sources of support, material and in kind.

However, the renunciation of inheritance rights by women across a range of Muslim societies has nothing to do with Islam, and is a socio-cultural practice that requires close scrutiny. It is ironic that while the half inheritance share is justified on the basis that women are supported by their husbands, the rationale for renouncing the remaining half is that they may still need the support of their brothers (Chaudhry 1997: 544). This suggests that apart from the quantum of shares, the quality of inheritance rights in terms of articulation and assertion is different in practice. Muslim women's access to inheritance, therefore, cannot be made in the abstract and is best understood through the interplay and constructions of custom, gender, kinship and property (Moors 2000). Therefore, any change must come from within the communities concerned.

In the Islamic framework, the compulsory inheritance rules are only a part of the inheritance system that has the potential of either enhancing or repudiating fully fledged property rights. Agarwal (1994: 282–4) draws an interesting contrast between Pakistan and Bangladesh. In each case inheritance is formally governed by the *Shari'a*. However, she points out that a number of researchers have found Bangladeshi village women, particularly poorer women, being increasingly inclined to claim their inheritance shares, although no such phenomenon can be observed in Pakistan. She concludes that widespread landlessness and scarce resources in Bangladesh, alongside the breakdown in traditional support networks, may explain women's willingness to stake their claim, whereas in the more prosperous agricultural areas of Pakistan there are no such push factors. The motivation, therefore, is contingent on a variety of social, economic, cultural and political factors.

In the Palestinian context, Moors (1995) found that a woman's likelihood of inheriting was based upon her class position, her location and her family relationships. A wealthy woman in an urban environment, whose brothers stood to gain social prestige for giving their sisters their allotted shares, was more likely to inherit from her father's estate than a poorer woman or a woman in a rural environment. However, the group of women who were most likely to receive their shares were those from families with a high level of education, particularly education in Islamic doctrine, whose fathers often held important positions within the religious hierarchy. It is suggested that this is an area, particularly regarding renunciation, where advocacy is possible to empower women. The widespread popular consciousness of, and pride in, the compulsory rules means there is potential through education and advocacy work to enhance women's access to property through inheritance. Nevertheless, any strategy for empowerment should be rooted in the knowledge that the fact that a woman makes a claim to her inheritance share does not necessarily say very much about her relative power or powerlessness within the family or even in the wider community.

Conclusions

In devising strategies designed to enhance security of tenure and to relieve poverty within Islamic societies, inheritance law and inheritance systems, particularly as they pertain to women, should not be regarded as a peripheral matter. Inheritance is an essential component in access to land. General knowledge of the basic legal system with respect to inheritance appears to be embedded within Islamic communities, but the specific rights are not necessarily publicized, and certainly not widely articulated or discussed. This is due to several factors: a perception that the rules are complex, which is deliberately reinforced by authority figures, widespread illiteracy particularly amongst Muslim women in some societies, and the marginality of certain categories within families and communities. However, dissemination of knowledge about the Islamic inheritance rules is important. Where implemented in letter and spirit, the rules provide a solid starting point for women and other members of the family in asserting the full range of their property rights. Where they are not implemented, or rather are avoided by various means, the system of classical rules on compulsory inheritance may provide a point of reference from which discussions and debates can move forward. In many political and social contexts the full implementation of the inheritance rules under Islamic law could be a realizable goal and create the basis upon which to enhance rights in land for less powerful members of society. However, the inheritance process is not dependent merely on formal legal norms, which are just a part of the picture.

Inheritance rules are presented as a complete divinely ordained code without room for compensation through other tools, but the transfer of property through inheritance cannot be considered in isolation. Legal techniques, notably *hiba* and the establishment of a *waqf ahli*, have developed to enable individuals to determine the devolution of their property to meet perceived social needs such as avoiding fragmentation of agricultural land and family businesses. The deployment of these techniques has a gender dimension. In some communities the lifetime transfer is seen as a means of adjusting for discrimination against women under the inheritance rules, but in other contexts to prevent family property moving out of male control or into the hands of 'outsiders'. Given the propensity towards consolidation of family property and its smooth intergenerational transfer, property, particularly farmland or a family business, is likely to be transmitted and retained in the hands of men. This expresses a social convention to the effect that men, as the producers, should manage and control both the business and the land it sits upon. Where these 'legal' techniques serve to achieve progressive and inclusive results, efforts to enhance their social legitimacy must be facilitated.

There are also compelling pressures on women – of affection, notions of honour and shame, and economic necessity – which have a bearing on whether they will assert a claim upon a share in an inheritance, agree to sell a share, whether for cash or symbolically, or renounce a share. These are not Islamic principles but socio-economic and cultural practices that have to be tested for utility and legitimacy, in view of evolving family and community structures. Therefore, the specifics of the inheritance system in any context should be demystified, including the dominant legal techniques of estate planning, the motivation for using those legal techniques and the social meanings attributed to the use of estate planning methods. Similarly, the subsequent processes of consolidation and renunciation of inherited property should also be queried. With regard to entitlement of shares and the impact of estate planning, consolidation of property and renunciation of shares, those involved and affected must have the opportunities to discuss and deal with the impact of their decisions.

Given that Islamic inheritance is closely associated with Islamic identities and social structures and a general concern about secularization as a threat to Islam, there is widespread resistance against anything other than very limited state intervention into this area, even amongst women. The reforms geared towards materializing the egalitarian and distributive aspects of Islamic law have to come primarily from within the community and be compatible with the Islamic frameworks. The main features of the inheritance rules appear to be clear-cut, particularly when they are deemed to be *qat'i* (unambiguous) and not readily open to any modification. However, any set of Islamic principles is to be reinterpreted and applied against the backdrop of the *maqasid al Shari'a.* Despite the limited forays into the realm of Islamic inheritance rules, the return to first principles and continuing development of these principles suggest that several inheritance practices may in the near future be subjected to *ijtihad* leading to newer forms of interpretation. This is particularly true since inheritance falls under the category of *mu'amalat* (social relations), more amenable to rationalization than matters falling within the *ibadat* (matters of worship), where there is less scope for *ijtihad.*

Inheritance rules are not, therefore, on the periphery of discussions about enhancing rights to land and must be understood as part of wider inheritance systems of legitimate methods of estate planning. However, some commentators caution against excessive concentration upon inheritance, particularly in relation to women, arguing that attention should also be paid to other means of accessing property. Inheritance rules also need to be considered within the broad, complex and myriad systems of property relations. They are, as it were, only one point, albeit an important one, in the property cycle. As will be considered in the following chapter, other avenues of obtaining property – such as maintenance, as a beneficiary under a *waqf* or from gifts – could be deemed compensatory for women's lesser inheritance shares. For example, the transfer of property from husband to wife at the time of marriage (*mahr/mehr*) may be as important in some women's lives as inheritance. In short, women's property rights in the Islamic framework should be approached holistically.

6

Muslim Women and Property

> [History] ... shows, no doubt, that [Muslim] women were property holders, a fact which has been pointed out for various Islamic societies and should be reiterated here ... that this certainty was not the case in many other civilizations, including many Western societies. The question is whether it also disproves the view of the subservient role of women in traditional Islamic society.... (Baer 1983: 9)

Within the Islamic framework, a Muslim woman possesses independent legal, economic and spiritual identity; she also has independence, supported by Qur'anic injunctions with respect to access to land. However, it is widely presumed that Muslim women are frustrated in their pursuit of property rights because those rights, particularly as to inheritance, are limited under the Islamic legal system; they lack agency in the face of oppressive family and social structures and have an absence of conviction in their articulation of gender rights. At an international level, the refusal of Muslim states to permit the inclusion of words in resolutions giving women equal land rights, preferring the language of equal access to land, is highlighted in the deliberations of international institutions such as UN-HABITAT's governing council. In this regard the reservations entered by Muslim states to CEDAW, particularly to Article 16 ensuring equality between the sexes in matters of marriage and family, are raised as illustrations of the barriers to the implementation of women's property rights. Women activists, including Muslim feminists, recognize the guarantees of land rights in Islamic human rights documents such as the UIDHR, but they stress also the lack of gender mainstreaming of rights and the difficulties in realizing those rights on the ground in the face of discriminatory social and cultural norms presented as rooted in Islam.

In the pursuit of authentic land tools from within the Islamic framework, the assumptions about Muslim women's property rights, including the orientalist notion of women operating under a rigid patriarchal system, are challenged. At the same time concerns about the origins and realization of gender land rights need to be interrogated. These issues are explored here through an analysis of the legal status of women with regard to property under the Shari'a, including their apparently deficient entitlement to shares in inheritance; the socio-historical background to women's property rights; and an appraisal of modern legal reforms. This exploration acknowledges both the dynamic nature of families in Muslim societies and the role of women as active negotiators within those families about matters that include access to both real and personal property. In encountering the Islamic property regime for women it is speculated specifically that a revival of the integrated and holistic compensatory property regime, as laid down in the *maqasid al Shari'a*, can be deployed to enhance women's economic security. Gender land rights may appear discriminatory, as with respect to inheritance, but there is the potential within the Islamic framework for women to receive other property rights by way of recompense. Elsewhere, where women's property rights fail to reach equality standards they may be subject to *ijtiha*. Such strategies have the potential for being viewed as legitimate in modern Islamic societies, especially where statutory changes of a secular nature struggle for acceptance.

Debunking Stereotypes Regarding Muslim Women

There is a common and enduring Western assumption that constructs all Muslim women as 'passively accepting their bleak lives, either because they know of no alternative or because they have no means to fight this faith prescribed by God and administered by their male masters' (Hoodfar 1998: 112). However, this representation of Third World women through a narrative of the victimized, with their governments demonized as men who are necessarily resistant to gender rights, underestimates the capacity of women and the potential for reworking state gender policies. Tucker has pointed out, from her historical research concerning Muslim women, that 'most scholars have come to understand that such images have far more to do with the historical process of Westerners constructing and exploring their own gender system than with dominant realities in Islamic history' (Tucker 1993: 37). An increasing number of Muslim women across the globe do not share in resignation regarding their inferior rights in practice or their helplessness with respect to misogynist versions of Islamic rights. They are combating both the traditional restrictive practices as well as challenges to their identity and empowerment through neocolonialist yardsticks (see Bhabha 1994; Al-Azmeh 1993; Ahmed 1992). Muslim women have found room to articulate their own distinctive standpoints while pragmatically embracing selected Western feminist strategies. Caught between the extremes of Western cultural imperialism and intractable conservative absolutism, these Muslim women work to neutralize both kinds of prejudices and misconceptions.

Difficulties for Muslim women may arise where conservative readings of the Shari'a are intertwined with gender-discriminating customary norms, which are presented as God's immutable word. Muslim women are concerned with both their worldly life in the here and now (*duniya*) and their salvation in the eternal life after death with God (*akhira*). The woman striving to be a good Muslim, while also wanting her legal rights, is likely to experience frustration and conflict when faced with patriarchal constructions of law and custom. Al-Hibri argues that these conflicts can be resolved only through a solid jurisprudential basis, 'which clearly shows that Islam not only does not deprive [Muslim women] of their rights, but in fact demands those rights for them' (1997: 16). This approach is particularly important in relation to women's property rights in Islam. The reiteration of the demand that these rights should be fulfilled is an important element in empowering women in contemporary societies.

Not all Muslim women are necessarily religious but the religious or cultural choices that women make, such as the adoption of the *hijab*, are sometimes seen as self-deprecating actions or choices. A dilemma for most Western feminists, whether they are atheist, agnostic or secular, has been what is commonly perceived to be a bundle of anachronistic religious patriarchal beliefs and practices. However, such an approach not only alienates believing women but also misses a wide range of practices that have positive implications for women's lives. Women may also choose to work within the Islamic framework while at the same time seeking egalitarian Islamic objectives through *ijtihad*, which is an acknowledged Islamic interpretative process. As Badran notes (1999: 180):

> [In recent decades] highly educated Muslim women, armed with advanced educations, including doctoral degrees, are applying a combination of historical, linguistic, hermeneutic, literary critical, deconstructive, semiotic, historicist, and feminist methodologies in their reading of sacred texts, pushing *ijtihad* to new limits.

It is obvious, of course, that the diverse lived experience of Muslim women all over the world cannot be essentialized through a universal and natural female subjectivity and the extension of a constructed homogeneity of the female subject (Basu 1999: 3–4). Women's status is determined not merely by religion but as much by their race, ethnicity, class, literacy, age, marital status, and other classifications such as 'fairness', beauty, rural/urban background, displacement or sexuality. As in other societies, a woman's access to land in the Muslim world is often frustrated by stereotypes of biological roles, her construction as a temporary member of the family (through marriage), interests in the consolidation of family properties and kinship relations. Nevertheless, a review of women's individual property rights within the Islamic legal framework may help to counter any such damaging suppositions or residual images. Subverting stereotypes of Muslim women would seem to be a prerequisite for developing meaningful strategies for women's access to land.

Addressing Gender Rights through International Human Rights Law

One of the ways to evaluate land, property and housing rights of Muslim women is through international human rights law standards. However, the relationship between universal and Islamic human rights is complex. Even within the international human rights framework, gender rights are not always prioritized (Gallagher 1997; Cook 1993). As Freeman (2002) notes:

> [As] has been documented by countless scholars and activists in the last two decades, women's human rights have been at best ignored, and more often overtly denied, since time immemorial. And given their historic invisibility in the 'mainstream' of human rights activity for the last 50 years, general progress in human rights does not automatically benefit women. It cannot be assumed that changes in law and policy, made without attention to women's specific circumstances and the consequences in their lives, will have a positive impact on their situation.

Until the 1993 Vienna World Conference on Human Rights, women were most likely to be subsumed within the category of 'family and children'. The movement for mainstreaming women's rights as human rights developed in most part through lobbying at successive women's conferences, Mexico (1975), Copenhagen (1980), Nairobi (1985), Cairo (1994) and Beijing (1995), giving rise to a series of resolutions from a variety of groups on women and property. Though the conclusions of such conferences can be seen as reflecting the consensual statements of governments, such platforms are no substitute for the more laborious process of finding or creating binding legal norms, because the mega-conferences are largely aspirational. Such meetings raise the public profile of human rights but also allow states to avoid legal engagement. Therefore women's rights to access land need to be clarified as well as acted upon (Medina 1993).

CEDAW (1979) in Article 1 has specified discrimination to include both 'indirect discrimination' and direct discriminatory effects, and sought to establish proactive duties for states aimed at protecting rights. These include the obligation not to tolerate gender discrimination; legislation and other necessary measures towards the vindication of gender rights; and policy initiatives to counter the social, economic, and attitudinal biases in the society that underpin and perpetuate gender-deprecating practices. In response, several Muslim governments have entered reservations, effectively opt-out clauses, in ratifying CEDAW's proclamation of gender rights.

Fundamental human rights have long been seen as male-oriented priorities, given a masculine interpretation with the privatization of gender rights deliberately operating to exclude state responsibility (Charlesworth *et al.* 1991: 63). CEDAW itself has not escaped criticism on these grounds. Thus Farha (2002) notes in the context of housing rights that:

> [A]lthough considerable attention has been paid to the right to housing in international law, the meaning of the right to housing for women has not been fully explored. Perhaps this lack of attention is due, at least in part, to the male-specific language of Article 11 (1) of CEDAW, which, in one fell swoop, assumes that all women cohabit with men or that men are the heads of households, thus rendering women's housing rights invisible.... [T]his is not surprising given that, on the one hand, the economic, social and cultural rights field was and continues to be dominated by men, who only rarely demonstrate an appreciation of women's experiences as they relate to human rights.

Western feminist legal scholarship on human rights has made a critical contribution by challenging gender bias in the formulation of human rights treaties, the male-oriented establishment of priorities and the lack of gender sensitivity in the work of human rights mechanisms and even NGOs. For example, feminist scholars have worked hard to dissolve the public/private dichotomy that allows most women's issues to be considered within the private domain and therefore not subjected to public accountability. Enhancing state responsibility for toleration of gender violations is already having an impact in Muslim societies. There may be disquiet over the manner in which some First World feminists have set about using their privileged position to fix the international human rights agenda, replicating the civil and political rights emphasis at the expense of Third World developmental issues. However, the increasing human rights scholarship among Muslim women is beginning to remedy that, although Islamic feminists believe that, despite appearances, the potential scope of Islamic gender rights reaches far beyond the fragile and tentative international women's rights paradigm.

Women's Rights to Property under Islamic Law

The scope of Islamic law relating to female ownership of property emerges from its main textual sources. The key texts are the *Qur'an*, read alongside the *Sunna*, as well as the theoretical debates and evidence of policy and practice through land registers, court records, *fatawa* and laws. There is explicit recognition of women's acquisition, utilization and alienation of property in the *Qur'an* through purchase, inheritance and *mehr* or *mahr* transferred to the wife from the husband at marriage and other transactions. The *Qur'an* notes that women 'shall be legally entitled to their share' (*Qur'an* 4: 7) and that 'to men is allotted what they earn, and to women what they earn' (*Qur'an* 4: 32). Only if women choose to transfer their property can men regard it as lawfully theirs (*Qur'an* 4: 4). The Islamic laws relating to property rights of women are drawn from a variety of fields such as family law (marriage/*mahr*, inheritance, and guardianship), property law (gifts, *waqf*, sale and hire) (Shatzmiller 1995) and economic law (right to work, income) as well as public law.

All the key Islamic legal materials generally support women's right to acquire, hold, use, administer and dispose of property. To take an obvious example, the legal disabilities of married women, which were a feature in the past of Anglo-American law are not found in Islamic law. Until legislative changes towards the end of the nineteenth century in England, the common law did not recognize the legal existence of the married woman; both her identity and rights to property were merged or rather submerged into those of her husband. In contrast, Muslim women throughout history, whether married or not, have enjoyed an autonomous legal identity and separate property rights. The *Qur'an* addresses men and women as distinct persons, different but equal individuals. In some contexts – as in the rules concerning inheritance, which award women smaller shares in property than men – the differentiation between men and women may be regarded as contributing to the latter's social inequalities. However, from a legal perspective the recognition of a woman's distinct identity leads to equal treatment between men and women in some very fundamental ways in relation to their property rights. There is no doubt that the Muslim woman retains control, according to Islamic law, over her pre-marital property and finances through marriage, and where applicable beyond into divorce and widowhood (Shatzmiller 1995: 253). The Muslim woman has no restrictions on the property she can purchase out of her earnings, on the gifts she may receive from her natal family or her husband's family, or on the endowment she may enjoy as a beneficiary of a *waqf*. In all these respects she is entitled to equal treatment with male members of the family.

Unequal Shares in Inheritance and the 'Compensation' Argument

There could be a net material flow from men to women within the family. For instance, *mahr* is a payment or promise of such a payment that a husband makes to the wife as a consequence of the marriage. In addition, a husband is under a legal duty to support and maintain his wife. There are no corresponding obligations on the part of the woman to provide for her husband or family, even if she has property and her husband does not. However, when it comes to inheritance, the woman's share is generally half of that of the male members. As has already been argued in the previous chapter, Muslim women's lesser rights in inheritance, under Islamic compulsory succession, have for long been regarded as a marker of the inferior status of women under Islamic law. Undoubtedly, these rules violate the non-discriminatory provisions of CEDAW. However, there is a robust viewpoint within Muslim societies, supported by many Muslim women, which argues that the totality of arrangements within the Shari'a is realistic and equitable (Wadud 1999; Hassan 1982; and Barlas 2002). Commentators who support the view that women's property rights in the Islamic framework should be approached holistically, point to the Qur'anic stipulation that 'men spend out of their property for the support of women'. The argument continues to the effect that women have no concomitant financial obligations. Other avenues of obtaining property such as gifts, dower, maintenance, and as a beneficiary under a *waqf* could be deemed compensatory. The argument is made by Al-Faruqi (2000: 81), for instance, who regards the legal system taken as a whole to be fair. She argues that the whole scheme is supportive of the family and fosters its interdependence, while at the same time ensuring that women are properly taken care of by their male relatives.

Powers has argued persuasively, without any specific focus on women, that because of the clear distinction between lifetime transfers and transactions that take effect upon death it is important that the system of compulsory inheritance rules should not be viewed in isolation. Rather, the rules on inheritance shares should be seen as part of a wider flexible system for the transmission of property across the generations and within the family (Powers 2002: 144; see also Doumani 1998: 7). As will be discussed later in this chapter, the impact of the actual practice on women of so-called 'compensation', via the transmission of property through *waqf*, *mahr* and rights to maintenance is uneven and variable. However, Muslim women's access to property is best understood through the dynamics of custom, family, kinship and the construction of property itself. Conservative interpretations of Islamic law and customary/traditional structures/practices often combine to diminish or altogether extinguish women's rights to property. The most obvious example is the recourse to *tanazul*, the customary practice of renunciation of even the reduced female inheritance share in favour of a male member of the family, such as a brother or son, which has over time been incorporated into the Islamic legal process (Moors 1995: 75). While there is justifiable concern over women being forced to renounce their limited property rights, even with respect to *tanazul*, as explored in the previous chapter, the reality may be far more complex. In itself neither an inheritance claim nor renunciation of an inheritance share should be assumed to be either empowering or an act of submission. The decision to surrender an inheritance share depends on a wide variety of factors, sometimes serving to enhance a woman's status within the family rather than weakening it. Voluntary renunciation of inheritance rights on the part of a woman may serve also to underline a woman's claims upon her brothers' social and family responsibilities.

Social History of Muslim Women's Property Rights

The present-day struggle for gender rights in Muslim communities is in sharp contrast to the apparent status accorded to women in other periods of Islamic history. Accounts of women's treatment under the law as equal with men and examples of women controlling and managing property provide powerful illustrations that the mechanisms exist within the Islamic legal framework to enhance the position of women in contemporary societies.

In early Islamic history, Muslim women played a variety of public roles and certainly exercised property rights. The Prophet in his farewell sermon spoke of property rights for both men and women and his wives had their own separate property. The Islamic division into Sunni and Shi'a sects is considered to have been triggered by the Prophet's daughter Fatima's claim for inheritance rights, which was rejected on the basis that the Prophet had no personal property.

The first convert to Islam (Khadija), its first martyr (Sumayya), the first to grant refuge to the Prophet at Madinah when he fled from persecution at Makkah (Umm Sa'id), the keeper of the keys to the Holy Ka'aba, the custodian of the first copy of the *Qur'an* (Hafsa), the manager of the first hospital (Rafidah Aslamiyya), one of the Imams appointed to lead the prayers of both men and women (Umm Waraqa) and a superintendent at the market at Madinah (Samra' bint Nuhayak al-Asadiya) were all women. It is Hagar (bondswoman of Prophet Abraham) who is considered the founder of the Makkan valley civilization and her discovery of the desert aquifer Zam Zam is still commemorated through the ritual of *sa'y* as an integral part of the mandatory Muslim Hajj pilgrimage. Three female personalities of the Prophet's household – daughter Fatima, first wife Khadija and the woman he married after Khadija's death, A'isha – yield a fascinating insight into feminism at the beginning of Islam.

Roded describes recent findings on the ownership and management of property by Muslim women in earlier ages as 'provocative' (1999: 142). New histories have emerged from studies of Ottoman records covering different regions and time periods (Sonbol 2003: 59–60, 66–9; Fay 1998: 118–40; Shatzmiller 1995). Particularly with respect to the *waqf*, these records show that Ottoman Islamic society was not as rigidly patriarchal as commonly assumed (Powers 1999). It is a history that some commentators regard as an important source of legitimacy for current strategies and processes designed to enhance women's empowerment with respect to property rights (Sonbol 2003). Marsot, in her research into eighteenth-century Egypt, concludes that 'women of all strata owned property; bought, sold and exchanged property; and endowed it at will' (1996: 37; Sonbol 2003: 68–9).

Shatzmiller's study of Ottoman records concludes that the implementation of women's rights was 'effected by mechanisms embedded in the Islamic legal system and by the latter's recognized personnel: notaries, witnesses, judges, muftis and male jurists who attempted to link actual socio-economic conditions with legal rights' (1995: 254). Jennings notes that '[W]here an Islamic inheritance was practised and where a strong court system guaranteed the implementation of these legal divisions, women property holders might well be nearly as numerous as men' (Jennings 1975: 98; Guity 1999: 70). Ottoman court records show that 'no one, including the husbands or even fathers, could make use of women's property without their consent, and women appealed to the courts when anyone tampered with their assets. The judges consistently upheld women's property rights' (Jennings 1975). Sonbol also notes that '*Qadis* and courts treated women the same way as they treated men when it came to all types of transactions. A woman's word in the court did not need corroboration any more than a man's' (Sonbol 2003: 73).

Ahmed (1992: 111) has warned, rightly, that the Western scholarly establishment is too quick to hail the documentary evidence that women undoubtedly did inherit, manage and own property, and were even willing to pursue their interests into the public space of the courts. Baer (1983: 13) found that in sixteenth-century Istanbul one-third of all founders of *awqaf* were women. However, he questioned the significance which may be attributed to such a finding, for women's *awqaf* were in the main fewer and smaller than those of men and did not usually include the most important asset, namely land. It is the case that some women were the *mutawallis* of *waqf* property, administering and managing it for the beneficiaries and receiving in that role a proportion of the total income. Nevertheless, in the majority of cases female founders appointed men as managers and at a later stage, when religious officials were designated to take on the administrative role, management passed formally into the hands of men. In most countries, *awqaf* were eventually abolished, nationalized or highly regulated, which removed from women an important way of accessing land.

The colonial encounter undoubtedly led to deterioration in both the legal status of Muslim women and their ability to exercise their rights. As Marsot (1996) argues, in specific relation to Egypt in the eighteenth and nineteenth centuries, when trade with Europe was extended the standing of élite and middle-class Muslim women declined. In the eighteenth century, in order to conduct business a woman had to deal through a male, but the documentation registered her legal existence as the active participant; he was merely a conduit. On the arrival of European institutions, banks, insurance companies and the stock exchange, a different kind of legal and social ideology was imported. As indicated earlier, this imported Western legal culture did not acknowledge the legal existence of married women. Any Muslim woman still had to operate through a male, but he was no longer her agent and she lost her legal personhood – an example, no doubt, of the diffusion, albeit contested, of nineteenth-century Western legal culture into colonized space.

The gradual advancement of women observed in most Western societies, at least in terms of their property rights, access to land and their ability to enforce their interests, although arguably from a low base, has not necessarily been seen in Islamic societies. Yet in earlier periods it may be that Muslim women had greater rights, access and control over property than is the case today, at least in some countries and contexts. It is for this reason that reiteration of Islamic history in relation to women, showing them to have had considerable property rights and legal status, has the potential to empower contemporary women. It is equally appropriate to caution that too much emphasis can be placed on women's apparent legal status and property rights, as evidenced in historical documents. However, this history does demonstrate, in practice, a fundamental form of equality between men and women, in terms of their treatment under the law. Moreover, as can be seen from the historical records, Islamic law contains important tools that can be used to enhance the position of women and their access to property. The strategy of deploying and in some senses reviving these 'authentic' tools is at least potentially legitimate. This is especially the case when such a deployment is compared with legal reforms that are secular in form.

Custom, Family and Women's Property Rights

A woman's right to property is not just an abstract ideal or a mere matter of legal principles, but a crucial dimension of her identity, security and empowerment (Agarwal 1994). It is nevertheless one that is shaped by her social status, place in the life cycle and household/family dynamics. As is evident from the earlier discussion on inheritance, family life and familial politics play a part in constituting women's lives and their ability to realize scriptural rights to land. Popular and scholarly discourses project 'a traditional monolithic family type constituted as the bedrock of Middle Eastern societies' (Doumani 2003: 4). This follows the orientalist discourse within Islamic legal studies, which assumed that the family was necessarily 'rigidly patriarchal' (see Anderson 1967). Recent research, however, debunks this 'orientalist construct of the monolithic patriarchal family of classical family law', instead recognizing the Muslim woman as a dynamic family member (Moors 1999: 143). Tucker states that 'as part of the economic, social and political landscape, the family evolved in response to variations of its role … operating differently as an institution of social control in different environments' (Tucker 1993: 205). Thus, the family is a fluid amalgam of different fields of experience for differently situated members, with room for a variety of strategies by women, 'some of which may appear counter-intuitive but not any less effective' (Doumani 2003: 16). Therefore, a Muslim woman's experience of property rights, taking place within the context of familial and social politics, is complex and uneven. Property becomes a matter of implicit and explicit bargaining and negotiation.

In theory, a woman's access to property and land will come at various stages of life, most notably through her 'rights' to *mahr* and maintenance. *Mahr* is a payment, whether in cash or as property, which the husband pays, or promises to pay in the future, to his wife as a consequence of marriage (Siddiqui 1995: 14–24; Charrad 2001: 36) and is quite distinct from the social phenomenon of dowry payments from the bride's side to the groom's side. Payments in the form of money or luxury goods from the bride's family to the groom or his family have become institutionalized in some Islamic societies, particularly in South Asia. Such transfers of property or dowry payment may be socially more important than dower given the increasingly high demands that are often made upon the bride's family in some parts of the world, but nevertheless they are not required by, or part of Shari'a law. Under Islamic law *mahr*, in contrast, is the wife's entitlement and it is generally perceived to be an essential aspect of the marriage, without necessarily being an absolute legal requirement for its validity (Nasir 2002: 83–4). It may consist of land, a usufruct (use rights) with a pecuniary value, cattle or crops. The value of *mahr* is usually determined by the socio-economic circumstances of the parties to the marriage.

Mahr is for the wife's use and may be disposed of as she wishes. One of the ways in which women can empower themselves is through the Islamic right of a reasonable *mahr*, without fear of social consequences. However, there is considerable variation in the quantum and mode of transfer. Nothing limits a wife with full legal capacity from relinquishing all or part of her specified *mahr*, thereby discharging her husband from his obligation to make the payment. She can also make a gift of the *mahr* property to her husband or another. Only rarely does the right to *mahr* itself go to court. However, the institution of *mahr* is important, particularly with respect to dissolution of the marriage due to divorce; it may even serve to discourage divorce. Where negotiations between the families over the marriage contract stipulate that part of the *mahr* be deferred, the law provides that this portion must be paid in full where the husband divorces his wife by means of repudiation (*talaq*). The wife, unlike the husband, has no such right to divorce by repudiation. If the wife seeks a judicial divorce, through a decree of *khula*, she is likely to lose her dower amount, since she is expected to give some compensation to her husband (El-Alimi and Hinchcliffe 1996).

At certain points in history *mahr* has been regarded as an important part of a woman's wealth. Tucker (1985) indicates that estate records in Nablus, Palestine, during the eighteenth and nineteenth centuries suggest that women acquired wealth through *mahr* at the time of marriage, amounting to about 15–20 per cent of middle- and upper-class women's wealth at death. However, research carried out more recently with village women in Bangladesh by Huda (1996: 294) found a general lack of awareness of Islamic *mahr* rights, often viewed as 'a promise which the husband has little intention of fulfilling'. In Palestinian society, Moors (1995) indicates, there has been a decline in the importance of *mahr* as a social institution. Rising land prices since the 1960s have meant that the main expense for the family of a new husband is the provision of housing for the couple, as opposed to the *mahr* payment to the wife. Any house that is built or purchased is the husband's property. Another effect of the upward spiral in land prices is to limit women's ability to buy land from their *mahr* wealth. Until the mid-1960s the transfer of *mahr* to a Palestinian woman in the villages around Nablus marked the beginning of a series of sales and purchases made by her – of gold, farm animals and sometimes land – designed to accumulate wealth. Contemporary Palestinian women are more likely to sell all the property given to them as *mahr* and use it to help a husband into business, to travel elsewhere for work, or to build a home. Beyond the payment of *mahr*, which is a direct effect of the marriage contract, a woman can expect to receive gifts throughout her life from men, including her husband, father or brother (Hamza 2002). Often such gifts will be received at important points in a woman's life, such as the birth of a (male) child. However, these gifts will tend to consist of jewellery, cash or clothing, rather than rights in land. The ability of poor women to accumulate sufficient money through savings from gifts to purchase land is very limited indeed (Stauth 1990).

There is a legal expectation that a woman's fundamental daily requirements will be met by her husband, which is relevant to her immediate shelter but likely to have only an indirect effect on a woman's ability to accumulate or preserve property and wealth. The basis of the Muslim law on maintenance is a verse in the *Qur'an* (4: 34) and some narratives forming part of the Prophetic *Sunna*. It is not disputed that a wife is legally entitled to maintenance during the subsistence of her marriage. Most Arab legal codes provide for maintenance including food, clothing and housing (Nasir 2002), corresponding to the standard of living of the family. As Zubaida (2003: 149) notes, maintenance is increasingly important since the past practice of divorced women returning to the natal family is less evident in contemporary society. In a modern urban setting, where housing is scarce, crowded and costly, this option may not be available and a divorced woman can find herself destitute. In practice, a wife may lose her right to maintenance under several circumstances, including the controversial justification of lack of obedience to the husband (*nushuq*). In the main this refers to leaving the matrimonial home without a lawful reason, or where a woman denies her husband access to a home which she owns. In Egypt, for instance, a woman may work provided she was not expressly forbidden to do so by her husband and it does not conflict with her family's interest.

Controversy surrounds the provision of maintenance in relation to the position of the divorced wife. Other than a right to specified *mahr*, conservative jurists hold that the divorced wife has no financial rights against her former husband, even in a case of *talaq*, since the marriage contract is dissolved. In other words there is no equivalent to the Western concept of alimony. Husbands may be enjoined to provide *mutat* (compensation) in some circumstances. Where the husband is found to have repudiated his wife without good reason, in some jurisdictions including Egypt and Jordan compensation may be required of him. Even in the most generous of these compensatory provisions, however, the sum to be paid to the wife does not exceed the value of a few years' maintenance. The contentious Shah Bano case demonstrates how women may suffer as a consequence of the principles of maintenance. The case involved a husband, a senior advocate by profession, repudiating his elderly wife by *talaq*, and claiming that he no longer had any financial obligations toward his former wife since he had already paid the *mahr* to which she was entitled (Akhtar 1994; Bhatnagar 1992). The wife made a claim for maintenance under Indian legislation and was awarded a very small monthly payment. On appeal from the husband, the Supreme Court in India held, on an analysis of Islamic law and other factors, that such an obligation on the part of the husband to pay maintenance did exist.

In the aftermath of the Supreme Court's decision, riots and demonstrations took place. The Shah Bano case acquired a political dimension, not least because all five of the judges in the Court were Hindu and their legal opinion appeared to raise a potential threat for the future in terms of Muslim law governing family matters. It led to the state passing the Muslim Women (Protection of Rights on Divorce) Act 1986, which shifted the maintenance responsibility to the extended family, *waqf* institutions and the state. However, the Supreme Court has shifted the position again recently, with an interpretation of Section 3 of the 1996 Act that the requirement that the husband make 'a reasonable and fair provision and maintenance' is to be read as the obligation to secure the future of his former wife. The resistance to subjecting maintenance to *ijtihad* seems to be more to do with patriarchal tendencies and inequitable gender structures, but it is likely that this could change with the shifting dynamics of family relations within Muslim societies.

Impact of Modern Legal Reforms

In the twentieth century a variety of legal reforms in Islamic societies have had an impact on women, their property rights and access to land. While these reforms were often legitimized by linking them to Islam and Islamic law, many were driven by secular considerations and influenced by the legal formulations and reform mechanisms of former colonial powers. Rarely was the enhancement of women's rights a particular objective. Modernist land reforms initiated across the Middle East did not achieve much by way of redistribution, and certainly bypassed most women. In fact, the changing patterns of the economy –

the shift from sharecropping to mechanized forms of production, as well as urbanization – consolidated land in the possession of males. With regard to land classified as *miri*, where Islamic law did not apply, rural women found that customary laws, with a pattern of male preferences, effectively made them landless (Tucker 1979: 245–71). Writing in the context of Egyptian land reforms, Hatem (1998: 88) noted that the main beneficiaries were rural middle-class men and to a lesser extent some rural working-class men. The small number of women who gained access to land was largely confined to widows as guardians of young sons, although not divorced women in a similar position, who were moved to protest about the law's application in 1952. Amawi (1996: 157) describes how during campaigns for land registration in Jordan in the 1930s and 1940s women went to the courts and the land department to complain that 'land which their male relatives were trying to register in their own names had been unlawfully taken away from them'. She adds, however, that both the department and the courts often sided with the women.

The process of codifying, harmonizing or modernizing personal codes, as family law reforms were otherwise called, was triggered by colonial influences but carried forward by postcolonial Muslim states. Thus fluid legal content developed in local Shari'a courts was transformed through state intervention into a Western-inspired form — the Code. The potential in such a process for norms to change and mutate is obvious. Legal reform of an area perceived as governed by detailed religious regulation is hotly contested and involves struggles for legitimacy. Not surprisingly, therefore, codification has been accompanied by 'painstaking efforts ... to portray the codes and any modifications as consistent with the Shari'a' (Ziai 1997: 72). For instance the Tunisian lawmakers, who devised what is widely regarded as the most radical and bold of these Codes, the Tunisian Personal Status Code, emphasized its source and spirit as lying with the Shari'a, despite the fact that the Code itself makes no such reference (Charrad: 2001). As Minault (1997: 7) notes, modern reforms have been based on 'scriptural authority as interpreted in the colonial context – increasingly restricted to certain specific texts and clearly defined readings from them'. If these reforms did little to enhance women's rights it is scarcely surprising, for this was not their purpose. The aim was to establish appropriate behavioural norms for the societies in question and thereby establish 'an irreducible Muslim identity within the political process' (Minault 1997: 7).

Codification of personal status law as a frame for women's rights or the lack of them, across diverse Muslim societies from Morocco to Indonesia, has been contested and remains a matter of vibrant public debate, even conflict. These debates are connected with wider concerns about the family, adherence to religious law, Western influences and arguments about the rights of women (An-Naim 2002). The Maghreb, specifically Morocco, Algeria and Tunisia, provides an example of how even countries with several shared historical and cultural features could have varied codification experiences (Charrad 2001). The Algerian Family Code of 1984 is largely faithful to the Shari'a, despite what have been termed some small 'concessions to modern social conditions' (Mitchell 1997: 198); unlike its Tunisian equivalent, it fully reinforces the bonds of kinship. The Moroccan Code of Personal Status, the Moudawana, drafted at the same time as the Tunisian Code, had more in common with that introduced in Algeria. However, recent changes in Morocco through the new Moudawana (2004) have the objective of 'freeing women from the injustices they endure, protecting children's rights, and safeguarding men's dignity', (King Mohammed VI 2003), within the tolerant spirit of Islam. The thorough reforms contained in the Moudawana (2004) offer substantial changes to the formal status of women and are to a degree supportive of the nuclear, married family. There are several features in the Maghreb reforms that are striking: for instance, the Tunisian Code holds that a wife should also contribute to the family's maintenance where she has the means to do so. The new Moudawana in Morocco completely excludes from its provisions the concepts of *ta'a* (a woman's obedience towards her husband) or *nushuq* (disobedience); joint decision making between the marriage partners is envisaged; and the Code conceives of joint ownership of property within marriage.

Most commentators confirm that the experience of these family law reforms, whether substantive or procedural, cannot be generalized (Welchman 2000). There are several positive and negative features. Others argue that the reforms have actually caused deterioration in the status of women (Moors 1999: 143). For Sonbol, the reforms are not innocent and have the effect of creating new institutions and practices which deny previous freedoms, while emphasizing earlier discriminations (Sonbol 1996: 7, 11). A major concern for some commentators has been the legal methods of *takhayyur* (selection) and *talfiq* (patchwork) among the various schools of Islamic jurisprudence infiltrated with Western ideas, leading to inconsistency and confusion (Hallaq 1997: 211). As Esposito notes: 'However salutary or substantive legal change may be, and as noble as reformers' motives may have seemed, their solutions have been of an *ad hoc* and piecemeal nature and their legal methodology has been deficient' (1982: 102). With further secularization inconceivable in most Muslim states, and the changes offering merely an amalgam of superficial reforms which do little to advance women's rights, the call to revisit Islamic sources is gaining momentum.

Conclusions

A number of international interventions as well as state programmes are deferential towards existing socio-cultural gender-deprecating norms in many Muslim societies. The root of the differential treatment of women arises out of their exclusion from public spaces where they can be a part of the decisions which affect them, their families and communities. Despite the democratic deficit in several Muslim countries, there is now an increasing role for civil society in asserting an indigenous framework of gender rights, in the same way as anti-poverty and microfinance programmes recognize the potential for women to be part of their own solutions and empowerment, enhancing the opportunities for the participation of women. Women theorists, lawyers, students, academicians, activists and ordinary women have taken on virtually every contested area of gender rights. They have campaigned against the practice of polygamy, *ar-raqid* (honour killings), female genital mutilation, restrictive behavioural codes based on the concepts of female obedience and domestic violence. The results of this engagement in the public sphere have not merely made women more visible but had an impact on society. But this is only the beginning and more needs to be done.

Islam is the dominant validating force in Muslim societies and the potential of Islamic gender empowerment needs to be explored and opportunities for its establishment identified. The Islamic framework can yield contemporary strategies which are innovative in terms of enhancing and securing women's property rights. Whether it is the faithful with reverence, the agnostic with respect or the secular out of pragmatism, women themselves are striving to transform the structures of gender oppression into processes of liberation. One approach is through *ijtihad* or independent reasoning within the Islamic framework (Wadud 1999; Barlas 2002; Hassan 1982). There is nothing to suggest that maleness is a criterion for becoming *mujtahid* (a person who practises independent reasoning). A new genre of *mujtahidat* has emerged, from among theorists, lawyers, students, academicians and activists (Webb 2000). As suggested in the previous chapter, explicit Qur'anic rules may render certain aspects of the Islamic property regime such as the compulsory inheritance rules unsuitable subjects for *ijtihad* (Amawi 1996: 155). However, other Islamic doctrines that influence the Muslim woman's ability to make choices and access land are being clarified. These include the right to work, travel alone, vote and stand for public office, be appointed as judges, and attend prayers in mosques; custody; *mahr* and maintenance; reproductive choices; the practice of polygamy; *mut'a* (temporary marriage); *talaq*; *qiwama* (male guardianship); domestic violence; and *wali* (the prerogative of the guardian). The methodology is to weed out suspect gender-deprecating customary norms projected as Islamic truisms by invoking the gender-empowering Qur'anic stipulations.

In working toward an effective woman-sensitive *ijma*, which validates *ijtihad*, the problem for Muslim women has been not merely exclusion from public space but, equally, the limited opportunities for interaction among women themselves. Politicized religion drives a wedge right across women, estranging the 'true believers' from the rest and creating divided loyalties (Jefferey 1999:

226–8). Maligned by the state and religious forces as disruptive surrogates acting against Islam, the state and the vital interests of Muslim women, women activists are always at risk of losing the support of the majority of Muslim women. Networks such as the Sisters in Islam in Malaysia and Women Living Under Muslim Laws (WLUML), or dedicated gender rights journals such as the Iranian venture *Zanan*, the Lebanese *Al-Raida* or the Cypriot *Shahrazad* show that women can effectively debate issues that concern them. However, the mobilization of women at the grassroots level can provide opportunities for greater gender-sensitive consciousness.

It may be obvious but it is also important to emphasize that substantive rights require enforcement through women's access to courts. Women in general have restricted access to formal law-generating mediums, whether legislation, judicial redress or *fatawa*, which are all at the command of a patriarchal religious state apparatus. Given the opportunity many Muslim women do access the legal system, whether customary, Shari'a or state courts (Bowen: 2003), but nevertheless the need to strengthen and gender-sensitize Islamic legal institutions, like their non-Islamic counterparts, is obvious. Currently family courts are being promoted within several Muslim countries; they are designed to be less legalistic and to encourage a mediation approach, drawing on the input of psychologists and other social experts. In Morocco, for instance, the Ministry of Justice has promised properly funded family courts to accompany the new Moudawana. Family courts have also made a recent appearance in Egypt, providing a one-stop shop for family disputes. No doubt they may avoid some of the endemic delays in the Egyptian legal system, but the question is whether they can deliver more equitable decisions. A recent Human Rights Watch (2004) report doubts whether, without substantive change on a grand scale, such courts can make any real difference in terms of enhancing women's rights.

While the fragile nature and limitations of the international human rights discourse is acknowledged, promoting human rights advocacy within local communities could empower women to assert their Islamic and international human rights. Muslim countries are increasingly ratifying international human rights treaties, thereby acknowledging their legal obligations to respect the basic rights of women. Beyond treaties, it is not contested that basic human rights arising out of the 1948 Universal Declaration of Human Rights have become the yardstick for the legitimacy of every government, and the demand in all societies. Most constitutions and national laws formally accept them. With respect to land rights, there is equally a plethora of international standards. Rather than negotiate with states or devise programmes and projects on the basis of states' willingness to accept, those seeking to advance land tenure rights must articulate them as enforceable and justiciable rights. Commentators have shown that there is no irreconcilable difference in human rights expectations between international human rights norms and Islamic principles (Ali 1999; Khaliq 1995).

However, states often offer conservative and patriarchal interpretations of religion as justifications for their failure to uphold rights or for their reservations in ratification, particularly with respect to CEDAW. Mayer (1999c), among other commentators, argues that evolving political contingencies and not Islamic beliefs determine most Muslim states' CEDAW reservations. These so-called Islamic reservations need to be confronted to distinguish the levels of religious imperatives, socio-cultural practices or 'folk religion', and contrived patriarchal policies.

Finally and, it is argued here, most importantly, there is potential in the integrated and cohesive property regime for women within Islamic jurisprudence. A question was raised: can the holistic approach to property rights for women in Islamic land law compensate women, through the life course, for their reduced inheritance rights through other means of wealth generation? These methods include a woman's equal access to purchase through earnings, *awqaf*, gifts and special supplements such as savings (from lack of financial obligations within the family), *mahr* and maintenance. In current practice, the system fails to deliver equitable access to land for several reasons. First, there is no mechanism to ensure that the woman is compensated for her inheritance loss in other ways, as there are different interests and relationships in play at various stages of the woman's life. The legal ideology may be holistic, but choices are often made in a vacuum, in the sense that they are made on the basis of current demands or needs, rather than in a 'life course' perspective. Second, while inheritance shares are often land rights, the others – such as *mahr*, maintenance and beneficial interests under a *waqf ahli*, the last now largely abolished – are at best limited to usufruct rights or wealth. Property tends to flow away from women, not towards them. In any event under social or familial pressure women may give up that inheritance right to land, or 'exchange' it for cash or other property, which may or may not actually be paid. Third, customary norms through family and kinship structures seem to have trumped Islamic principles by making earnings and savings difficult, the *mahr* and maintenance rights nominal, conditional or non-enforceable, and inheritance rights often merely theoretical. However, Islamic principles and early practice demonstrate that it does not have to be this way and that a reappraisal of Islamic law could empower Muslim women and enhance security of tenure. A key element in that reappraisal should be a fresh assessment of the *waqf* institution. It will be argued in the following chapter that the revival of *waqf* should not be underestimated in strategies to enhance the property rights of women and many other groups, including the most vulnerable such as the landless and children.

7

The *Waqf* (Endowment) and Islamic Philanthropy

> The *waqf's* contribution to the shaping of the urban space can hardly be overestimated.... A major part of the public environment in (Islamic) towns actually came into being as a result of endowments. (Hoexter 2002: 128)

The *waqf* is a highly significant legal mechanism and a key Islamic institution. It has been recognized and developed under the Shari'a for more than a millennium. Under the *waqf*, an owner permanently settles property, its usufruct or income, to the use of beneficiaries for specific purposes. At its heart the Islamic endowment is connected firmly with the religious precept of charity. The investment of the Muslim community over time into the *waqf* institution is enormous, including hundreds of sultans and rulers, thousands of affluent families and millions of anonymous ordinary citizens making little contributions of whatever they could. *Awqaf* grew to a staggering size, amounting to about one third of the Islamic Ottoman Empire and a substantial part of Muslim lands elsewhere. Wherever there was an established Muslim community, one was likely to find a *waqf*. *Awqaf* dot the Islamic landscape, from monuments such as the Indian Taj Mahal to the Bosnian Mostar bridge, from the Jerusalem Al-Aqsa mosque to the Egyptian Al-Azhar university, from Shishli Children's Hospital in Istanbul to Zubida's Waterway in Mecca. Each *waqf* is influenced by the political, economic, and social conditions of its environment. Under the Shi'a practice, the *auqaf* (Persian, singular *vaqf*) were also numerous. *Awqaf* are also found in the West, in Sicily, in Cyprus, in Andalusia, in Greece and in the Americas.

Despite the widespread presence of the *waqf* institution, debates persist as to its effectiveness in achieving development goals and the modern period has seen its economic decline. In several Muslim countries reforms have abolished, nationalized or highly regulated *awqaf*. The legal sources, structure and types of *waqf* are explored in this chapter, along with a consideration of the reasons behind its decline. However, the eclipse of the *waqf* has left a vacuum in the arena of public services, which the state has been unable to fill easily in many Muslim countries. Moreover, a closer study of these 'religious lands', which are mostly in disuse, unaccountable or kept out of development plans, is required. Both the 'idea' of the *waqf* and the *waqf* doctrine itself remain influential and the reinvigoration of the *waqf*, as an indigenous philanthropic mechanism, has taken hold in some Muslim societies. The *waqf* served and continues to serve as an instrument of public policy and has an impact on all aspects of Muslim life, including access to land. Its future potential cannot be underestimated. An evaluation of any future role for the *waqf* in strategies to improve security of tenure should be built upon an appreciation of its legal foundations, history and socio-economic impacts. The revival of the idea at the local, national and international levels requires that its past is narrated and lessons are learnt.

A Unique Islamic Institution

The *Qur'an* contains no specific reference to the *waqf*, and its legal parameters have been developed through centuries by jurists. It is inspired by the repeated emphasis on charity as an act of devotion to God (for example *Qur'an* 51: 19; 2: 215; 3: 92; 2:177). Charity towards economically dependent members of family, community and society is one of the five fundamental principles of Islam. For instance, every Sunni Muslim is obliged to pay an annual *zakat* in monetary terms, calculated on the basis of annual profits or income above and beyond living requirements, though the manner of its payment varies. It could be paid to mosques, needy individuals, charitable institutions or the state. In countries such as in Pakistan, Sudan, Libya and Saudi Arabia an obligatory tax is levied. In others such as Jordan, Bahrain, Kuwait, Lebanon, Malaysia and Bangladesh, the collection of *zakat* is organized by the state and regulated by law (Kogelmann 2003: 68). *Zakat* serves to purify both wealth and the person who makes the charitable payment and Islam condemns certain behavioural patterns widely associated with some persons who have achieved riches, such as arrogance, greed and love of wealth (*Qur'an* 89: 15–24; 92: 1–13; 100: 1–11; Behdad 1992: 77). Under the Shi'a doctrine there is a similar charitable obligation (*khoms*). Though *zakat* is not directly related to the *waqf* institution, the *waqf* and *zakat* arise out of the same Islamic principles. Devotion to the way of God or the way of goodness or piety and a strong desire to win divine approbation have been the root cause of the origin and development of this institution. Land settled within a *waqf* may be colloquially referred to as 'religious land', thereby demonstrating the vital relationship between the religious charitable precept and the institution.The *waqf* is one of the vehicles to comply with the charitable expectation, although as discussed below there could be other incentives for setting up a *waqf*.

The tradition of statements and practices attributed to the Prophet (*Sunna*) promoted the *waqf*, from the earliest period within the Muslim world. However, the *waqf* as an institution evolved more systematically from the seventh–eighth centuries (Çizakça 2000) and was a key public institution for the Ottoman city (Gerber 2002). Gerber argues from a sociological perspective that it is possible to classify *awqaf* as either large, such as those founded by the sultan or members of the ruling élite, or small, such as those established for the benefit of a group of residents in a particular locality. Large *awqaf* were 'like a branch of the central government' (Gerber 2002: 75), providing the main services: the *imaret* (soup kitchen), *madrassa* (school), Friday mosque and so on. In seventeenth-century Bursa, the records show that in a city of 30,000 residents there were 374 separate small *awqaf*, serving particular neighbourhoods, again providing local public services.

Aqwaf were largely created through *waqfiyya or waqfnama* (written legal documents). In earlier times these documents were not centrally deposited with the state and were seen largely as private matters unless disputes arose (Hamza 2002). The interest of the state, however, began with the search for additional funds in the form of land taxes, though the idea of taxing *awqaf* must have first sounded radical given its immunity from state supervision. Over time, particularly during the Ottoman rule, *waqf* properties were part of cadastral survey and registered in the same manner as other land. Pennell (2005), using historical records, notes that a register of *waqf* properties devoted to mosques, foundations, alms, and charitable works was reorganized in 1809. A special office for *awqaf* with a number of bureaucrats over time led to the establishment of an office for registration and control which was linked to the supreme judge who used to be called the 'judge of judges' (Kahf 1999). *Awqaf* were incorporated into the extensive land information record, though it was by no means complete or perfect. *Waqfiyya*s are an important source for the study of the social history: they describe not merely the buildings and what goes on inside them, but also their environment and surroundings, and mechanisms for their use and maintenance. Further important information emerges from the registration and revenue process, land reform and settlement case studies, and court records. These sources from places such as Istanbul, Cairo, Fez, Mosul, Damascus, Jerusalem and Isfahan, from as early as the fifteenth–sixteenth centuries, provide a fertile documentary base from which to challenge stereotypes and point to vibrant economic and civil society structures and activities.

The development of the *waqf* was largely due to a conservative view of the role of government, which was seen as supporting and subsidizing but not carrying out welfare activities. Therefore services like health and education in the Ottoman Empire were privately financed and organized through the *waqf* system, as a part of public policy (Arjomand 1998). The Ottoman rulers saw themselves as primarily responsible for security, defence and tax collection, and the *waqf* was a crucial vehicle for welfare support of the people. Throughout the Middle East, it long served as a major instrument for delivering public goods in a decentralized manner. As Kuran notes, 'Even a lighthouse on the Romanian coast was established under the waqf system.' This is particularly noteworthy in view of the modern intellectual tradition that treats the lighthouse as the quintessential example of a pure public good that must be provided by the government out of tax revenues (Kuran 2001).

Whether the *waqf* was able to deliver services of quality and whether it was a preferable provider have been debated. Huff, for example, frowns on what he considers the intrusion of religious dogma in what ought to have been secular activity (such as science education), referring to the influence the *Ulama* came to exert over the institution (Huff 1993: 3–4). Ihsanoglu, on the other hand, argues that the *waqf* system facilitated 'scientific autonomy' and learning far ahead of European learning (Ihsanoglu 2004: 49). Others point to the perpetual nature of *awqaf* as one of the causes of the decline in agricultural productivity (Watson 1983: 139–46). Yet others point to the *waqf* institution as coinciding with a golden period (though it continued into the 'dark' periods) in Muslim history, protecting aristic freedoms and rights as well as stimulating growth (Iqbal 2002: 140–52; Ihsanoglu 2004). This debate over the past contribution of the *waqf* continues, and even though for a variety of reasons the *waqf* has been abolished or highly regulated, it is a debate that remains relevant to assessing this institution's future potential for facilitating access to land.

Legal Framework for the Waqf

Islamic endowment has been developed by the practice, development of principles and regulations over centuries. The Islamic *waqf* arrangement permits the owner to settle his 'property to the use of beneficiaries in perpetuity' and the property becomes '*waqf* upon a declaration by its owner (the *waqif*) permanently reserving its income for a specific purpose'. Ownership is thereupon 'arrested' or 'detained': the *wāqif* (founder) ceases to be the owner of the property; it cannot be transferred or alienated by him or her, by the administrator (*mutawalli/nazir*) of the *waqf* or by the beneficiaries; and it does not devolve upon the owner's heirs (Cattan 1955: 203). This 'tying up' of property also signifies that is protected from sale or seizure and its use or benefits given to others. Ultimately, all *awqaf* must be dedicated to charity, but this purpose need not be immediate. It is possible to found *waqf ahli* in which the income or usufruct of the property is utilized for the benefit of the founder's descendants, and upon their extinction devolves to charitable purposes. There are opportunities for outsiders to challenge a *waqf*, as illusory or abusive of others rights, as in a case where a dedication undermines the rights of creditors or causes a person's rights to be defeated or delayed.

All of the Islamic *maddahib* (jurisprudential schools) agree that the essential components of a valid *waqf* include a founder/creator, a declaration, a beneficiary and specific property. The essential (*arkan*) components of a *waqfiyya* include a *waqif* of mature and sound mind, *qurbah* (pious purpose) and *ghah* (a declaration), *waqf fi-sabilillah* (endowment in the way of Allah) to set up a pious endowment, *mawquf 'alayh* (a beneficiary or beneficiaries) and *mawquf* (specific property) to be converted into a *waqf*. The *waqf* deed itself needs to be legally authenticated and kept with a *qadi*. Some *waqfiyya*s were carved on the exterior or interior walls of the buildings. Clearly the *waqf* was more than a legal arrangement as some of the *waqf* properties also have inscriptions warning of curses on anyone who alters any of the *waqfiyya's* conditions. In contrast to buildings where details of the *waqf* are put up, there are also traditions of oral *waqf*, though these are rare. Benthall refers to Oman where 'almost all *waqf* property is held on trust by word of mouth tradition ... and this tradition continues even in the modern state, though gradually the legal status of *waqf* property is being formalized. Disputes over such matters are apparently rare' (2002: 153).

The laws relating to the *waqf* are an integral part of Shari'a law. Given the relationship between *waqf* and other areas such as inheritance, bequests, gifts and marriage, it is sometimes dealt with as part of family law. The context of the recourse to the *waqf*, whatever the pious motives of the property owner, includes the compulsory inheritance rules. Since the *waqf* is indivisible, it offers opportunities to owners who wish to evade the splitting up of their property due to inheritance (Powers 1999: 1167; Layish 1997; Doumani 1998: 26–7). As Gerber (2002: 75) has commented:

> From very early on, people from all walks of life bequeathed all types of property to diverse beneficiaries, familial or charitable, for motives ranging from a deeply religious desire to perform charitable acts to a narrow, selfish wish to disinherit one's daughters.

There are generally held to be two basic forms of *waqf*: public and family/'private'. First, there is the *waqf khairi*, which involves the 'permanent' dedication of the property for charitable purposes, such as a *madrassa*. When created during the *waqif's* lifetime, such an endowment takes effect immediately and may consist, should he or she desire, of all, or just part of, the *waqif's* property. If a *waqf* is designed to take effect upon the death of the *waqif*, it can be revoked or changed at any stage until death. However, such a *waqf* is subject to the established limits on Muslim wills in that the endowment may not exceed one-third of a person's assets. The second form, the *waqf ahli*, is sometimes misleadingly referred to as the private endowment. Here the property, with its usufruct or income, is held for the family of the *waqif* or other specific individuals, until the extinction of his or her descendants, whereupon it is diverted to a charitable purpose. It is a sound mechanism for safeguarding family properties from the uncertain upheavals of economic and political life. Since the property is perpetually endowed it cannot be confiscated by 'the whims of the powers that be' (Doumani 1998: 26). For the same reason it also provides a protection against other families or competitors intent on property grabbing, for instance through marriage or extortion (Doumani 1998). This form of endowment is known as *waqf ahli* or *waqf dhurri* in Arab countries. It is termed a *waqf al aulad* in South Asia, where it was widely used and actively encouraged during the nineteenth century as a method for preserving landed estates. Land was placed under the management of a single male successor, usually the eldest son, with allowances made to other members of the family (Carroll 2001: 257–9).

Some commentators include a third category, the *waqf mushtarak*, best described as a quasi-public endowment, which primarily provides for particular individuals or a class of individuals including the *waqif*'s family, but also serves certain outside public interests, such as a mosque which is convenient for, but not exclusive to, family members. Another type of *waqf* is the *waqf gayri sahih*, a state endowment created either because it was established from the state treasury (*bait al-mal*) or because the *waqf* has been taken into state control.

The basic principles on *awqaf* remain the same throughout the Islamic world. However, there are variations in Islamic jurisprudence between the different Sunni *maddahib* – Hanafi, Maliki, Shafi'i and Hanbali – regarding the theories of the *waqf*, as well as diversity in social practices, judicial attitudes and implementation by states. Shafi'is insist that particular words be used to signify intention to create a *waqf* and that the beneficiary must accept the *waqf ahli*, while other schools do not. Though Shafi'is and Hanbalis do not insist on this, other schools of law require the delivery of the possession of the property for completing the *waqf* and some insist on the appointment of the *mutawalli/nazir*. Moreover, practices were modified over time to adapt to different situations and regions because of the particular socio-political contexts and the varied legal traditions. Rules can vary, therefore, according to geographical area and depending on the dominant jurisprudential school. This leads to 'somewhat different approaches depending on whether the relevant jurisdiction is Sudan or Africa west of Egypt, Saudi Arabia, part of Central Asia, or within a band stretching from Egypt and East Africa through parts of the Persian Gulf area and on to southern Asia' (Schoenblum 1999: 1191).

On the particular issue of ownership of the *waqf*, juristic opinion is divided. While in theory the *waqf* property is dedicated to God, its temporality raises issues over ownership. *Waqf* denotes the tying up of property in perpetuity in such a way that proprietary rights cannot be exercised over the property itself but only over the usufruct or income. As Hoexter argues, 'continuous charity' (*sadaqa jaaria*) provides security and irreversibility to the charitable act (Hoexter 2002: 122, 130). However, even within the dominant Hanafi tradition, the *waqf* doctrine has raised complex jurisprudential issues since the earliest times (Hennigan 2004). Shafi'is argue that the property is simply owned by God, which in practice restricts human choices. Hanbalis say the ownership is transferred to the beneficiaries. However, Malikis consider that ownership rests with the *waqif* and is inherited from her/him by legal heirs. Thus, Malikis did not insist on the perpetuity and continuity of the endowment in the way Hanafis, Shafi'is and Hanbalis required. Therefore, when reformers sought to modify the *waqf* institution in Hanafi or other jurisdictions, they favoured the Maliki position. Since Malikis did not insist on perpetuity, the nature of the *waqf* could be altered or varied. There are variations also in the Shi'a legal position, for example, allowing the sale of family *auqaf* (Persian) on the basis that the beneficiaries were owners, although not in the case of public *auqaf*, where the beneficiaries cannot be the owners.

Property and the Cash Waqf

The majority of *awqaf* are real property, where the security of the act of 'continuous charity' is easily evidenced. Some moveable assets, such as furniture, books or farm animals, may be settled in a *waqf* and classical Muslim jurists refer to *waqf* of mobile assets as a practice from the Prophet's times (Kahf 1999). However, as the perpetuity of *waqf* is the general rule, money has not always been regarded as valid subject matter. During the Ottoman period, in the fifteenth and sixteenth centuries, a particular form of endowment or trust fund, the cash *waqf*, by which money was settled for social and pious purposes, came to be approved by the courts. The very nature of a *waqf*, with the word literally meaning detention, is that property is being permanently tied up and endowed to charity. Proprietary rights cannot be exercised at any time over the body of the endowed property, but only on the income or usufruct, and it must be settled in perpetuity. The concept of a cash *waqf* of this kind, thus, presents some difficulties within Islamic law, since money does not have the enduring qualities of, for instance, real estate. The long-term survival of a cash *waqf* may therefore be called into question. However, Kahf (1999), who points out that the Maliki school recognizes *manafi* (usufruct) *awqaf*, notes:

> The 'running' feature of *waqf* can be manifested in different forms. It may be shown in terms of pledging the income/usufruct of an asset for a period of time at the end of which the asset and its income/usufruct return to the founder, in terms of distributing both its income and parts of its asset over repeated instalments to the

> beneficiaries, hence temporality comes from depletion of the asset, in terms of a perpetual asset that produces a repetitive flow of income or services, or in terms of a right granted to the beneficiary to receive periodically, at repeated intervals or when needed, a flow of mobile objects/usufructs. All are Waqf and there is no need for excluding any of them from being a Waqf without valid rationale or support from an original text.

Çizakça (2004) indicates that through a three-fold process Ottoman jurists came to legitimate the cash *waqf*: 'the approval of a moveable asset as the basis of a *waqf*, acceptance of cash as a moveable asset and, therefore, approval of cash endowments'. This did not put an end to debate about the legitimacy of this form of *waqf*, which continued with some vibrancy amongst leading jurists within the Ottoman world through the sixteenth century (Çizakça 2004). Through study of the court registers for the city of Bursa, Çizakça estimates that at least 20 per cent of cash endowments in the fifteenth- and sixteenth-century Ottoman sphere survived for more than a century. This suggests that in practice cash endowments could be as 'perpetual' as those involving real estate. The fact that the endowed capital can be added to year by year in the cash *waqf* through the addition of income, and by further contributions, may go some way to explaining their resilience.

Cash endowments were an important source of credit, with the endowed capital lent to borrowers. The returns were used for charitable purposes, after any deductions for expenses incurred by the *mutawalli* or *nazir* and any taxes. Money earned through provision of credit that was not distributed according to the terms of the *waqf* in any particular year was added to the endowed capital. Çizakça (2004) estimates that about 10 per cent of the total eighteenth-century population of the city of Bursa, which averaged about 60,000 inhabitants during that period, borrowed from cash *awqaf*.

This credit provision aspect of cash *awqaf* raises interesting questions for Islamic law and has proved a modern debating point for jurists and historians. Did cash *awqaf* violate the Islamic prohibition on *riba* (interest)? Some historians have claimed that the cash *awqaf* lent money on interest, or used transactions which were designed to get around the strict legal prohibition on *riba* but produced an 'interest-like' payment (Çizakça 2004, citing Barkan and Ayverdi 1970, Mandaville 1979 and Gerber 1988). On the other side of the debate it is argued that since the Ottoman courts examined these endowments they must be legal and that the return paid to the *waqf* by the borrower was a share of profit as opposed to interest. This form of credit declined, as did the endowments themselves when they came under increasing state control, being replaced by modern banks. However, there is a renewal of interest in the cash endowment (*waqf*), as will be discussed in the following chapter on Islamic credit and microfinance.

Accountability of the Waqf

In the Ottoman period, large imperial *awqaf* founded by a sultan or a sultan's wife, were managed by a *mutawalli* (or *nazir*) with no personal connection to the *waqf*. The *mutawalli* was required to run the *waqf* according to the terms within the founding deed, particularly its charitable purposes, and according to the general expected standards of behaviour and values within Islam. Gerber (2002: 76) discusses the likely response from within the community where a manager, for instance, did not meet these requirements in relation to an endowment of an *imaret*:

> If the manager failed to provide food measuring up to the traditional standard in the kitchen, he immediately found himself sued in court by a group of respectable citizens, invariably headed by *ulama*, usually teachers in *madrassas*, the real public opinion leaders in [an Ottoman] city.

He goes on to explain that accountability in relation to these large *awqaf* was also provided by the courts, with the records showing that citizens often brought 'supervisory' cases in relation to a *waqf*. Repairs and renovations to endowments, certainly in the records of Bursa, were conducted only with the licence of the court and under the direction and supervision of the *ulama*. Individuals drawn from the religious élite also managed smaller *awqaf* – in seventeenth-century Bursa, for example – with the *qadi* having a supervisory function.

Reiter (1994) has studied the records of the Shari'a court in twentieth-century Jerusalem and these, too, show cases brought against *mutawallis* (or *nuzzar*) of *awqaf*, including allegations of neglect, mismanagement and embezzlement, sometimes leading to the dismissal of the *mutawalli*. The documentary evidence also reveals that the *qadis* had a supervisory role in relation to *awqaf*. This can be seen from the very large number of applications by *mutawallis* to renovate and repair existing buildings, undertake new building, purchase new properties, and develop *waqf* land.

Socio-economic Impact of the Waqf

While the millions of *awqaf* spanning the world varied, the majority of foundations fell into the five basic welfare categories of food, housing, health, education and religion. The beneficiaries of *awqaf* could be exclusively family members, but the governing charitable ethos is demonstrated in the high proportion devoted to general welfare. Yediyildiz (1982b: 28–33) finds from the Ottoman *awqaf* records that during the eighteenth century no more than 7 per cent of *awqaf* were held exclusively for the benefit of the founder's family. The *waqf* provided services that the modern welfare state today offers, and this had the tacit support of the state. In fact the Ottoman rulers seemed to have preferred this arrangement, with the sultans frequently creating *awqaf* for public purposes (Hoexter 2002). These charitable foundations, providing income in perpetuity for designated purposes, generally worked well except when there was state interference or poor management (Ihsanoglu 2004: X, 46–7). The *waqf* after nationalization may be indistinguishable from state bureaucracies, but during the time of their autonomy they provided decentralized planning and a dynamic civil society, which in turn affected the nature of the *waqf*.

The *waqf* was intended by classical Islamic jurisprudence to be a 'third sector' of philanthropy or civil society, which existed independently of both the state and the profit-making private sector. As Bremer (2004: 5) notes, 'The oldest civil society institution, the *waqf* or Islamic endowment, combined the features of a philanthropy, a social service agency, and albeit indirectly, a political voice competing with that of a ruler.' *Awqaf* were an integral part of the neighbourhood economy and society and 'affected … by a whole range of local factors, from weather to urban development' (Singer 2002: 169–70). Gerber (2002: 77) comments: 'it is obvious that small charitable *waqfs* constitute a major example of the autonomous working of civil society and the public sphere in the Ottoman Empire'. The integrity of the *waqf* objectives, the quality of services it offered and the transparency of its functioning were in large part due to the effectiveness of civil society institutions. It was also civil society that resisted the governmental encroachments on the autonomy of the *waqf* institution.

In the nineteenth century, the founding of European-inspired municipalities marked a formal repudiation of the *waqf* system in favour of government-coordinated systems for delivering public goods (Kuran 2001). While some states preferred reform of the institution to deal with what was widely regarded as wastage, mismanagement and corruption, others nationalized it or abolished it. Most Muslim countries now directly or indirectly administer *waqf* lands in separate ministries, leading to the demise of the *waqf*'s non-governmental identity – making *awqaf* virtually indistinguishable from state lands. However, unlike state lands, *awqaf* are usually outside the regular land information systems and may have different management structures. A real casualty has been a social order allocating certain rights and obligations and the demarcating of public spaces for government and civil society. However, as will be argued below, there are signs of the revival of the *waqf* concept through initiatives within civil society.

Baskan (2002: 23) comments that through the great variety of recipients and players the *waqf* system was a practice that 'succeeded for centuries in Islamic lands in redistributing wealth, as a product of state–individual cooperation'. Shaham finds that freed slaves were more often than not the sole beneficiaries of *awqaf* in eighteenth- and twentieth-century Egypt (2002: 162–88), and they were also their founders (Fay 1998). Though the *waqf* is an Islamic institution, the beneficiary, the administrator and the process could and did involve non-

Muslims. *Awqaf* supported many churches and synagogues and these were equally admissible in the Muslim courts of law. *Waqf* law, after all, insisted only that the property be given into the ownership of God for the benefit of mankind. Several non-Islamic states with substantial Muslim communities have also allowed for the *waqf*, and the 'secular' administration has not undermined this institution any more than reforms by Muslim states.

The substantial literature on how *awqaf* improved the status of women was alluded to in the previous chapter. Recent research suggests that women in the Ottoman world, in various cities and through a range of historical periods, were deeply involved in the active management of their own wealth, particularly as recorded in the previous chapter in the creation and administration of *awqaf* (Sonbol 2003; Fay 1998; Shatzmiller 1995). Some very famous endowments by women of high rank involved the sponsoring of monumental public works. One of the most famous was Hurrem (or Khurrem), the wife of the Ottoman sultan Suleyman the Lawmaker, who endowed philanthropic institutions in her own name in Mecca, Medina, Jerusalem, Edirne and Istanbul. The first of these to be established, the Istanbul *waqf*, was built between 1537 and 1539. It included a mosque, a religious college, a soup kitchen, a hospital and a primary school (Peirce 1993). However, the creation of *awqaf* was not confined to the ruling élite. Tucker (1985: 96) points out in her study of Egypt that, while women from either the ruling or commercial sectors of society settled the majority of *awqaf*, women from the artisan class also endowed property.

It is certainly the case that women did, unlike their contemporaries in many other parts of the world, administer and manage their *waqf* property, with some women, some of the time, serving as *mutawallis/nuzzar*. Tucker (1985) found that women in nineteenth-century Egypt frequently acted as the *mutawallis/nuzzar* of *awqaf*, receiving, as did most of those who held this position, about 10 per cent of the total income. This administration involved 'a number of possible business transactions, including the keeping up or renting of the ... property, the overseeing of the income, the supervising or repairs to the endowed mosque or school' (Tucker 1985: 96). However, as has already been argued, it is important not to overemphasize the documentary evidence and it may be that, as Ahmed (1992: 112) has argued, Muslim women's relationship to property was 'derivative and marginal'. However, with respect to the *waqf*, the Ottoman records support the argument already presented to the effect that Islamic society was not as rigidly patriarchal as commonly assumed (Powers 1999).

Debating the Contribution of Awqaf

The role and the performance of the *waqf*, which comprised such an important part specifically of the Ottoman lands, has been the subject of intense debate.

Despite its role as a welfare mechanism, it has been argued that the *waqf* institution, being resistant to market forces, created evolutionary bottlenecks locking vast resources into unproductive organizations for the delivery of social services (Singer 2002: Goldstone 2003; Kuran 2004). Shatzmiller analyses the legal material arising out of advisory opinions from *muftis* (*fatawas*) from North Africa and Muslim Spain to contend that the economic performance of the public good *waqf* was flawed. She finds that 'problems were expressed in two ways: in procedure, in the everyday operation of the system, which was conflict-ridden and prone to come to a halt; and in the lack of economic growth' (Shatzmiller 2001: 70).

However, these unflattering appraisals of *waqf* doctrine and practice outlined above, and the role of traditional Islamic law, have been disputed. Gerber (1999: 100) challenges general assumptions about the moribund Ottoman economy and its static intellectual society. His research into the economic literature, particularly in the eighteenth century, suggests a period of 'dynamic development, rather than one of decline'. Hoexter (2002: 102) also challenges the 'oriental despotism' theory by offering *awqaf* not as the problem but as a concrete means by which Islamic doctrine was expressed and implemented for the *umma*.

Recent analysis of the systematic records of the Ottoman Empire, relating not just to the creation of *awqaf* but also to their management and administration, is informative. It indicates 'that the condition of being endowed was a more fluid state, less permanent and, as a result, less of a trap or snare than is often assumed' (Singer 2000: 163). Singer points to evidence of properties being traded in and out of a famous charitable endowment in Jerusalem, which was established in 1550 by the wife of Sultan Suleyman I (Singer 2000: 163–4). For instance, properties that provided uncertain revenue and required considerable attention were exchanged for more reliable sources of revenue. Singer concludes that while it is the case that *awqaf* were intended to be perpetual, in any individual *waqf* where the revenue-producing properties no longer served the beneficial purposes of the particular institution they would be exchanged 'for something more useful' (2000: 163).

The growth of *awqaf* in the Ottoman era can be attributed to the fact that they provided the majority of social services in the Ottoman state. But they also expanded in direct correlation to the risk of expropriation of private land by the state, heightened in the seventeenth and eighteenth centuries, being largely immune to confiscation because their services were considered sacred. Johnson and Balla argue that 'Ottoman holders of capital were protecting their assets the only way they could – through the *waqf* system' (Johnson and Balla 2004), yet the proliferation of endowments provided a large number of cases of mismanagement and nepotism, and made them a visible target for governments.

Colonialism and the Waqf

Several factors, both economic and political, led to the decline of the *waqf*, including attacks on the institution by the colonial powers, which had a paradoxical relationship with the *waqf*. In some cases they preferred a *status quo* which ensured stability as well as social legitimacy. However, they found the *waqf*, which was neither private nor public land, inscrutable, particularly because it differed from Western models of charitable trusts. The colonial powers, particularly the British, began to reconstruct *waqf* law through an elaboration of common-law family, trust or public laws (Lim 2000). An example is South Asia, where the Privy Council tried hard to reconcile the Islamic *waqf* with the English trust before, in 'the notorious' (Mahmood 1988) Abul Fata case of 1894, declaring the *waqf ahli* to be invalid (see *Abul Fata Mahomed Ishak v. Russomoy Dhur Chowdry* (1894) 22 IA 76). However, the statute titled the Mussalman Wakf Validating Act 1913 restored the institution, responding to Muslim outrage and pressure from the leading Muslim institutions and leadership (see Kozlowski 1985). The Act remains in force in India to this day, although it has been drastically amended and the institution has been affected by socio-economic legislation of a more general nature (Mahmood 1988).

Waqf land was seen as a vast resource of 'non-private' land that could easily be harnessed by the colonial powers for other purposes, particularly where religious dissent could be disregarded. Despite earlier assumptions about their perpetuity, *awqaf* had their status altered or extinguished, although the experience varied between the Muslim countries. Where there was any lack of certainty about the status of *waqf* property, as was the case where old Ottoman records were incomplete, lands were siphoned off by the colonial and later the postcolonial state (Raissouni 2004). The main argument of colonialists was that the *waqf* was inefficient, inequitable and uneconomic, and thereby a cause of backwardness. Specific cases of maladministration fuelled the growing perception that the institution was unsuited for the development of modern economies. As the welfare role of the Muslim states (influenced by trends in Europe) expanded, the state regarded the *waqf* as the property of entrenched political classes, particularly the *ulama*. However, as Kogelmann (2002: 66) notes, the vast majority of the population continued to be dependent on the generosity and benefits of family and wholly charitable foundations.

The institution of the *waqf* was, in fact, often a power base for the *ulama*. Islam does not have a priesthood, nor do the religious clergy perform sacramental roles in interceding between God and man. The status and authority of the religious clergy arises out of their role as Islamic scholars and the public face of formal, orthodox religion. They are often the spokespersons for Shari'a law, sometimes being perceived as representing the consensus (*ijma*) of the *umma*. Ghozzi (2002: 317) suggests that 'the adaptability of the *ulama* groups to environmental changes highly depended upon their relative acquisition of three institutional and symbolic capitals – group consensus, institutional autonomy, and charisma'. One of the factors which facilitated the growth of the religious sector in Islam was the *waqf*. Although the *waqf* was envisaged as a private pious act, a large number of endowments were dedicated to mosques and schools which were run by the religious scholars and clergy. Furthermore, the informal consultations regarding the setting up of *awqaf* empowered the Islamic scholars and made them central to the functioning of the *waqf* institution. The administrator appointed by the *waqif* in a substantial number of cases was chosen from among the personnel of the mosque. Over the years, *waqf* landholdings grew considerably, providing the *ulama* with a degree of economic independence from the central government and social legitimacy through taking credit for the benefits of the *waqf* system.

The *waqf* institution developed relatively freely in early Islamic periods because there was no formal division of the church and the state. During the Ottoman period, the state did not see the *waqf* as a threat, although it did institutionalize the role of the clergy. In the Ottoman political culture the clergy acknowledged the ultimate supremacy of the state over both religion and welfare, despite their important role in delivering some of the services which otherwise would have been in the state realm (Mardin 1983). However, with the advent of less secure or colonialist governments and the growing scrutiny of the role of the *ulama* in modernizing societies, the *waqf* institution came under attack as the embodiment of the incompetence and misuse of priestly or scholarly power. For example, French colonial rule over Tunisia from 1881 was marked by a conscious effort to control the institutional and financial autonomy of the religious sector. This trend continued in some postcolonial Arab states as they sought to secularize their societies by following the example, in varying degrees, of Kemal Ataturk, who in 1924 sought to dismantle the already weakened religious sector (*ilmiye*) in Turkey.

In a number of Muslim countries, however – notably Iran and Saudi Arabia – the religious scholars continue to exert considerable influence. Whereas the *ulama* in Saudi Arabia are part of a state-religious apparatus, the religious sector in Iran has directly asserted power. The politics of *vaqf* has been central to the fortunes of the religious leadership in Iran. For example in 1978 Iranian students demonstrated againt the Shah's expropriation of *vaqf* lands. Under the Shi'a socio-religious order, the *ulama* have a far more extensive role and are perhaps the most important layer of society (Keddie 1964: 52). In Iran, despite protests from the *ulama* particularly, the Endowment Organization (*Sazeman-e-auqaf*) was created in 1964, with the administrators (*mutavallis*) being incorporated into the government as deputies (Kamali 1998: 148). However, the *ulama* were able to sustain their autonomy and activism because of another arrangement, 'share of the Imam' (*sahm-e-Imam*). Under this practice, 'every good Muslim should pay 10 per cent of his annual income to the *ulama* for religious institutions' (Kamali 1998: 148).

Decline of the Waqf

While Western trusts, themselves inspired by the *waqf* (Lim 2000), are flourishing and extending their reach, the *waqf* has declined in importance. The vital difference between the two types of endowments, trust and *waqf*, is the Islamic emphasis on perpetuity. The perpetual nature of the *waqf ahli*, for example, meant that as generation succeeded generation, the number of beneficiaries increased to a point where the benefits accruing to an individual were insignificant. As a consequence 'interest in maintaining the property diminishes; the property falls into disuse and ruin' (Carroll 2001: 261). Similarly, even the office of the *mutawalli* was passed down through generations. This process of neglect was exacerbated where the administrators over time became the principal beneficiaries in the property, drawing income from the dedicated property for their management work (Layish 1997: 356). It was these economic disadvantages that led to the widespread abolition of the *waqf ahli*, though it once had the approval of all schools of Islamic law, both Sunni and Shi'a (Carroll 2001). Kuran (2001) argues that 'the states of the Middle East might have tried to compensate for the rigidity of their *waqf* systems by pressuring the courts to play fuller roles in the management of existing *waqfs* and coordinating the formation of new ones. However, these tasks were hindered by two basic principles: static perpetuity and the founder's freedom of choice.' Kahf (1998: 14) suggests that perpetuity is not an absolute condition for the creation of a *waqf* and calls for the reconstruction of the *fiqh* of *awqaf*. He constructs a complex argument to the effect that the contemporary *waqf* can be temporary. While perpetuity may not be an absolute condition, however, the endowment of temporary property must be the exception as opposed to the rule (Kahf 2001).

Schoenblum (1999) argues that 'to a large degree, [the decline] is ascribable to the legal doctrine associated with the *waqf*', which has been rigid as well as over-regulated by Muslim states, in contrast to the natural responsiveness of the Western trust. The dominant view, spearheaded by orientalist commentators such as Schacht (1986) and resonating in recent works, including Kuran (2004), holds traditional Islamic law and the institution of the *waqf* to be among the main causes of the Islamic world's economic disappointments. Baer (1969: 81–3), for instance, regards the *waqf* in twentieth-century Egypt as responsible for 'economic and social ills' with respect to the agrarian structure, since the preservation of wealth in land in the hands of the few has contributed to high prices for land and high rents. This is not the view, however, of those who reject the idea of Islamic law as monolithic, static and autonomous, pointing instead to the deep evolving legal pluralism. The *waqf* does have Islamic origins, but it is a doctrine shaped by the prevalent political, customary and economic forces (Singer 2000: 161). For Meier (2002), the *waqf* institution was a flexible category under Islamic law and Ottoman Sultanic law, but it was eventually corrupted by centralization and over-regulation under the impress of modernizing nineteenth-century reforms.

Postcolonial Attitudes Towards Awqaf

Modernity brought about significant changes to social service structures and the institutions of the Ottoman era began to evolve into modern institutions in the form of public or privately funded schools, charity organizations and modern hospitals. Rather than modernize the *waqf* institution, the postcolonial Muslim states sought to abolish or nationalize them. In the countries of the Middle East both abolition and restriction of family *awqaf* have become commonplace. Kuran (2001) argues that 'by the nineteenth century the system's rigidities made it appear as a grossly inadequate instrument for the provision of public goods; and this perception allowed the modernizing states of the Middle East to nationalize vast properties belonging to *waqfs*'. The logic was that the *waqf* system was 'reasonably well-suited to the slow-changing medieval economy into which it was born, [but] unsuitable to the relatively dynamic economy of the industrial age' (Kuran 2001).

Shortly after independence, several Syrian newspapers carried articles suggesting that the country's economic potential could not be realized without the dissolution of family endowments. The reformers recognized that 'public' *awqaf* should be left intact, not least because of their perceived importance in the minds of more traditional sections of the *ulama* (Deguilhem 1994). Syria abolished family *awqaf* and prohibited their future creation in 1949, with the approval of leading Syrian jurists who provided authorization for their abandonment from within Shari'a doctrine (Mahmood 1988). The new law was widely explained in the newspapers, in general placing the reforms in a positive light and emphasizing the view that this was a step forward in terms of social justice. At the same time public *awqaf* were brought firmly into the state apparatus. Public *awqaf* came under the surveillance of the Ministry of *Awqaf*. Other countries that went down a similar road include Tunisia (1958), where some four million acres of formerly endowed land was transferred to private owners as part of a wider process of reform, Libya (1973) and the United Arab Emirates (1980). Severe limitations were placed upon *awqaf* elsewhere, as in

Lebanon (1947) and Kuwait (1951) (Carroll 2001: 261–2; Layish 1997: 356–7). This administrative pattern was repeated in most Muslim countries and India.

Family *awqaf* were abolished in Egypt (1952), in conjunction with far-reaching land reform, including redistribution of land and rent control. The Ministry of *Awqaf* in Egypt was also given wide-ranging powers over *khairi awqaf*, with agricultural lands held by these institutions taken into the Ministry, their revenue spent according to the Minister's decision. Lesser numbers of people were now interested in creating new *awqaf* (thus defined), given the increasing danger that eventually the properties would come wholly under governmental control. Commenting shortly after these reforms, Baer (1969: 92) expressed the view that 'the income from these extensive properties will no longer be spent on purposes some of which are anachronistic curiosities and on other objects opposed to the interests of the state'. Strategies developed over time to support the *waqf* as a dynamic and flexible institution also came under legislative attack. The use of legal techniques utilizing long leases with advance lump sums (*hikrs*) or 'two rents' (*ijitarayn*) was no longer permitted with respect to *waqf* lands in Syria following Law 163 of 1958. Egyptian reforms in 1960 deemed that all such rights were to be terminated within a certain period (Ziadeh 1985). To take another country where the institution survives, all *awqaf* in India are subject to wide and strict administrative regulation, drawing them firmly into the control of the state. The effect, at least in relation to the family *waqf ahli*, is that, according to Mahmood (1988: 6), it is 'a speedily dying institution', although it is noteworthy that the institution remains in existence at all in this non-Muslim country.

The abolition of the *waqf* or its nationalization by postcolonial Muslim states is ironical. It was welcomed in the West as a move towards land market economics and private property. However, the states already possessed large tracts of state land that were unproductive, and the limited land reform through redistribution was not very significant. Instead, the 'anti-*waqfism*' was prompted by socialist ideas of state-led development and anxieties over the state-rivalling political power adhering to *awqaf* (Bremer 2004: 1). However, the decline of the *waqf* may also be attributed to efforts at 'consolidation of power by political movements intent on gaining control of private capital' (Schoenblum 1999).

States' efforts to control *awqaf* as a means of extending their power have been evident throughout Islamic history, although such efforts have met with resistance (Kuran 2001). Under Ottoman rule, organs of state authority initially sought to administer the orderly functioning of the *waqf* institution and to derive some revenue from it, but increasingly came to rubber stamp its authority (Johnson and Balla 2004). In the beginning, the state levied taxes on *awqaf* to finance its bureaucracy, but the need for liquid funds to fund military and other needs soon led to *awqaf* lands being treated almost like any other property. Eventually in modern times states' main justifications for interference were public interest, in that the *waqf* did not serve the purposes for which it was originally intended and the state was better positioned to administer them efficiently.

Several states – such as Egypt, Turkey, Tunisia, Syria and Algeria – sought to redistribute the *waqf* lands among the landless but there is insufficient evidence on the overall impact, beneficial or otherwise, of these land reform initiatives. Equally there is little research on the administration of these nationalized properties still held by states. It is difficult to compare the state administration of the *waqf* with the earlier arrangements of *mutawallis*, if any generalizations can be made at all. On the contrary, it is a widespread belief that these nationalized *awqaf* have virtually 'disappeared', appropriated by the state without distinction as to their origin or special nature or siphoned off by private individuals. It is for this reason that most countries with substantial *waqf* property have ministries or departments of *waqf* that monitor these lands and their management, either directly or indirectly. There are two major concerns about this monitoring process relating to lack of transparency and lack of integration of these lands in the land registers, as well as perceived corruption in the state administration of these properties. The challenge therefore is to release the potential of the *waqf* either for the original intention of the *waqif* or in the public interest.

Contemporary Revival of the Waqf

While *awqaf* are in disarray – having been abolished, nationalized or mismanaged – there is growing evidence of a resurgence of interest, promotion and rethinking on the subject. Mahmood (1988: 20) suggests, for instance, that the *waqf khairi* as well as the *waqf ahli* should be up for 'reconsideration by the jurists, economists and social scientists of the contemporary world of Islam'. The idea of the *waqf* did not lose its appeal, despite its official eclipse, for several reasons. The *waqf* concept is rooted in classical Islamic doctrine and practice, which appeals both to those who seek a holistic approach to Islamic principles as well as to those who seek a return to an idealized past. Many would argue that the *waqf*, apart from facilitating estate planning in the face of fixed inheritance rules, is an essential vehicle for the Islamic charitable ethos. The state in most Muslim countries has failed to live up to the welfare support standards evident in Western countries. Equally, Western models of philanthropy as well as humanitarian support have proved inadequate. There is an impetus towards not only 'releasing' *waqf* properties now controlled by the state but also encouraging newer ones (Baskan 2002).

An increasing number of non-governmental organizations are using the *waqf* model to solicit and manage funds, cashing in on the appeal of the institution's authenticity. The North American Islamic Trust (NAIT) was established in 1971 in the USA and Canada. NAIT provides protection and safeguarding for the assets of the Islamic Society of North America (ISNA) and other communities by holding their assets and real estate in *waqf*. The World Waqf Foundation, a member of the Islamic Development Bank, has as its stated mission to 'activate the role of Waqf as a socio-economic institution in order to contribute to the plans and programmes of sustainable development that aim at civilizational uplifting of Muslim Peoples and communities and end the suffering of the poor'. The National Awqaf Foundation of South Africa (NAFSA) and the Awqaf Fund for the Disabled and Individuals with Special Needs (AFDISN) are examples of a growing movement which includes transnational as well as local actors.

This interest in the *waqf* is mirrored by the platforms of socio-political groups across a range of Muslim countries. Many view the *waqf* as an element of their Islamic identity and its revival as signifying a return to holistic Islamic principles. There is also a proliferation of material in the academic literature relating to *waqf* which generally revisits the experience of the institution (some with new empirical research into historical documents). This material also offers analyses of the institution's strengths and weaknesses and proposes newer approaches to a modern, efficient and responsive endowment. For example, the American University in Cairo organized its annual History Seminar on 17–19 March 2005 on 'The Uses of *Waqf*: Pious Endowments, Founders, and Beneficiaries', and the Islamic Studies Programme at Harvard Law School has also hosted a conference on the subject.

The *waqf* is also attracting considerable attention from economists and the corporate sector. The Saudi-owned Rusd Islamic Investment Bank, with a capital of US$50 million, announced in 2004 that it seeks to re-engineer and re-introduce many of the great Islamic concepts such as the *waqf* in developing its Islamic trust and asset management products (Parker 2004). Some Islamic banks, for instance in Malaysia, are offering products which combine a cash *waqf* with a partnership (*mudaraba*) principle, whereby the wealthy may deposit funds as an endowment with the bank, which manages the fund and ensures that the depositor's share of the profits is used for benevolent purposes. Thus, the idea of the Islamic *waqf* endures, even where its position within some legal systems remains questionable.

The Organization of Islamic Conference (OIC), an influential group of 57 member states which also reaches out to Muslim communities in other parts of the world, has prioritized the promotion of the *waqf* on its agenda. The distinctive contribution made by the *waqf* to the educational and health fields and in eradicating poverty is highlighted (OIC 2000). It has urged 'member states to pay further attention to *waqfs* in the legislative and administrative fields and pave the way for them to develop their societies'. To this end the OIC is facilitating, through the initiative of the state of Kuwait, the 'exchange of expertise, information and experiences'. This process includes capacity-building workshops as well as the preparation of 'a comprehensive strategy for promoting and developing *waqf* institutions and activating their role in the development of Islamic societies'.

The Islamic Development Bank, an organ of the OIC, has also been paying attention to the *waqf*, holding seminars and 'meaningfully contributing towards investing and developing *waqf* assets' (OIC 2000). The Islamic Development Bank has a substantial *waqf* fund (formerly known as Special Assistance Account), with a target capital of US$1.5 billion. This is used for emergency aid, assistance to member countries affected by locusts, floods and earthquakes, assistance to mitigate refugee problems, and scholarship programmes as well as other educational, health and social projects for Muslim communities in non-member countries in Asia, Africa, North America, Australia and Europe (Islamic Development Bank Group 2003). The Islamic Educational, Scientific and Cultural Organization (ISESCO) also has a specific programme for promotion of the *waqf*.

In a politically charged world, however, the ideologies of the beneficiaries and the founders/creators of *awqaf* alter the perception of neutrality of the charitable endowment (Benthall 2003). The *waqf* may be seen, particularly from a Western perspective, as an undesirable stronghold of economic and social power wielded by influential political or religious groups. This is a particularly sensitive matter when it resurfaces in parts of the Middle East during the War against Terror and the Arab–Israeli conflict, where Palestinian *waqf* lands are very important to the dispute. Philanthropic actions are not regarded as politically neutral acts of piety.

Waqf *in the State Discourse – Kuwait Case Study*

The Muslim states that are members of the OIC have reiterated their commitment to the *waqf* institution, with Kuwait and Saudi Arabia leading this initiative. Most Muslim countries have ministries of *Awqaf*, which are being streamlined. Recent reforms include King Mohammed VI's announced plans in Morocco for 'reviving the *waqf* institution and rationalizing its policies so that it may go on fulfilling the objectives for which it was legally established, as well as carrying out its social solidarity mission, as it continues to develop and grow, thanks to the generosity of benefactors'. However, the experience of Kuwait, as the leader in *waqf* management, is worthy of especial notice in demonstrating the kinds of innovation that can assist the institution to make progress.

This case study relies entirely on the Islamic Development Bank report by Salih (1999). After independence in 1965, Kuwait upgraded its department of *awqaf* into a ministry, mirroring the actions of many other Muslim states. In 1993, however, it established the Kuwait Awqaf Public Foundation (KAPF) with the express aim of developing *awqaf* in a strategic fashion, continuing its overall management role while building on past experience by using modern institution-building techniques. KAPF created a network of specialized bodies to carry out specific tasks and adopted a simpler overall control system. Salih (1999) identifies the key elements of the system as

> separation between *waqf* assets, management outcome and the management of *waqf* service programmes; effectiveness of organizational communication lines and the smoothness of administrative movement; and striking a balance, when distributing powers, between the necessities of taking initiatives and control requirements. In addition to KAPF, the institutional network includes the specialized funds in the *waqf* sector, *waqf* community development, *waqf* projects, *waqf* investment staff and private *waqf* administration.

The network established by KAPF includes both domestic and local relationships, and those with partners, bodies and institutions outside Kuwait. Locally KAPF focuses on organizational relations with government bodies, charitable and investment institutions and private entities. Its foreign relations campaign includes exchanges of good practice and technical cooperation with other Muslim countries, locating and coordinating international support for promoting *awqaf* and collaborating with its partner bodies to develop foreign *waqf* investments. KAPF's investment strategy is 'to maintain a balance between financial and development criteria', while 'diversifying its Shari'a-compatible resources and commitments both locally and internationally' (Salih 1999). Considerable growth in 1993–6 in the volume of newly established *awqaf*, revenues from *waqf* investment and expenditure on development projects suggests that KAPF has been successful in meeting the objectives of both the investment strategy and its wider mandate (Salih 1999).

KAPF has used modern computerized information systems, including an integrated database for *awqaf*, linked into other Islamic and global systems. It is active in research and development, 'feeding and refining its strategic planning, management and investment functions' (Salih 1999). Knowledge dissemination on the *waqf* as a modern institution is also part of KAPF's programme of work, including the issuing of a *waqf* bibliography and a periodical. As Salih (1999) states: 'In short, information technology and R & D are helping KAPF to achieve its objectives and to renew itself to meet challenges of promoting *waqf* and revitalizing its community role.' Whether Kuwait provides a useful model that can be transferred to other contexts is considered by Hamza (2002). He identifies a problem surrounding land information systems and *awqaf* in the context of Bahrain. Two *waqf* departments were established there in 1926, one relating to Sunni *awqaf* and the other to Shi'a *awqaf*. Interviews with the directors of both of these departments in 2002 indicated that for many years these were not properly managed and they are 'facing a backlog of problems inherited from the last seventy years' (Hamza 2002: 39). Hamza also highlights a lack of coordination between ministries and a need for greater use of computer systems. He adds that most *waqf ahli* are not registered with the departments and that there is little or no legislative or administrative regulation of *awaqf* generally. Hamza looks to the 'modernization' of *awqaf* in Kuwait as the way forward in terms of giving the *waqf* a role 'in solving some national problems such as the provision of land for housing, industry and investment' (Hamza 2002: 41).

Innovation in the Administrative Structure of Awqaf

Over centuries the *waqf* has been subject to innovative legal mechanisms. Imber (1997), for example, explores the contribution of Ebu's-su'ud (c. 1490–1574), who creatively harmonized Hanafi law, the dominant school of law of the empire, with Ottoman sultanic law. Some argue that these legal reforms were *ad hoc* and insufficient but others point to the *waqf* as a remarkably vibrant and flexible institution. Further, Islamic law also developed rules equivalent to the English doctrine in charitable law of *cy-près* (near or close to). According to these rules the income of *awqaf* would be applied, where the original purposes were impossible to carry out, to similar objects, as near as possible, to those set down by the founder of the endowment (Mulla 1990: 151). It is well recognized that although the *waqf* administrator cannot depart from the terms set by the *waqif*, he or she has wide powers to protect and enhance the property, seeking administrative or judicial ratification where necessary.

Western commentators have long been concerned about the 'lack' of legal personality of the *waqf*. It has also been argued that classical Islamic law did not recognize juristic personality or a collective individual such as a business corporation. Yet the concept of the *waqf* comes very close to a manifestation of a legal entity, as it has a separate and independent financial personality (*thimmah*) of its own, which is not intermingled with that of its manager. The *mutawalli/ nazir* is only a representative of the *waqf* and the relations between the institution and the manager are very well elaborated in Islamic law (Kahf 2001). The *waqf* could and did provide, therefore, a vehicle for the development of law pertaining to issues such as the legal personality of the city, the committee and the mosque.

Several Muslim scholars have queried whether the Western concept of a corporation suits the *waqf* institution, particularly given its charitable nature and the limited rights of the manager, *mutawalli/nazir*, in respect of alienation of property. However, this is now largely an academic question as modern legislation regulating *awqaf* in Muslim countries was quick to assign them legal personality. As Kuran argues:

> Today, in the early twenty-first century, the *waqf* institution is equipped with adaptation facilities it traditionally lacked. Most significantly, it now enjoys juristic

> personality, which means that it can sue and be sued as a legal entity. Traditionally, it was the manager who had been standing before the courts as an individual plaintiff or defendant. Another major reform is that a modern *waqf* is overseen by a board of *mutawallis* endowed with powers similar to those of a corporate board of trustees. (Kuran 2001)

Efforts at capacity building by *mutawallis/nuzzar* and enhancing transparency and accountability are important, but the real challenge lies in improving and rendering more efficient the structures of *waqf* administration.

There are many examples of how the *waqf* institution in its contemporary manifestation has adapted to modern management and regulatory frameworks. The most telling is the 'statute' of the *waqf* for the Islamic University in Uganda set up recently by the OIC. After setting out its objectives, the statute delineates its organizational structure: a supervisory group, a board of directors, a board of trustees and an office of experts overseeing finances. The *waqf* of the University is to have an independent juridical personality and is subject to 'Islamic Shari'a provisions'. While this is a unique international collaboration, it also shows the sophistication in structure of which the *waqf* is capable. What is certain is that the *waqf* worked best in the past where local actors had a say in its functioning and the revival of this institution will depend on emphasizing its role in the public sphere amongst those who are best equipped to run it (Hoexter 2002).

Ijtihad *and the Perpetuity of the* Waqf

The main difference between the *waqf* and other forms of charity in Islamic theory is the former's perpetuity as *sadaqa jaaria* (continuous charity). Thus, *awqaf* can maintain their original objectives, resisting manipulation by the state or individuals. This perpetuity of the *waqf*, however, has been attacked as excessively rigid and inefficient. Contemporary Muslim jurists point out that while perpetuity may be the general rule, there is room for the exception of a time-bound *waqf*. Ideally perpetuity means until the Day of Judgement, but realistically it means 'as long as the property lasts'. A *waqf* may turn out to have limited duration either because of the will of the *waqif* or the nature of the property. The Maliki School of Islamic jurisprudence explicitly accepts temporality in *waqf* if the founder so wills it, although other *madhahib* do not.

Kahf (1999) argues that 'everything in *waqf* is subject to *ijtihad* and there is no single ruling in it that gained unanimity except that the *waqf* purpose must be *birr*' (benevolent). Apparently all schools of *fiqh*, including the Malikis, failed to anticipate cases in which the *waqf* answers real but time-bound needs. Kahf points out that 'contemporary experiences of Muslim societies and communities indicate that temporality by will of the founder and by nature of certain objectives is part of social life as all societies need it as much as they need perpetuity and glorify it'. He gives the example of the *waqf* of usufructs and financial rights, which may turn out to be time-bound.

> Contemporary life has many forms of usufructs that can be made into *waqf* such as driving a car on a toll way or passing through a tunnel or bridge that has fees on it. Similar to that is the use of a parking lot given a *waqf* for two hours for the Eid prayers twice a year. These kinds of *waqf* need to be recognized by the contemporary *fiqh* as well as by the laws of *awqaf* in the Muslim countries and communities.

The *waqf* is a post-Qur'anic institution developed by jurists and governments over centuries: there is potentially fertile ground for revisiting the model in view of past experiences and contemporary expectations. *Ijtihad* or personal reasoning within the Islamic jurisprudential framework is an integral part of establishing the dynamism, adaptability and relevance of the institution.

Access to Land through the Waqf *Model*

It is generally recognized that vast tracts of *waqf* lands, particularly those under government control or supervision, lie waste. In India, for example, *awqaf* are estimated at over 100,000 properties and many establishments are derelict or have been encroached upon (Indian Express News Service 1999). Innovative approaches to *waqf* lands (and state land) can release the potential of a high proportion of these lands in the public interest. Muslim governments in the past have nationalized and then redistributed large areas of *waqf* lands, but the impacts are unclear. However, where redistribution of the ownership of these unused lands to the landless poor poses problems, the *waqf* model itself can provide alternatives. Even properties that are not currently endowed can be designated as a *waqf* for the benefit of vulnerable groups. The Islamic concept of endowing state land to benefit the welfare of the needy is known as *al-irsadat* and governed by the law of *waqf*. There are special rules under Islamic law relating to *mawat/mewat* land, so-called dead land which is not used or owned by anyone. This can be redistributed to those who use the land through *Ihya' al-Mawat*, an established Islamic economic and legal principle for the revival of dead land. There are strict rules as to what may be considered as waste (*mawat/mewat*), but an analogy to the principle of reviving dead land could pave the way for unused lands to be used by the landless. A state *waqf* is one possibility.

An example of what may be achieved comes from discussion regarding large-scale modern 'squatting' in Al-Madinah in Saudi Arabia referred to in Chapter 3. In the 1970s, squatting was 'viewed by the squatters as a continuation of their traditional and legal rights', based upon the *hadith* that 'he who turns dead land into life becomes its owner' (Bukhari 1982: 555). Bukhari recounts that squatters occupied 'virtually dead' land, building a fence, putting up a shelter, then going 'to the religious court for legalization of their possession' (Bukhari

1982: 556). Where the court deemed the land to be 'useless' and unclaimed, after investigation, it was registered in the name of the occupier. Later the occupants invested in the property and erected permanent homes. Despite his use of the term 'squatting', Bukhari records that no such 'popular' word was used to describe these occupations, because they were part of the legal and social tradition. The state has the power to promote access to land through the *masalah marsala* (Islamic public interest principle) and the *waqf*, with its charitable ethos, may well prove to be an appropriate institutional vehicle, which can be adapted to particular localities. For example, Thier and Chopra (2002: 27), writing in the context of Afghanistan, note that:

> The idea of an independent village-based foundation like a *waqf* (an endowment for religious institutions which governs and manages separately from civil authorities) may be worth investigation. A small resource base for projects and individual or group loans to communities, along microfinancing lines, could generate greater local initiative.

Conclusions

Rather than the narrative of the *waqf* as a historical or virtually extinct model, its revival offers the potential benefits of an inclusive, non-élitist and authentic economic institution. There are two obvious implications of the renewed focus on the *waqf*. First, existing *awqaf* could be better managed and used for enhancing security of tenure, and also for the urban poor. Second, future *awqaf* could assist resource mobilization and redistribution, and strengthen civil society. Given the apparent support for the idea at the local, national and international levels among Islamic communities, the *waqf* need not operate at the margins of socio-economic and philanthropic activity; instead, it should be mainstreamed within state legal and economic systems. Several Islamic institutions, such as the OIC and its subsidiaries, as well as international development institutions could play a vital role in ensuring that the *waqf* fulfils its development potential.

The state has been unable to serve all of the public purposes undertaken historically by the *waqf*. Apart from capacity, the ability of the centralized state to deliver speedy aid and humanitarian support to vulnerable groups is questionable. The endowment *waqf* served as a bulwark for civil society and has the potential still to play that role. Sajoo (2001) argues that since social traditions such as those relating to *awqaf* are deep rooted in Muslim consciousness, 'the potency of these ethical affinities becomes all the more evident in times of crises, when official institutions prove inadequate'. The current reappraisal of the role of the *waqf* offers opportunities to learn from the mistakes of the past and to construct a modern legal and administrative framework. Although it is a matter of debate amongst scholars, since the *waqf* is not a Qur'anic creation it is more easily subject to creative interpretation and change. There is no reason why a modern and responsive doctrine of *waqf* should not emerge from the personal reasoning recognized by classical Islamic jurisprudence as *ijtihad*, a confluence of foundational Islamic principles and modern management techniques.

The eclipse of the *waqf* has left a vacuum in the arena of public services, which has not been filled. Students, health patients, the homeless, travellers, the poor, the needy and prisoners are only some of the vulnerable people who have lost the cover of the *waqf*. This has made Muslim societies further dependent on uncertain foreign donation, which is widely resisted both for its inherent instability and as unwanted foreign intervention. The call to harness indigenous philanthropic traditions aims to tap into the considerable 'social capital' which has survived through the institution of *zakat*. The endowment *waqf* is an embodiment of the principles of self-sufficiency, egalitarianism and learning that mark Muslim societies. Although for Muslims there is an annual obligatory charity obligation, the *waqf* serves as an additional and appropriate mechanism for effecting other philanthropic objectives. In fact, *zakat* can be used to finance and strengthen *waqf* institutions. Similarly, as will be argued in the following chapter, cash *awqaf* provide much needed credit and other financial services.

The increasing popularity of the *waqf* does not necessarily imply a nostalgic return to a traditional model. Modernization of the *waqf* can deliver a transparent and responsive institution with modern management structures that can rival Western charitable institutions and improve access to land. The *waqf* should be seen as a civil society institution providing public space, thereby capable of promoting democratization and good governance. Given the number of Muslim and non-Muslim countries where the *waqf* is used, there is ample scope for sharing of good practice and their experiences. International Islamic institutions such as the OIC, civil society in general and international agencies have a key role in providing the fora for the sharing of experiences and the development of norms relating to efficient management. The example of Kuwait could be considered a best practice, with its efficient *waqf* administrative processes and efforts at sharing experience and technical know-how.

It is a widely held view that 'reforms' of *awqaf* that took them within the public sphere of government have squandered valuable material and human resources. More research is needed as to how those lands are being currently managed. At least two problems can be perceived in relation to reviving *awqaf*: the first is the creation of appropriate information systems to enhance transparency; and the second is finding the means to finance a revival. If endowed lands are to remain within the public sphere, the integration of information regarding state-endowed lands is necessary if these are to be transparently managed and factored into general development. In some instances the only information available is the historical *waqf* records, dating back to the Ottoman period, although in some Muslim countries such lands have to be registered under specific legislation. Perhaps the Ottoman practice of surveying and registering *waqf* land could serve as an inspiration for modern Muslim states.

There is a deficiency of funds for regenerating the productivity of the endowed lands and also a lack of public finance instruments to secure the development of *waqf* properties while offering the owners a market-determined return. This is not a simple matter given that *riba* (interest) is prohibited under Islamic law. It has been suggested that re-privatization may be a way forward and the traditional *waqf* model contains within it methods by which the endowment can finance or refinance itself. These include creating a new *waqf* to add to the old one, and using the mechanism of a long lease with a large advance lump sum and a nominal rent (*hikr/hukr*). A long lease can enable the *mutawalli* of a *waqf* to circumvent the prohibition on the sale of endowed property and use the lump sum to purchase new revenue-producing property or perhaps to repair existing buildings belonging to the *waqf*. The rise of Islamic finance and banking, which is explored in the next chapter, provides a suitable environment for the renovation and reinvigoration of *awqaf*. Shari'a-compliant financing modes could be utilized by energetic *mutawallis/ nuzzar* in partnership with Islamic banks, such as the *murabahah* (mark up/cost plus sale), allowing the purchase of materials and equipment to improve endowed property.

Certainly, Islamic endowments should not be ignored in debates about land regularization and security of tenure as they often comprise extensive tracts of land. The revival of the *waqf* could in the end depend on the commitment of stakeholders through recognition of the benefits of freeing up the dead capital held in *awqaf*. Where there is a shortage of land for distribution, derelict land could be redistributed to landless poor such as squatters, as a new state *waqf* in the public interest. There is also potential, discussed in the next chapter, for the *waqf* to be used to facilitate microfinance and other initiatives. This may well be an opportunity to facilitate the development of indigenous models based on modern benchmarks and capable of responding to contemporary challenges.

8

Islamic Credit and Microfinance

> [An] important function of Islamic finance that is seldom noted ... is the ability of Islamic finance to provide the vehicle for financial and economic empowerment ... to convert dead capital into income-generating assets to financially and economically empower the poor .... (Mirakhor 2002)

Acquisition of land and the access to, improvement and enjoyment of property are often predicated on the ability of individuals to access financial services and secure easy and affordable credit. The significant and increasing demand from within Islamic communities that financial services be compliant with Shari'a law has stimulated a diversification of banking activities by both Islamic and Western commercial banking institutions. Islamic banks are seen as having several interrelated benefits, particularly when compared to commercial interest-bearing banking (Mills and Presley 1999). They are able to mobilize funds and savings amongst those who are excluded from conventional banks because these institutions do not conform to Islamic values. Equally, conventional commercial banks are not always easy to reach, particularly in rural areas with few local branches. Islamic banking also provides a system for those who wish to assert their identity through using Islamic methods and institutions. It suits those who may distrust or be intimidated by large conventional banks and who prefer mutual cooperation between bank and customer, which is implicit in the Islamic banking value base (Chapra 1992). Finally, Islamic banks potentially offer more responsible and profitable financial services due to the closer bank–customer relationship.

Islamic banking is now a boom industry owing to its increase in global market share and fast-paced growth. With over one billion Muslims worldwide, annual growth rates of over 15 per cent in Islamic finance are not surprising.

Islamic Credit and Microfinance

There is increasing and diverse interest in the interface between microfinance initiatives and banking methods governed by Islamic values. Microfinance is the process of building financial systems that serve the poor. The United Nations has deemed microfinance a priority and 2005 was designated as 'Microcredit Year', with microcredit recognized as making a valuable contribution towards attainment of the Millennium Development Goals. Undoubtedly, microfinance is a powerful tool to fight poverty, though it might not be the appropriate strategy for all poverty alleviation programmes. Microfinance has also become a key concern of national governments, including those of Muslim states, non-governmental organizations and, more recently, commercial banks. Microfinance in Muslim countries offers a choice of conventional, informal and Islamic financial products. However, unlike conventional finance, which is preoccupied with profit maximization within a given regulatory framework, Islamic finance is also guided by principles aimed at human development and poverty alleviation that provide a fertile environment for innovative microfinance initiatives.

Islamic microfinance tools can enhance security of tenure and contribute to a transformation in the lives of the poor. Little is known, in mainstream discourse, about what stimulates such alternative credit systems, the key distinguishing features of Islamic finance and credit, the development of Islamic microfinance models and the practical challenges to these innovations. As will be demonstrated, the origins and development of Islamic financing, together with the present market for Islamic financial products, must be understood within the larger context of Islamic religious, ethical and economic systems. It will also be shown that Islamic principles are being applied effectively to microfinance with appropriate legal and financial instruments, although only to a limited degree with respect to housing microfinance. The potential for further development in suitable contexts is explored through experiences in two particular Muslim countries that have yielded lessons for strategies of empowerment through Islamic microfinance, especially for women. Both Yemen and Bangladesh reveal conditions that make Islamic microfinance better suited to some Muslim societies.

Islamic finance is an outcome of the demand for financial products that are in compliance with Shari'a law, most obviously with respect to the prohibitions upon *riba* (usury) and *maisir* (gambling). Islamic microfinance has not been developed systematically, however, though it too has been generated by these and other fundamental Islamic values. As Islamic microfinance upscales and diversifies, as with Islamic banking, there is a need for better regulation to provide transparency and protection for those using these services. Regulation is of particular importance in regard to housing microfinance, which involves relatively large loans and requirements for collateral or guarantees. For many, the overarching imperative may well be that beneficiaries of microfinance are assured that products claiming to be distinctively Islamic are authentic and deserving of the name. Islamic microfinance thus presents challenges to both conventional and Islamic bankers as they seek to generate models which cater to the demands of this world and the hereafter.

Modern Revival of Islamic Finance

Islamic financing principles, which are said to have propelled Muslim dominance as an economic and trading power in the Middle Ages, have made a dramatic comeback in recent decades (Iqbal 1997). The largely rural Mit Ghamr bank in Egypt, created by Dr Ahmad al-Najjar in 1963, is credited with being the first modern institutional initiative with Islamic financing principles, though it was experimental and short-lived. The early success of this bank with savings and investments, as well as its rural outreach (Donohue, 2000: 140; Mengers 2002: 7–9), led to other more stable Arab institutions such as the Egyptian Nasir Social Bank, established in 1974. Since then, Islamic financial institutions have expanded to over 75 countries and a preliminary count identifies over 250 institutions (Asian Development Bank 2004). However, the roots of modern Islamic banking do not lie solely in the Arab world. Comprehensive and far-reaching efforts to reorganize national banking in accordance with Islamic law and replace conventional interest-based commercial banks were seen in Pakistan, Iran and Sudan.

Experiences are diverse, with different objectives and trajectories of progress. The policy in Pakistan, for instance, was fairly cautious and the banks concentrated on financing short-term trade transactions. By contrast, in Iran policy makers were prepared to advance the process of Islamization energetically. At government level Islamic banking in Iran was and is viewed as an essential strategic component in achieving a fully developed Islamic economy, not least because it shapes the attitudes and the behavior of clients (Khan and Mirakhor 2003: 22). In Sudan, the first Islamic bank was established in 1977 and interest-based banking was prohibited only six years later, leading to a rapid expansion in Islamic banking. Malaysia saw its Islamic banking sector rise to 8 per cent of the local market in 2001 from virtually nothing in 1993, with plans to expand in the near future to 20 per cent. In contrast to the generally hostile reception to the 'Islamic' brand in the West, Islamic finance has won many converts. For example, a Western bank, Lloyds TSB, opened its Islamic banking services in the UK on the basis that there is a 'demand from over two-thirds of the two million Muslims in the UK who want Islamic banking' (BBC 2005). Global financial institutions that have established Islamic banking with Shari'a-compatible services include Citibank, BNP Paribas, UBS and ABN Amro. This is matched by the increasing number of national and local providers in the field.

Total holdings of Islamic finance institutions are estimated at approximately 10 per cent of global gross domestic product (El-Hawary *et al.* 2004; Institute of Islamic Banking and Insurance 2005; Anwar 2003: 64–5). Islamic capital invested in global financial institutions is currently estimated at US$1.3 trillion, and over 105 Islamic equity funds globally manage assets in excess of US$3.5 billion in total (Asian Development Bank 2004). Islamic finance encompasses banking, mutual funds, securities firms, insurance companies, and other non-bank institutions. Rapid growth in Islamic banking has led to an explosion of Islamic banks or financial institutions in most Muslim countries. Countries with substantial Muslim populations, including European and North American countries, have also seen a steady increase in Islamic banks (Institute of Islamic Banking and Insurance 2005). Islamic banks are thus a global phenomenon, with their spread across the world estimated as follows: South and South East Asia (47 per cent), the Gulf States and the Middle East (27 per cent), Africa (20 per cent) and Western countries (6 per cent) (Anwar 2003: 64).

This trend towards a new and innovative set of financial institutions is particularly impressive given the pressures of the global market in the latter part of the twentieth and the beginning of the twenty-first century. Islamic banking is seen largely as a success story, despite some failures, both commercially and in terms of customer satisfaction (Kamal, Jamal and Al-Khatib 1999; Metawa and Almossawi 1998). In some countries, such as Iran and Sudan, Islamic banks are the only ones allowed to operate owing to their conformity with Islamic law (Shari'a). In other countries, ranging from Bahrain, Bangladesh and Egypt to Indonesia, Jordan and Malaysia, Islamic banking competes with conventional banking and finance. In addition to Islamic banks, there is an increase in the number of global financial institutions offering Shari'a-compliant products through Islamic 'windows', or through separate banks, branches, or subsidiaries specializing in Islamic financial products. Kuran argues, however, that these Islamic institutions have not revolutionized the economic lives of Muslims but merely created vibrant sub-economies that offer cultural and interpersonal bonding (1995: 155–73).

One key growth area is in the provision of Islamic mortgages, both within the Muslim world and in Europe and North America. Bahrain, for instance, saw considerable expansion between 1980 and 2000 in the number of mortgaged parcels of land and in the percentage of properties purchased through an Islamic bank (Hamza 2002). Another area experiencing expansion is Islamic insurance (*takaful*), which emphasizes mutual interest, cooperation, joint indemnity and shared responsibility (Bhatty 2001; Yousef 2005). The first modern *takaful* company, the Islamic Insurance Company of Sudan, was set up in 1979. While there are more than 50 operators worldwide offering *takaful*, with total assets standing at over US$1 billion, their penetration even in Muslim countries remains fairly small, particularly with respect to life insurance. Malaysia has seen the most obvious and rapid expansion of Islamic insurance and one of its key financial companies, Takaful Malaysia, has entered into joint ventures to expand Islamic insurance activities in Sri Lanka and Saudi Arabia (2005). The D8 group of developing countries has a five-year strategic plan to move Islamic insurance forward in their countries by 2006, with Malaysia again taking a key leadership role.

Foundations of Islamic Economic Activities and Behaviour

Although the modern reinvigoration of Islamic finance coincided with the account surpluses of oil-exporting Islamic countries, its maturity is rooted in a desire for socio-political and economic systems based on Islamic principles (Asian Development Bank 2004). The *Qur'an* and the *Sunna* encourage, respect, praise and regulate productive economic activities and the quest for material possessions and profit, as a means for providing human sustenance as opposed to a goal in itself. The Prophet was himself a successful trader and his first wife Khadijah provided finance for these trading ventures and was involved in their management. The first community of Muslims, being traders who had to journey and move goods over large distances and inhospitable terrain, required substantial risk capital and borrowings. Therefore the *Qur'an* commends trade (2: 198, 73: 20) and repeatedly refers to 'loaning' as 'beautiful' in the context of man's relationship with God (2: 245, 73: 20).

Islamic financing principles emerge from a broader economic ideology. Discussing the foundations of an Islamic economic system, Chapra points out that Islam 'is not an ascetic religion' and encourages man to enjoy earthly gifts from God, while seeking to promote social welfare and just income distribution (Chapra 1970: 3–4). Economic activities are not considered a separate part of human behaviour within the Islamic framework. Material pursuits occupy a sphere linked to spiritual values and religious beliefs (Behdad 1992). Commercial activities conducted in order to provide for individual, family and loved ones are both *halal* (permissible) and in many circumstances commendable. There are narratives within the *Sunna* in support of trade as preferable human activity. One saying is to the effect that 'the sincere, the faithful merchant will on the Day of Judgement be among the prophets, the righteous and the martyrs', another that 'Merchants are the couriers of this world, and the faithful curators of God on earth' (Rodinson 1978: 33–4 quoted in Gran, 1998: 51). Such was the influence of Muslim trading principles that many historians argue that Islam spread more by the example of its trading standards than by the sword.

While the *Qur'an* celebrates good trading practices, it is also conscious of those who are unable to trade (2: 73) and praises charitable acts towards the poor and destitute (see for example *Qur'an* 9: 60). It demands compassionate treatment of poor borrowers – 'If the debtor is in difficulty, grant him time till it is easy for him to repay' (2: 280) – even calling for a waiver, where necessary, as an act of piety. This is supported by the charitable obligation which finds expression in *zakat*, one of the five pillars of Islam, which is a levy on Muslims for distribution to the poor and needy. Islam also deplores certain behavioural patterns widely associated with some persons who have achieved riches. The *Qur'an* condemns greed and love of wealth which lead to arrogant behaviour (89: 15–24; 92: 1–13; 100: 1–11; Behdad 1992: 77). Economic gain should not, therefore, be achieved at the expense of spiritual and moral values and the textual sources of Islam are concerned with setting out in considerable detail the boundaries of permissible economic behaviour. Islamic law lays down the conditions for valid business and financial transactions and practices. For instance, the *Qur'an* gives guidance as to the necessity for written business contracts, duly witnessed (2: 282). Whether a business or transaction is *halal* or *haram* (impermissible) is not merely a question of substance; its legitimacy is also connected with the ethical quality of the procedure by which it is carried out.

Most pro-faith commentators would argue that the Islamic economic system has to be adopted in its entirety through Islamic social, political, and economic conditions (Chapra 1970). It is seen as a third way between capitalist and socialist economic models (Abdul-Rauf 1979). Khan (1994) suggests that these economic principles also require individuals in pursuit of individual wealth to spend in the way of God (*infaq*), abstain from dealing with *riba* (interest), observe sanctity of covenants and trusts, comply with justice, facilitate enterprise and respect the environment. Yet it is readily accepted that 'most of the literature on Islamic economics assumes an ideal Islamic society which does not exist anywhere and the possibility of its coming into being in the near future is also remote' (Khan 1994: 73). The close ties between Muslim countries and the global economic, trade and financial regimes ensure that Islamic financial systems survive alongside and compete with Western financial institutions and products. The conundrum for believers is how the Islamic economic system and financial arrangements can apply in such a 'mixed economy', where the religiously permissible coexists with the impermissible (*halal–haram*). The role of religion in the making of modern economics is controversial. As was indicated in the previous chapter in relation to the *waqf* institution, several commentators such as Kuran (2002) and Guiso, Sapienza and Zingales (2002) consider Islamic principles as the reason for the economic backwardness of the Muslim countries. However, among others, Noland (2003) argues that, if anything, Islam promotes growth rather than acting as a brake on development. While the *Qur'an* offers fundamental principles and modes for economic behaviour, it does not provide details regarding financial services themselves. There is space, therefore, for 'inductive reasoning' in the development of Islamic economics (Khan 1994: 64), which may explain why innovation has a key role in the Islamic financial framework, by comparison with its contribution in other Islamic fields.

Distinguishing Features of Islamic Finance – the Prohibition on Riba *and* Gharar

During the flourishing of Islamic trading and business activity in the medieval period, Islamic merchants interacted closely with Europeans and others. A number of 'techniques and instruments of Islamic finance were later adopted by European financiers and businessmen' (Iqbal 1997). Gambling is one form of *gharar*, which although difficult to define implies hazard and deceit and excess, all of which are to be avoided. It may also be equated with the uncertainty and speculation which are features of conventional banking and finance. The modern development of Islamic financial products has been about both indigenous Muslim ideas and the material interests of national and commercial Western banks. It has thus emerged as a confluence of practices – although based on Islamic principles including the avoidance of interest, upholding of the sanctity of contracts, and prohibition of activities connected with gambling or alcohol (Iqbal 1997). Essentially, there are two interrelated principles with respect to financial transactions that are the pillars of Islamic finance and banking. First, the relationship of creditor and debtor which identifies interest as the price of credit and the location of pressure/risk entirely on the borrower (as in the Western models of commercial banking) is not permitted. Second, persons or institutions, in providing capital, should not receive a reward from financing any venture without exposure to the risks involved in that venture (Mengers 2002: 10). Furthermore, Islamic values encourage entrepreneurship while promoting economic and social development (through *zakat* or charity).

The condemnation of usury as moneylending for interest is well established within the Islamic framework (Choudhury and Malik 1992). The *Qur'an* prohibits 'usury' or *riba* in several different contexts (2: 275, 3: 130, 30: 39) in emphatic, clear and unambiguous language, including the verse (dated late in the Prophet's mission) which reads: 'Those who devour *riba* will not stand except as stands one whom the Devil has driven to madness. That is because they say: "Sale is like usury", but Allah has permitted sale and forbidden usury' (2: 275). This prohibition derives from the concept of money in the Islamic framework as representing merely purchasing power. Money is not an earning asset and therefore cannot earn interest. Money is merely a medium of exchange. It has no value in itself, and therefore should not be allowed to give rise to more money unless it is invested. Money advanced to a business as a loan is regarded as a debt of the business and not capital. It cannot accrue any return (i.e. interest). However, while *riba* is sometimes translated for Western consumption as simply a prohibition on interest, according to Behdad (1992: 86), *riba* more literally means 'over and beyond', while others have translated it as 'increment', 'increase', 'addition' and 'growth' (Chapra 2003: 2). In other words, the prohibition on *riba* may be wider than a mere condemnation of interest.

The concept of *riba* also covers all transactions that give one party more than 'fair exchange' value (*riba al-fadl*), which are designed to produce an 'interest-like' payment (Chapra 2003). An arrangement by which one party purports to sell one pound of salt, in anticipation that the other party to the transaction will make a future transfer of two pounds of salt in return, would not be permitted. Such a transaction sets an artificial higher price on identical goods in order to produce an extra payment that is equivalent to interest in a loan transaction, although there remains some debate amongst scholars on the precise scope of *hadiths* in this regard (Chapra 2003). Any transaction between lender and borrower such that the lender receives gains on capital through an additional excess payment, small or large, in money or another commodity is considered *riba*. Even a condition that the loan shall be preceded by some service by the borrower to the lender falls under the scope of *riba*. On the other hand, profits are distinct from *riba* and not prohibited. Labour and effort, including the efforts of merchants or entrepreneurs through their initiative and risk, are the creators of value and the profits from trade are not considered unlawful. In any business the human effort is more important than the money invested in the business. The gains from trade, profits, are in part a return on financial investment, but the rate of return is not fixed or predetermined and carries with it a risk. Reward should not come simply from a 'premium' for postponing the repayment of a loan, without the creditor taking on any risk as to the possible negative outcomes of the venture (Behdad 1992).

The prohibition on usury is often explained further as a corollary of both the Islamic prohibition against hoarding or an excess accumulation of personal riches (*Qur'an* 102: 1–4 and 104: 1–9) and the injunctions in favour of charitable acts. Trade and financial gain may be lawful, but beyond a certain point gain becomes excessive and 'immoral' profiteering (Behdad 1992). Savings, the difference between what has been gained and what is needed for sustenance and charity, are encouraged to be put to good use. Therefore, an individual should not hoard money, nor should a trader hoard goods in order to corner a market (Behdad 1992: 85). Moreover, El-Gamal (2001) uses classical Islamic jurisprudence, particularly the writings of Ibn Rushd, to argue that the prohibition on *riba* is not just a concern about exploitation but a sound economic argument which is based on economic efficiency. It operates to 'fairly compensate each party for the value of its goods as determined by the marketplace'. Under this reasoning, fixed, predetermined interest rates are not merely exploitative, but socially unproductive and economically wasteful. In the absence of interest, the preferred mode of financing is profit and loss sharing. In the practice of Islamic banks, the contractual agreement between the bank and the depositor determines the proportion of share or loss to be borne by the investor.

The dominant view, arising out of classical interpretations, therefore, is that the spirit of the prohibition on *riba* covers all forms of interest. However, there is some debate among Muslims as to whether this is a total prohibition on employment of fixed interest in moneylending or merely on excessive interest charges (Mallat 1988, Karsten 1982). The prohibition of interest has been interpreted differently by a range of scholars of *Shari'a* law and there are various schools of thought on the topic. Consider the impact the debate over the prohibition of *riba* had on cash *waqf*, discussed in some detail in the previous chapter and arguably an important source of money for the needy during earlier periods of Islamic history. It is contended by some that these cash *awqaf* charged 'interest' or an 'interest-like' payment, albeit at rates well below those prevailing amongst contemporary moneylenders (Johnson and Balla 2005).

A common example of a questionable device was holding the borrower's house as collateral for credit from the *waqf* (Çizakça 2004). The borrower would be allowed to continue living in the property, but would have to pay rent to the *waqf* until such time as the borrowed sum was repaid. At that stage ownership in the house would return to the borrower. Such methods, as Çizakça (2004) explains, could be viewed as 'within the letter of the law while violating its spirit', with the rent being a form of 'pseudo-interest' levied by the *waqf* on the borrower. However, it can also be argued that the Ottoman courts of the time, which had the opportunity to examine many cash *awqaf*, were of the view that they were legal and that the payments made by borrowers to the *awqaf* were a legitimate share of profit and not interest. The borrower was expected to use the capital sum received from the *waqf* for investment, and the payment by the borrower to the endowment did not include interest, but the return of the principal plus a share in the profits earned from that investment (Çizakça 2004).

More recently, Sheikh Dr Tantawi, the current head of the influential traditional Islamic university Al Azhar in Egypt, has joined others in arguing that conventional banking interest is a share in the profits of growth-inducing investments, and not the forbidden *riba*. This follows a line of thinkers, such as Sir Sayyed in the nineteenth century, who have argued that there is a difference between usury, which is prohibited, and interest when it is for commercial lending, which is not prohibited (Ahmad 1958; Visser and MacIntosh 1998). By comparison, in a significant decision which appears to reflect a more general standpoint, the Supreme Court of Pakistan declared in 1999 that all types of interest fall within the purview of the Qur'anic prohibition on *riba* (*Dr Mohammad Aslam Khaki v. Syed Mohammad Hashim*, PLD 2000 SC 225, see Usmani 2000).

Social and Developmental Roles of Islamic Banks

Islamic banking aims to facilitate commerce, investment and legitimate socio-economic activity while contributing towards the overall growth and expansion of the economy. At the same time, it consciously works towards the alleviation of poverty and the more equitable distribution of economic opportunities (Loqman 1999). Several Islamic banks, for instance, offer interest-free benevolent loans, on which the bank has no expectation of making any profit. The customer must simply return the original principal sum, free of any additional charges (*qard hasana*) other than, in some cases, a basic administrative fee. Islamic banks make these loans available for welfare purposes to needy individuals as an act of compassion (Wilson 1987: 215). Those who benefit from the loans include students who require help to pursue their education, but occasionally the loans are granted to small farmers or the like. Some banks also take deposits for social purposes which are to be used, in the same way as the modern cash *waqf*, exclusively for the welfare of those in need (Wilson 1987: 215).

Many Islamic banks have taken their place as participants in the global market-place, albeit in accordance with Shari'a principles. This competitive positioning with conventional commercial banks, at least in part, may be enhanced by the increasing interest of conventional international banks in the Islamic banking system as a means of growth and expansion (Naser, Jamal and Al-Khatib 1999). In Europe, North America and across the Arab world international non-Islamic banks have developed branches or sectors operating within the requirements of Islamic law, a momentum no doubt fuelled by the development of Islamic financial products comparable to the traditional offerings of international banks. The Islamic financial system seeks to integrate market-based financing principles with non-market ethical principles derived from Islamic economic principles, thereby bridging the gap between a market economy and a traditional system. As a result, it is widely considered as a 'moral economy' which offers an alternative and effective approach to banking.

Competition is accompanied, then, by a deeper responsibility for social welfare through financing, rooted in Islamic values and economics. The Islamic bank aims to ensure that individuals' surplus wealth is not hoarded, but directed as savings into investments within or upon worthwhile ventures. The Jordan Islamic Bank, for instance, has been involved in investing in the development of housing projects for both middle-class and lower-income groups (Wilson 1987). In addition, some banks, such as the Sudanese Islamic Bank, have placed great emphasis on the needs of the poorest sectors of society and the role that an

Islamic institution should play in seeking to meet those needs. It has financed farmers to grow potatoes in schemes whereby the profits and losses are shared between the bank and the farmers on an agreed basis, as well as purchase and resale agreements to fund a range of small businesses (Osman 1999; Harper 1994).

Application of Islamic Principles to Microfinance

Islamic microfinance has emerged from the same principles of Islamic financing that have been applied to trading, business and investing within Muslim communities. Poor households use financial services to raise income, build their assets, and cushion themselves against external shocks (Brandsma and Hart 2004), but estimates indicate that fewer than 5 per cent of the world's poor have access to financial services, and Muslim countries do no better. However, microfinance institutions, which aim to provide financial services including credit, savings, cash transfers and insurance to the excluded entrepreneurial poor, are widespread throughout the world, including Muslim countries, although the emphasis continues to be placed on the provision of credit, at least in the early development of such institutions (Ledgerwood 1998). Despite criticism, microfinance is a promising strategy with increasing success in making the poor bankable, although perhaps less successful in enabling the very poorest sectors in society. Such credit and savings approaches, including Islamic microfinance initiatives, have the potential to make a significant contribution to the financing of housing, land and property rights for the poor.

The Islamic principles of equal opportunity, entrepreneurship, risk sharing, charitable obligation and participation by the poor are supportive of microfinance principles (Ferro 2005). As Dhumale and Sapcanin have argued, 'many elements of microfinance could be considered consistent with the broader goals of Islamic banking. Both systems advocate entrepreneurship and risk sharing and believe that the poor should take part in such activities' (1998: 1; Dhumale and Sapcanin 1999). In its ideal form, an Islamic bank is much more than just an institution guided by Islamic principles and avoiding interest payments; it seeks to achieve a just and equitable society (Molla *et al.* 1988). With their distinctive values, Islamic financial schemes can reach out to groups excluded by conventional banks and 'catalyze economic development and reduce poverty' (ADB 2004: 2).

In particular, the poorest of the urban poor, including squatters on remote or unutilized land and those living in rental arrangements in overcrowded inner-city slum tenements, tend to fall outside the net of the general finance industry. A Harvard University study argues that the development of appropriate financial instruments to meet the shelter needs of this latter population group is without doubt the greatest challenge facing the housing microfinance industry today (Harvard Research Group 2000). In this context, Islamic programmes can play their part.

Although currently less widespread than those providing entrepreneurial credit, initiatives for the purchase, construction or improvement of homes, for installing basic services or even to fund land-titling processes can also fit within the Islamic framework which supports private ownership. The *Qur'an* explicitly commands respect for the property rights and houses of others (2: 18; 24: 27), with the Prophet encouraging land ownership. As Kahf (1998) has argued, the rise of Islamic finance and banking has led to a contemporaneous development of Islamic jurisprudence, producing a range of new financing modes, in accordance with these principles, to support individuals in acquiring property. As will be discussed in more detail later in this chapter, the urban middle class in Muslim countries throughout the Arab world, Asia and countries in Europe and North America with substantial Muslim populations are increasingly utilizing Shari'a-compliant mortgages, provided by banks, in order to fund home purchases and improvement. This raises possibilities for using similar mechanisms as vehicles for housing microfinance to enhance access to land and security of tenure for other less-privileged sectors of society.

Mirakhor (2002) points also to the possible release of 'dead capital' through documentation of physical assets in order to convert them into productive, income-generating, assets, holding out considerable opportunities for empowerment. In this he is consciously echoing the influential thesis of de Soto in *The Mystery of Capital* (2000), with his message that the formalization of property rights for the poor in developing countries will enable them to mobilize their assets, liberating their economic potential. Using the example of the Housing Bank of Iran, which helps people without homes to own one, Mirakhor notes that these homes can then be used to generate additional capital for the owners to undertake other productive activities. Thus, Islamic finance has an important role to play in widening the provision of funds to enable the purchase of, or building of, homes for those without them, and in enabling their owners to use the property for further income generation. A wide range of products exists within the Islamic banking and finance sector, some of which have potential for developing Islamic microfinance, despite concerns over their authenticity, integrity and regulation.

Islamic Financial Objectives and Products

Any Islamic financial system or Islamic financial institutions such as a bank or microfinance institution (MFI), which is governed by the principles of Islamic law, will have a number of distinctive objectives that are consistent with the broader goals of Islamic banking and finance (Dhumale and Sapcanin 1999).

These include the requirement that only business activities that are Shari'a-compliant qualify for investment. For example, businesses dealing with alcohol, gambling and immoral activities are prohibited. Furthermore, it envisages development of appropriate contractual instruments in financing individuals that avoid speculative risks, through the profit- and loss-sharing principle. Freedom of contract in Islamic law enables the continuing development of new instruments, provided they are in accordance with legal principles and free of interest (Al-Amine and Al-Bashir 2001: 26–7).

The deposit and lending products of conventional commercial banks have been remodelled to comply with Islamic principles as well as being competitive. For instance, instruments have been found to enable people to purchase homes with mortgages, or buy goods, such as cars, or start/expand a business, for which conventional banks would offer an interest-bearing loan, secured or unsecured. Some of these instruments are not entirely uncontested. As will be discussed in greater detail later in this chapter, there are those who express concerns as to their accordance with Islamic values and consequently their validity (Anwar 2003: 67–71). Nevertheless, there are a variety of financial products which have been developed by commercial Islamic banks to be compliant with Islamic law. Anwar (2003: 62) finds 21 types of interest-free instruments for conducting banking transactions. However, only a small number of these instruments are used regularly, with some rarely used in practice and remaining largely theoretical. Four in particular are fairly common in practice: *murabaha* (mark-up/cost-plus sale); *mudaraba* (trust financing); *musharaka* (joint venture) and *ijara* (lease).

First, there is *murabaha*, which is a common form of trade financing, particularly in short-term trade finance. It is a financial product similar to trade finance in the context of working-capital loans and to leasing in the context of a fixed capital loan. The institution buys goods and resells them to entrepreneurs for the cost of the goods plus a fixed mark-up for administration costs (Donohue 2000). The financing entity owns the goods until the last instalment is paid. This is a two-stage process of financing purchase of goods by banks and the sale of those goods to clients at mark-up prices, on a deferred payment basis. The first stage in this transaction is where a financier (such as a bank) purchases goods, including machinery, raw materials, equipment, or a house, from a third party on behalf of, and at the request of, a client. At the second stage, at a later date, the client purchases the goods on a mark-up or cost-plus basis, thereby giving the financier agreed profits on the transaction. The deferred payment may be in instalments, under an agreed payment schedule, rather than in a single lump sum.

Each stage is to be kept separate with the financial intermediary (the bank) bearing the risk of loss, even if only momentarily, to satisfy the requirement that it owns property that it is selling to the client. This has become the financing technique most widely used by modern Islamic banks, particularly to help customers to purchase consumer durables such as cars, but also, as will be discussed in more detail below, to provide finance to purchase a house. Some estimates suggest that as many as 90 per cent of all transactions undertaken by Islamic banks are on the basis of *murabaha* (Anwar 2003: 64). Its popularity is due to the short-term nature of the financing, limited risk, and guaranteed profit. Islamic law allows a buyer to cancel a deal at any time. *Murabaha* is a flexible model widely used for microfinance clients. Its advantages are that it does not require conventional collateral for credit, since the commodity or asset itself serves as collateral. It is easy to manage since it does not require accounting records.

Second, there is the *musharaka* arrangement, comparable to common law partnership where partners control rights proportional to their capital contribution, which also determines their returns (Donohue 2000). In contrast to *mudaraba*, discussed below, where only one partner (such as a bank) provides capital, here all partners agree to invest. The venture may be jointly managed and the share of profits is determined again by the parties together in advance, while losses are shared according to respective contributions. Versions of this form of contract have been used to permit both short-term and long-term financing for business, including farming. All partners have a financial stake in the company and the right to a pre-determined percentage of the profits. Investment is not required to be paid back at a predetermined date and the bank remains a partner in the operation. This is not a common financing mode among Islamic banks, as the banks are typically not involved with enterprise management. However, it has been used for commercial real estate investment, for the development of offices and modern apartments for rental. For instance, in Singapore the *musharaka* structure has been used, in conjunction with other Shari'a-compliant financial instruments, to develop a number of sites (Rahman bin Kamsani 2005), although there appears to be no specific evidence of its use with respect to the provision of housing for low-income families or those living in informal settlements, or with the aim of enhancing the property rights of the poor.

Third, the *mudaraba* product is one in which the investor bank contributes capital and the entrepreneur provides management, with the entrepreneur and investors splitting profits according to a contractual formula (Fadel 2004). Thus, the *rabal-maal* (the financier, such as a bank) exclusively provides the capital monies for a project, while the *mudarib* (client) provides know-how, labour or management expertise, and they agree together in advance how to divide the profits. The provider of the capital (the bank) carries all the risk of the loss of capital funds, although the other party risks the deprivation of a reward for time, effort and so on. While it does not lend itself to financing in relation to housing, trust financing in farming (*muzar'ah*) involves harvest sharing between the bank and the entrepreneur, and the bank provides funds or land. In *mudaraba* the provider of the capital has no control over the project management, which makes this a preferred mode for banks. In addition to being used for individual business ventures a more complex version of the *mudaraba* is used for some Islamic investment funds. Some banks are also offering products which combine a cash *waqf* with the *mudaraba* principle, whereby the wealthy may deposit funds as an endowment with the bank, which manages the fund, while the depositor's share of the profit is used for benevolent purposes. Like the *musharaka*, the actual return on the *mudaraba* is unclear, since it depends upon the final profit. However, a major difference between the *mudaraba* and the *musharaka* is that in the former case the entrepreneur is not required to invest his/her own capital, and the total loan is paid back at a predetermined rate (along with any profit). The partnership is then closed.

Finally, an *ijara* arrangement has been fashioned as a financial product in which a financier purchases an asset and then leases it to the client for a fixed rental fee. The duration of the lease and the fee will be fixed and agreed in advance (Donohue 2000). A product is used for a specified period for a specified amount, without the user taking ownership of the product: thus the transaction is really the sale of a usufruct. Both rent and usufruct must be determined with sufficient specificity at the time of the lease to survive scrutiny for prohibition against speculative contracts. In one version of this instrument, the client is committed to buying the asset at the end of the lease and the fees paid constitute part of the purchase price. Under a lease-purchase arrangement, payments include a portion applied toward the final purchase of the product and ownership is transferred at the end of the lease period. This is an instrument that may be used for purchasing a home, in place of the prohibited mortgage on which interest is paid.

Islamic Mortgages

Mainstream lending institutions have developed *murabaha* and *ijara* specifically for financing the purchase of residential property within the Islamic framework, generally within developed economies (El-Diwany 2003). *Murabaha* is the mechanism used most widely for this purpose. As in a house purchase using a conventional mortgage, the prospective owner finds a property and agrees on a price with the vendor, but it is the lending body, such as the bank, that makes the purchase from the seller. The lending institution then sells the property to the purchaser for a higher price (including the profit mark-up), to be paid in fixed equal instalments, usually over an extensive period of 15 or more years. In some countries, this model has presented a particular problem under the tax system, which may require tax to be paid on both sale transactions, as was the case until recent changes in the United Kingdom. Hamza (2002) indicates that this is the prevalent form of Islamic mortgage, which he terms 'mutual contracts', in the Gulf States.

There are also mortgages involving the payment of rent, as opposed to interest. Again, the prospective owner finds a property and agrees a price with the seller. As with *murabaha*, the lending institution purchases the property at the agreed price, but agrees to sell it to the client at the end of a period such as 15, 20 or 25 years. However, during that period the client lives in the property, paying rent to the lender for its 'use value' (El-Diwany 2003). This product can be adapted to allow the client to make lump sum repayments each year, or pay off the mortgage in one payment when funds are available. On the other hand there is considerable uncertainty for the client in regard to the fact that the rent to be paid will be recalculated at the beginning of each year.

Both of the above methods developed to replace interest-bearing mortgages in a legal environment of secure titling with a formal land registration system; they may not be useful in the context of the developing world. They are generally somewhat more expensive in terms of transaction costs than conventional mortgages, because of the double-sale and accounting regulations (El-Diwany 2003). In the European context, banks tend to require from the client a fairly large deposit (about 20 per cent) as compared to conventional mortgage lenders. However, El-Diwany (2003: 5) describes a third model of cooperative Islamic home financing used over a considerable period in Canada, the diminishing partnership model, which may hold out greater possibilities for addressing the needs of Muslims outside the system of formalized property rights. The prospective purchaser (client) has to serve a prequalifying period in order to be permitted to apply for a mortgage, during which time he or she purchases shares in the financing organization:

> Funds raised by the organization in this manner are used to finance other clients who have completed their prequalification periods. When the client has qualified for house financing, Person A (the house financing organization) buys the house in its name from Person B (the house seller). Person C (the client) then becomes a partner of Person A in a nominal partnership vehicle which is deemed to own the property ('nominal' because the name of this partnership vehicle does not appear on the property's title deeds). For this purpose, Person C transfers the value of his prequalification shares in the organization to the partnership vehicle, and the relative size of Person A's and Person C's contributions determine the ratio of their shares in the partnership. Person C now lives in the house and pays rent to the vehicle. The rent is then distributed among the shareholders of the vehicle, which of course include Person C himself. Over time, Person C buys Person A's shares in the vehicle and eventually comes to own all of them. At this stage he is the full nominal owner of the house and therefore pays all of the rental on the property to himself. The final formal step is then taken of transferring title in the property to the client ... between Person A and Person C.

As El-Diwany's detailed description emphasizes, there are elements of mutual cooperation which underpin this method of housing finance; these, it could be argued, have a strong correlation with the model of the microfinance institution.

Takaful *(Islamic Insurance) and* Microtakaful *(Micro-insurance)*

While Islamic banks have developed instruments which can be used to facilitate the financing of house purchase, in the developed world mortgages are usually accompanied by life and building insurance as a protection against natural disasters and death. Less frequently, insurance is also used to ensure the continuation of mortgage payments in cases of sickness or the loss of paid employment. However, the Islamic prohibitions on *gharar*, *riba* and particularly *maisir* mean that conventional insurance, amongst Sunni Muslims at least, has been widely regarded as taboo. Life insurance as sold in the conventional fashion was declared unacceptable in 1903 by prominent Islamic scholars (Bhatty 2001). However, cooperative forms of Islamic insurance, known under the umbrella term *takaful*, have developed. The word literally means 'guaranteeing each other' or 'mutual guarantee'. At the heart of the cooperative scheme is the idea that each individual member sincerely intends to donate their contribution to the fund, or common pool, in order to support other participants who are faced with difficulties. In its commercial form several products have been created, some of which use the *mudaraba* model (Salih 1992). It has been recognized that the mutual and cooperative insurance movements in Western Europe have much in common with the Islamic *takaful* industry (Billah and Patel 2005).

Individuals on very low incomes and their families are acutely vulnerable to any rise in expenses or decline in financial resources due to death, sickness, or natural and other disasters. Such incidents lead to the depletion of savings and the forced sale of land. While microfinance institutions have demonstrated that poor people are able to save and service loans made to them, it is also the case that any economic downturn will quickly lead to a rapid depletion in any savings. Insurance has an important potential role, therefore, in poverty alleviation strategies: it can cushion the impacts on the vulnerable of death, illness and other hazards (Patel 2005). Conventional insurance in Muslim countries does exist, but is directed towards the needs of the large or medium-sized commercial sector. However, as Patel (2005) has argued, cooperative insurers, including those rooted firmly in Islamic financial principles, are well placed to meet the needs of the poor. He states:

> The cooperative structure makes it easier to win the trust of the members … and is better placed to tap into members' know-how, loyalty and ideas. The strong community relationship, good user networks, member involvement and democratic

> process encourage a growing feeling of trust and building of social capital to develop a better society.

Patel goes on to suggest that there is a largely unmet need for Islamic insurance products within the microfinance sector, what he terms *microtakaful* products, as an accompaniment to housing microfinance. He gives the example of the Agricultural Mutual Fund of Lebanon as a possible model for future developments. This fund was established in 1997. It provides health insurance coverage and educational scholarships for its members in 180 villages in southern Lebanon and is aimed at the 'economically weak'. The scheme provides health insurance for 5,000 families paying US$10 per month as a premium, with some who are unable to pay, or to pay the full amount, being assisted by other policy holders. There is considerable participation from policy holders in the management of the fund.

'Back Door' Conventional Banking and Microfinance

There continue to be debates, discussed earlier in this chapter, as to whether the lending practices of cash *awqaf* in the past were within Islamic principles. In a similar way, the question has been raised as to whether those instruments which are currently preferred by Islamic banks and their customers, as well as increasingly in the provision of microfinance, go beyond a change of name or terminology. Are these transactions within the letter of the law but not its spirit? While a significant proportion of Muslims use conventional Western-style banking, and to a lesser extent conventional insurance, there is an increasing demand for Shari'a-compliant financial products that are based on Islamic economic principles and Islamic financing arrangements (Fadel 2004). Islamic banks and Islamic enterprises are a cooperative venture between financial experts and Shari'a experts (or committees) who decide on the Islamic validity of a particular product. There is room for interpretive differences of opinion among jurists and different Shari'a committees may and do react differently to similar contractual provisions. However, some commentators have considered whether the financial products of the Islamic banks are little more than devices to circumvent the letter of the law, but which serve in practice to introduce *riba* by 'the back door'. Anwar (2003: 69), for instance, suggests that some of these financial products should be assessed against a particular *hadith*: 'A time shall come to mankind when they will legalize *riba* under the garb of trade.'

From time to time newspapers within the Arab world have carried articles doubting the Islamic credentials of banks that claim to be compliant with Shari'a (Donohue 2000: 138–9). This was particularly evident during the crisis over the so-called Islamic investment companies in Egypt during the 1980s, the best-known of which was al-Rayan. These companies promoted their Islamic credentials and reached out to customers who had little contact with the conventional banking sector. When these companies failed, they were found to have been involved in a form of pyramid investing, with new depositors providing the funds for fictitious returns to old depositors. However, there was also evidence that al-Rayan had incurred losses from speculating in gold derivatives on the international markets, thereby throwing considerable doubt upon its adherence to Islamic principles (Bahaa-Eldin 1999).

At a more general level, Donohue (2000) is concerned as to whether the predominance of *murabaha* products – the financing of the purchasing of goods by banks and their subsequent sale to clients at mark-up prices – amounts to little more than a change of labels driven by the market with the aim of producing products that match those of conventional banks. He argues that 'the man on the street cannot see the difference between Islamic banks and those which are traditional' (2003: 145), perhaps because of the prevalence of *murabaha* products which appear to mirror conventional forms of consumer credit. Fadel (2004) argues that in order to justify the label Islamic finance, Islamic products should be distinguishable from those provided by conventional banks. At the same time, Donohue (2000) emphasizes that modern Islamic banking is still at a relatively early stage of development and that criticism should be tempered by an appreciation of that fact.

Just as doubts have been raised about the Islamic credentials of mainstream Islamic financial institutions and products, so too it is questioned whether some MFIs truly deserve to be labelled as providing distinctively Islamic microfinance. In devising pro-poor strategies to enhance land and property rights, including the provision of housing microfinance, awareness of the strength and depth of local beliefs concerning matters such as *riba* are important. Microfinance clients should have access to Shari'a-compliant services, where such compliance is significant to them. However, Grace and Al-ZamZami (2001) in their report on microfinance in Yemen, are forthright in their assessment that the extent to which a microfinance product is altered to be Islamic depends on 'how strongly these beliefs regarding interest are held'. Therefore, where these beliefs are not as pervasive, institutions may make cosmetic changes to their operations and products, such as changing the term 'interest' to 'service charge'. In other cases where these beliefs are fundamental and widespread, more extensive adaptations have had to take place, which affect the core of an institution's systems, operations and beliefs.

In some contexts, the interest portion of the repayments made by the member of the microfinance initiative who has taken a loan is reformulated as an administrative or management cost. Islamic law does permit transaction fees that are used sometimes in relation to the zero-return loans made by Islamic banks to the needy, but such costs may not be linked to the amount of the loan. A *New York Times* editorial (21 March 2004) states for instance that such an approach was taken in Afghanistan by the microfinance project known as Parwaz, with the interest portion of small loans made to women entrepreneurs 'cleverly called an application fee'. Attempts to allay in advance any local fears that the loans being made are not permitted within the Shari'a, as in the Parwaz project, may meet with some success. However, as hinted at in the *New York Times* editorial, care must be taken to ensure that this amounts to more than a change of name or label. The success or failure of a scheme may be dependent upon local resistance, which may possibly be laid to rest by ensuring that the products offered are in accordance with Islamic law.

Need for Regulation

The relative infancy of Islamic financial institutions, in comparison to longer-established conventional interest-based banking, has led to several problems. Donohue (2000) points to a series of 'external factors', such as a lack of appropriate regulatory frameworks for Islamic banking in some countries. He refers to the spectacular bankruptcies of some Islamic investment institutions, such as al-Rayan in Egypt. He also points, however, to positive developments in regulation – in Egypt, for example, in the aftermath of the Islamic investment institutions crisis in the 1980s, and in Jordan. Donohue (2000) also points to concerns over the role of central banks in terms of setting credit ceilings and legal reserves, together with their lack of intervention when Islamic financial institutions encounter severe liquidity difficulties. In addition, he documents his concerns about 'internal factors'. These include a lack of sufficient expertise and training in Islamic banking amongst officials in some banks. There are also differences of legal opinion between various Shari'a committees, each of which exists to advise a particular bank as to whether particular transactions are permissible.

No uniform regulatory and legal framework has been developed for an Islamic financial system and Islamic banks form their own boards for guidance. Sundararajan and Errico (2002) and Timberg (2003) point to the special risks generally arising out of the profit- and loss-sharing modes of financing and the special nature of investment deposits where capital value and rate of return are not always guaranteed. Timberg (2003) suggests a modified CAMEL (capital adequacy, asset quality, management, earnings and liquidity) system of supervision for Islamic banking. The Asian Development Bank has taken the initiative with the Islamic Financial Services Board (IFSB) to provide a regulatory structure (Asian Development Bank 2004). In addition, the IMF, the World Bank and the Bank of International Settlements (BIS) in Basle are all observers/members of the IFSB, set up in Kuala Lumpur in 2002. An appropriate regulatory framework is especially critical for the robust financing of the housing, land and property industry, since housing usually forms a major part of the national assets of any country. Governments, too, are interested in regulating microfinance, and several countries have passed laws on microfinance, although some of these efforts risk jeopardizing rather than assisting the industry's healthy development.

Islamic Microfinance in Practice

It has been argued that there is considerable potential for the development of specifically Islamic microfinance strategies. There are considerable benefits to be accrued from such innovations in terms of providing access to financial products with religious, social and cultural legitimacy to those sections of society, particularly women, who are traditionally excluded from credit. The potential of Islamic microfinance, however, has hardly been tapped. A number of empirical reports carried out by specialist agencies have sought to provide a systematic overview and evaluation of microfinance in the Islamic world and/or Islamic microfinance itself (see Brandsma and Chaouali 1998). A World Bank report on the Middle East and North Africa in 1998 noted that 'several programmes in the region offering financial services based on Islamic banking principles show promising results' (Brandsma and Chaouali 1998: 2). A recent follow-up report notes that the 'Islamic finance methodologies are being applied by new microfinance programmes, and existing programmes that use Islamic finance – some of them very large – have become more visible' (Brandsma and Hart 2004: 2).

During the recent period, the outreach of the microfinance industry in the Arab world has almost quintupled in size since 1999, going from over 129,000 active borrowers at the end of 1999 to over 710,000 at the end of 2003 (Brandsma and Burjorjee 2004: 17). A network of microfinance institutions in Arab countries, known as Sanabel, was established in September 2002, drawing together institutional members from several countries including Egypt, Jordan, Lebanon, Morocco, Tunisia and the occupied Palestinian territories. It has produced regular surveys of the development of microfinance in the Arab states region, including the establishment of programmes based on Islamic finance principles. In a survey published in October 2004, Sanabel briefly recorded microfinance operations in Syria and Yemen (Brandsma and Burjorjee 2004: 30 and 84). Microfinance services in the area, some compliant with Islamic law, are limited largely to credit for enterprise, not consumer credit, the building or purchase of homes, or home improvement (Brandsma and Burjorjee 2004: 29).

Microfinancing has been referred to as 'barefoot banking' because of its ability to deliver financial services to rural women, and is of particular relevance in largely gender-segregated societies. Experience shows that providing financial services directly to women can aid empowerment. Women clients – with their generally high repayment and savings rates – are also seen as beneficial to the institution. A 2004 report on microfinance in the Arab world finds that the region has seen a significant improvement in terms of outreach to women borrowers. Up from approximately 36 per cent of borrowers in 1997, women currently make up 60 per cent of all clients in the region (Brandsma and Burjorjee 2004). Micro Fund for Women – a private non-governmental organization and leading provider of microfinance to Jordanian women entrepreneurs – is an example of a particularly innovatory scheme run by women for women. Its goal is to empower women as income earners and decision makers in their homes and communities, leading to improvement in the economic status of women's families.

The most common Islamic transaction according to the Sanabel report is the *murabaha*, although reference is made also to a 'UNDP-funded-village-bank-like programme' in Syria, which has 'taken the Islamic financial concept of risk and profit sharing one step further' (Brandsma and Burjorjee 2004: 30), in that the village members of the scheme acquired shares in it, with any profits divided annually between them. The same report notes that Egypt remains the region's leading provider but has lost market share, while Morocco is second, having experienced dramatic growth since 1997. However, other countries, such as Lebanon, and Palestine's West Bank and Gaza, saw their microfinance industries stagnate, or even shrink. This was mainly because microfinance providers in these countries went through restructuring and consolidation, or, in the case of the West Bank and Gaza, faced particular challenges arising out of the Intifada. In Morocco, however, which has seen rapid expansion generally in microfinance provision, three MFIs have implemented housing loan schemes, with further programmes due to be launched in the near future (CHF International 2005), although these do not appear to be consciously developed within the Islamic framework.

Despite this expansion, microfinance in some parts of the Muslim world is a relatively recent phenomenon and there appears to be an increasing gap between demand and supply of Islamic microfinance in different parts of the Muslim world. A number of specialized agencies and institutions – including the UNDP, World Bank, IMF, Asian Development Bank and the Islamic Development Bank – have offered recommendations for realizing the potential of Islamic banking and meeting the challenges. The Asian Development Bank noted, for instance, that an Indonesian White Paper clearly established the development of Islamic banking as a goal for 2004. In the Philippines, too, attention is turning to the Islamic market as an important potential source of public funds. In 1998 the UNDP's Regional Bureau for Arab States, together with the World Bank's Middle East and North Africa Region, published a technical note on *An Application of Islamic Banking Principles to Microfinance*. Since then there has been an increase in literature on standard setting for Islamic microfinance and the Consultative Group to Assist the Poor (CGAP), a consortium of 28 public and private development agencies, has provided some key guidelines. The remainder of the discussion in this chapter will seek to provide an understanding of the contexts, debates and challenges facing Islamic microfinance. To this end, the experiences in two countries will be explored: Yemen, an Arab country where seven out of 15 microfinance initiatives were recently stated to be applying Islamic financial principles (Alirani 2003); and Bangladesh, a Muslim country using microfinance which is not self-consciously Islamic. In particular this exploration includes a consideration of the gender dimension in the microfinance enterprise.

Islamic Microfinance in Yemen

Comparing conventional and Islamic microcredit schemes in Yemen, the Sanabel report expresses a concern as to whether the latter type of programme is 'efficient, sustainable [and] capable of achieving significant outreach' (Brandsma and Burjorjee 2004: 84), although several such schemes have been established. Brandsma and Burjorjee (2004) note that a 'premium' has to be paid by borrowers because of higher transaction costs on Islamic lending. The experience of the Hodeidah Microfinance Programme, established in Yemen in 1997, is fairly well documented and instructive. The project lends to the poor for entrepreneurial activities using a two-stage purchase and resale mechanism, with a fixed service charge and repayment schedule determined in advance, although the charge is paid at the end to avoid any appearance of interest. By this means both commodities and fixed assets may be acquired. It seems that costs are higher than with respect to conventional microfinance because a field officer has to investigate each purchase, buy the goods on the market and exchange cash for them (Grace and Al-ZamZami 2002).

From the outset, however, it was recognized that the religious beliefs of the people in Hodeidah were such that credit in accordance with Islamic banking principles would be preferred. Grace and Al-ZamZami (2002) state that some potential clients feared that the loans might be prohibited by Islam and that

> Some religious/mosque speakers announced that the project practices *riba* (charging of interest) which is prohibited in Islam. However, when the project management described details of the transaction, most of these speakers felt the product did adhere to the *murabaha* methodology and retracted their statements.

They document the administrative challenges which this Islamic financial product presents to the microfinance institution and its additional costs, but also acknowledge its strengths in reaching out to those otherwise excluded and in terms of acquiring broader local approval (Grace and Al-ZamZami 2002).

Bangladesh and the Grameen Bank

Bangladesh is overwhelmingly a Muslim country with an Islamic constitution, and its experience in combating rural poverty is itself worth studying. Its people are, to varying degrees, conscious of the authenticity or cultural specificity of the microfinance products. The history of the Grameen Bank of Bangladesh, which has served as the model for other institutions, demonstrates that it was derived from socio-cultural practices not in conflict with Islamic principles and helps in understanding the dynamics of microfinance choices and assertions of religious identity. Grameen was initially set up in a village in 1976. Under a law created for the purpose in 1983 it became a bank. It produced an easily understood system of microfinance, particularly the provision of small collateral-free loans to the rural landless poor for productive enterprise purposes, focusing on the landless or those with very small landholdings. Schemes centred upon villages, with members self-selected by the ability of neighbours to evaluate each other's creditworthiness. Members made weekly repayments on the loan, including interest. It may be described simply as solidarity group lending. In 1984 it began offering housing microfinance for the construction of homes.

Research has demonstrated that Grameen has positive short-term and long-term economic and social effects on the households of participants, including better nutrition for children (Hashemi and Schuler 1997). Women members of the Bank, when compared to other poor rural women, show a high degree of participation in the labour market, an enhanced status within their families with respect to decision making and greater freedom of movement. There is also evidence that membership of Grameen over a number of years leads to an expansion of assets for many women. Formerly landless women will purchase land for agriculture and for building or extending homes. Improvements to homes such as the addition of tin roofs to houses are also a visible outcome of membership (Momen 1996). Empowerment of women and the poor in general is widely viewed as a fundamental purpose by those in the Bank, although this is not necessarily emphasized at the grassroots level. However, the Grameen Bank has been subject to criticism and resistance both within and outside Bangladesh.

At first there were those who argued that collateral-free loans could not work or that microfinance was not a valid means of addressing the fundamental causes of poverty. However, from within the rural communities of Bangladesh itself criticisms came particularly from those sections of society who stood to lose from cheap collateral-free loans. These groups included the traditional money-lenders who involved their clients in a spiral of indebtedness from high interest rates and the village landed élite who benefit from cheap labour. The increased visibility in the public sphere of women who are members of Grameen may also be regarded as a particular irritant and challenge to some established authorities. Increasingly the concerns of local forces have been picked up and shaped by groups that have a wider national agenda. The argument is that the Grameen Bank is a dangerous manifestation of an imported foreign and secular culture that is designed to undermine and challenge Islam (Hashemi and Schuler 1997). This viewpoint has found expression sometimes through acts of violence against Grameen offices and personnel by at least one militant group. A spate of bomb and grenade incidents in early 2005, in which Grameen Bank branches were targeted alongside the offices and personnel of other NGOs concerned with poverty alleviation, represents the latest round of these attacks (*Daily Star* 2005).

Hashemi and Schuler (1997) suggest that Grameen has taken a nonconfrontational approach to its internal critics, adopting an approach, for instance, whereby its social transformation objectives, including the empowerment of women and the poor, are played down by its staff on the ground. At the same time, as these commentators note, the bank staff, like the majority of people living in the villages, pray, fast and take part in religious events, while expressing the Bank's activities in terms of well-embedded social obligations towards the welfare of the poor. The Grameen Bank, and the microfinance institutions based on that model, can be positioned within the Islamic framework, although it is the case that most members pay back their loans with interest. Some of its activities, such as the Struggling Members Programme for beggars, with interest-free loans, and its use of profits seem to be evidence of an underpinning of Islamic values and even Islamic banking principles.

The provision of housing microfinance by MFIs, whether for 'whole house' financing, house construction and improvement, buying land or the installation of services, despite a fairly long history, remains generally less widespread than provision of entrepreneurial credit, particularly in the Muslim world. The Grameen Bank moved into this field later in its history, only after full establishment as a bank. Housing finance forms a smaller part of its overall provision than entrepreneurial microcredit, although more than 600,000 houses have been constructed using small loans of about $250 (Younis 2005). However, housing microfinance may involve larger loans, require a guarantee or collateral, and be difficult to implement in informal settlements, where the MFIs' clients frequently reside. In Morocco, where housing microfinance has begun to show significant development, the microfinance law, which was changed in 2002 to permit loans for purchasing land, houses, improvements to existing homes, and the provision of utilities, has a relatively low ceiling for such loans of $3,456 (CHF International 2005). This limitation has been addressed by some institutions using the 'progressive building' method, in which a series of small loans is advanced as the process of house construction develops (CHF International 2005). It would seem that in Morocco all the existing providers of housing microfinance require loans to be backed either by a guarantor or by collateral, in the form of household goods or forced savings (CHF International 2005).

Experience in Yemen and Bangladesh suggests that Islamic microfinance institutions will face many of the same limitations and problems as conventional providers. Nevertheless, there is great potential to apply Islamic financial principles and banking practices in a concerted manner to the provision of microfinance. This has a number of obvious potential benefits. First, conventional banks and MFIs may shy away from lending to people living in informal settlements and a scheme compliant with Islamic legal principles may draw in poor entrepreneurs otherwise left out of credit markets but who would wish to avoid *riba*-based credit. The strong correlation between Islamic principles and the values underpinning microfinance, including the emphasis upon partnership, mutual guarantees and a concern for the welfare of the community of Muslims, may provide the basis for innovation even in seemingly inauspicious circumstances. It is possible that Islamic MFIs may through their social, cultural and religious legitimacy develop instruments such as the diminishing partnership model to meet the needs of clients without formal title but with some right to land or a *de facto* protection from eviction.

Second, such a scheme may be more acceptable to traditional and religious authorities whose support, or at least lack of resistance, may enhance the chances of successfully establishing the institution, particularly although not exclusively in rural areas. Aspects of good practice in relation to housing microfinance appear to correlate closely with the values and mutual cooperation that are the hallmark of Islamic financial institutions. The complementary aspects of microfinance and Islamic banking principles hold out considerable possibilities for social and economic transformation.

Conclusions

Modern Islamic microfinance institutions are still a recent phenomenon and have experienced haphazard growth. They are not yet fully evolved but their potential is significant. In particular, Islamic microfinance products are suitable to enable housing microfinance that is within Islamic law and to enhance security of tenure, particularly for the poor. Islamic jurisprudence, with its emphasis upon partnership and a concern for community welfare, together with the expansion in Islamic banking and microfinance, has the ability to respond creatively to the needs of the urban poor. There is an emphasis in existing microfinance schemes on loans to the 'entrepreneurial poor', rather than the full variety of financial services that the poor need. However, appropriate financial instruments have developed which avoid *riba* and can enable individuals to purchase homes, just as they can provide funds to start up businesses. While there are dangers in creating high expectations and the limits of macroeconomic poverty alleviation strategies must be recognized, sustainable and viable long-term programmes with the appropriate range of products for the target groups should be expanded.

Diverse models and practices are inherent in the choice and flexibility Islamic microfinance offers, but these services need to be regulated in order to provide transparency, instil consumer confidence and prevent fraud on beneficiaries due to unfamiliarity with the products. State regulation, though necessary, has been *ad hoc* and sometimes an obstacle to the evolution of effective microfinance mechanisms. In the case of microfinance, states should be encouraged to support MFI membership of the Islamic Financial Services Board and to provide fora for sharing best practice and success. An appropriate regulatory framework is required for a vigorous housing finance system, especially given the importance of housing as a key national asset in most countries. Housing microfinance programmes tend to involve larger loans, with guarantees and/or collateral, therefore effective regulation of Shari'a-compliant housing microfinance schemes is crucial. It may be the case that microfinance, including Islamic microfinance, will reach its full potential only if and when it is integrated into a country's mainstream financial system in order to standardize regulation and underpin outreach mechanisms.

The success of any microfinance project is dependent on the building of permanent local financial institutions that can attract domestic deposits, recycle them into loans, and provide other financial services. The failures of microfinance in general have occurred when MFIs have not been regulated or supported by either their funding bodies or government. Capacity building of MFIs depends on forming strong and transparent management structures, and merely espousing Islamic principles does not absolve them from creating a culture of accountability. Islamic MFIs which seek to enhance the position of the poor, including the realization of their rights to secure shelter, must develop their financial accountability in the same way as conventional microfinance institutions. Financial accountability is linked closely to social accountability and microfinance schemes work best with the full involvement of their members. Indeed this is an imperative for the survival of most microfinance projects. In order to pay for itself a scheme must reach out to very large numbers of poor people in order to be self-sustaining. Strategies to enhance opportunities for the poor to participate in, and become educated about Islamic microfinance products are an essential component of outreach as well as contributing to good management and financial stability.

Many customers of Islamic banks may have a history of banking in the conventional commercial banking sector. However, there is also evidence that an institution rooted in Islamic values and financial principles will draw in customers new to banking, and a similar case can be made for microfinance.

These customers may have excluded themselves at the prompting of their religious beliefs, but the behaviour of the bank or microfinance institution itself may also be a factor. The increasing demand for Islamic banking and financial products, the entry of a variety of financial institutions into the market and the sheer range of Islamic products raises the question of whether these justify the label 'Islamic'. Given that some microfinance projects, particularly those focused upon reaching out to women, have been accused of meddling with social codes, such questions could be fundamental to the continued existence of some projects. There are no easy answers, space must remain for diversity, and Shari'a experts will have different opinions about the same contractual relations. However, sharing best practice and harmonization of general Islamic products would enhance the credibility of Islamic finance and microfinance.

In many contexts Islamic microfinance and conventional microfinance coexist and distinctions are not immediately apparent. Therefore, the demand for the development of Islamic microfinance products may not be as obvious or as strong as the demand for Islamic financial instruments in the commercial banking sector. It is important, however, that the vulnerable, particularly those on very low incomes, are provided with the opportunities and fora to learn about Islamic microfinance products and ultimately to participate in their development. This is particularly the case with respect to schemes funding the purchase of houses, their improvement or services. If such schemes are both Shari'a-compliant and shaped by local communities, they can inspire consumer confidence while extending and enhancing land rights.

Postscript

From Strategy to Tools

Shortly after the summary of this research was disseminated by UN-HABITAT and its partners, the balance and utility of its findings came under focus from both a general and a Muslim audience. The objective of this research, as conceived by UN-HABITAT, was to produce a body of material and to propose strategies, thus enhancing the knowledge as well as augmenting the effectiveness of those working in Muslim contexts. The research was immediately made available to practitioners from Afghanistan to Somalia. More specifically, a new initiative, the Global Land Tool Network (GLTN) – aimed at developing innovative, pro-poor, gendered, affordable and scalable tools – began to apply Islamic tools to land, property and housing rights. This research was presented at several stakeholder meetings such the GLTN partner meetings attended by land professionals, civil society, researchers and officials in Stockholm, Sweden (November 2005) and Oslo, Norway (March 2006). It was also presented at the Expert Group Meeting (EGM) in Bangkok, Thailand on 'Secure Land Tenure: New Legal Frameworks and Tools in Asia and Pacific' (7–9 December 2005) organised by UN-HABITAT, the United Nations Economic and Social Commission for Asia and Pacific (UNESCAP), the International Federation of Surveyors (FIG) and the World Bank.

The biggest challenge came when the research was to be debated by Muslim land professionals, experts, civil society and government officials at the Arab Expert Group Meeting. The workshop held in Cairo on 17–18 December 2005 was part of a high ministerial conference hosted by the Government of Egypt and organized by the United Nations Economic and Social Commission for Western Asia (ESCWA), UN-HABITAT, and the League of Arab States. The organizers considered it prudent to refer the research to two important authorities: first, the Al Azhar, considered the highest seat of Islamic learning in the Sunni Muslim world; and, second, a committee of experts convened by the government of

Egypt. Both the committees returned the verdict that the research was fair, balanced, constructive and in line with highest standards of Islamic scholarship. The meeting of over 45 experts itself discussed and endorsed the research as a baseline study for future research and policy making. They adopted the Cairo Initiative on Islamic Land Tools, calling on UN-HABITAT as a focal point to garner regional and international support and resources to consolidate and further promote the development of Islamic land tools.

Islamic land tools, even in Muslim countries, cannot be a substitute for the continuing process of universal or generic land tool development because the complementary role or appropriateness of Islamic tools depends on particular demands and contexts. However, Islamic approaches do not reflect a preference for religious discourse over universal or secular land approaches but rather a pragmatic strategy. The relationship between Islamic and other tools facilitates valuable cross-fertilisation through best practices. The development of Islamic land tools, like the evolution of customary tools, is not an internal matter but a cross-cultural, interdisciplinary and global effort. Though Islamic principles are influential, they intersect in dynamic ways with state, customary and international norms. Their relationship with other systems of formal and informal land tenure is under further study. In clarifying Islamic principles and developing effective tools, injurious cultural practices carried out in the name of religion may be countered.

The multi-stakeholder discussions have focused on how to facilitate the development of innovative, pro-poor and gendered Islamic land tools which could be used appropriately in specific contexts. Three broad challenges face tool development in the Muslim world. First, the crystallization of positive strategies from the Islamic land discourse and best practices from the Muslim world, needs to inform the tool development process. Second, there is a need to prioritise specific processes of Islamic tools generation which can be innovative, pro-poor, gendered, affordable and scaleable. Third, interfaces between the various actors – whether tool developers, grassroots groups, civil society, states, development partners or scholars – are needed to harmonize universal, Islamic and professional land principles. The ownership of the process by Muslims is important but civil society and development partners must contribute to a process that is inclusive, objective, systematic and transparent.

There are several methodological questions relating to the process of developing land, property and housing tools from Islamic best practices. The stakeholder consultations have indicated that the process must be representative, focused, constructive and non-ideological. Every Islamic professional tool undergoes a rigorous process as do other tools. There is a need for consultations between representative groups of professional tool developers, civil society, Islamic scholars, policy makers and development partners. Harmonization of universal and Islamic principles, objectives and values enables systematic identification, upscaling, development and evaluation of Islamic tools. The Islamic tool development process generally follows stages similar to those in the development of other types of land tools, but adjusted to its distinctive sources, needs and sensitivities. The main players will be the community groups, including grassroots women, tool developers, state officials and development partners, with the addition of Islamic scholars and Muslim communities and institutions. At the launch of the Global Land Tool Network at the World Urban Forum in Vancouver, Canada on 20 June 2006, the development of Islamic land tools was highlighted as one of the priorities for the network. This book is but a small beginning in triggering networks, frameworks and dialogues aimed at converting the promises of Islamic principles into practical tools for women and men around the world.

Bibliography

'Abd Al-Fattah, N. (1999) 'The Anarchy of the Egyptian Legal System: Wearing Away the Legal and Political Modernity', in B. Dupret, M. Berger and L. al-Zwaini (eds) *Legal Pluralism in the Arab World*, The Hague: Kluwer Law International.

'Abd Al-Kader, A. (1959) 'Land, Property and Land Tenure in Islam', *Islamic Quarterly*, 5.

Abdul-Rauf, M. (1979) *The Islamic Doctrine of Economics and Contemporary Economic Thought: Highlight of a Conference on a Theological Inquiry into Capitalism and Socialism*, Washington: American Enterprise Institute for Public Policy Research.

—— (1984) *A Muslim's Reflection on Democratic Capitalism*, Washington: American Enterprise Institute for Public Policy Research.

Abed, S. (1995) 'Islam and Democracy', in D. Garnham and M. Tessler (eds) *Democracy, War, and Peace in the Middle East*, Bloomington: Indiana University Press.

Abu-Dayyeh, N. (2006) 'Prospects for Historic Neighborhoods in Atypical Islamic Cities: The View from Amman, Jordan', *Habitat International: Journal for the Study of Human Settlements*, 30, 1.

Abu-Lughod, J. (1980) *Rabat: Urban Apartheid in Morocco*, Princeton: Princeton University Press.

—— (1987) 'The Islamic City – Historic Myth, Islamic Essence, and Contemporary Relevance', *International Journal of Middle East Studies*, 19, 2.

Aga Khan Development Network (2000) *Philanthropy in Pakistan: A Report of the Initiative on Indigenous Philanthropy*, Islamabad: Aga Khan Development Network.

Agarwal, B. (1994) *A Field of One's Own: Gender and Land Rights in South Asia*, Cambridge: Cambridge University Press.

Ahmad, I. (1993) 'Islam, Liberty, and the Free Market', in M. M. Abul-Fadl (ed.) *Association of Muslim Social Scientists Proceedings Twenty-first Annual Conference*, Herndon, VA: International Institute of Islamic Thought.

—— (2004) 'The Challenge of Institutional Governance in Islam: Justice, Democracy, and Shariah', paper presented at the 5th Annual Conference of the Center for the Study of Islam and Democracy: Defining and Establishing Justice in Muslim Societies, May, Washington DC.

Ahmad, S. A. (1958) *Economics of Islam (a Comparative Study)*, Lahore: Sh. Muhammed Ashraf.

Ahmed, L. (1992) *Women and Gender in Islam*, New Haven: Yale University Press.

Akhavi, S. (1980) *Religion and Politics in Contemporary Iran*, New York: New York State University Press.

Akhtar, S. (1994) *Shah Bano Judgement in Islamic Perspective, a Socio-Legal Study*, New Delhi:

Kitab Bhavan.

Alam, M. N. (2003) *A Comparative Study between Islamic and Conventional Banking Systems. A Study Based on an Institutional-Network Theoretical Framework*, www.alternative-financing.org.uk, March.

Al-Amine, M. and M. Al-Bashir (2001) '*Istisna* and its Application in Islamic Banking', *Arab Law Quarterly*, 16, 1.

Al-Araki, A. M. (1983) *From Ibn Khaldun: Discourse of the Method and Concepts of Economic Sociology*, Oslo: University of Oslo, Faculty of Social Sciences.

Al-Asad, M. (1997) 'Ruptures in the Evolution of the Middle Eastern City: Amman' in M. E. Bonine (ed.) *Population, Poverty and Politics in Middle East Cities*, Gainesville, FL: University Press of Florida.

Al-Azmeh, A. (1993) *Islams and Modernities*, New York: Verso.

Al-Braizat, Fares (2002) 'Muslims and Democracy: An Empirical Critique of Fukuyama's Culturalist Approach', *International Journal of Comparative Sociology*, 43, October.

Alchian, A. A. (1977) 'Some Economics of Property Rights', *Il Politico*, 30, reprinted in A. A. Alchian, *Economic Forces at Work*, Indianapolis: Liberty Fund.

Al-Faruqi, M. (2000) 'Women's Self-identity in the *Qur'an* and Islamic Law', in G. Webb (ed.) *Windows of Faith: Muslim Women Scholar-Activists in North America*, Syracuse, NY: Syracuse University Press.

al-Ghannouchi, R. (2000) 'Traditional Muslim Society is a Model of Civil Society', in A. Tamimi and J. Esposito (eds) *Islam and Secularism in the Middle East*, New York: New York University Press.

Al-Ghunaimi, M. T. (1997) 'Justice and Human Rights in Islam,' in G. E. Lampe (ed.) *Justice and Human Rights in Islamic Law*, International Law Institute.

Al-Hibri, A. (1997) 'Islam, Law and Custom: Redefining Muslim Women's Rights', *American University Journal of International Law and Policy*, 12, 1.

Ali, S. S. (1999) *Gender and Human Rights in Islam and International Law: Equal Before Allah, Unequal Before Man?*, The Hague: Kluwer.

Alirani, K. (2003) *Islamic Microfinance – Yemen Experience*, First Annual Conference of Sanabel, Microfinance Network of Arab Countries.

Al-Maamiry, A. (1987) *Economics in Islam*, New Delhi: Lancers Publications.

Al-Mahmassani, S. (2003) *Al mabadii, al shariiya wal kanouniya fi al hajir, alnafakat, almawarith, wal wassiya*, Lebanon: Dar Al Elem Lilmalayin.

Al-Nowaihi, M. (1975) 'Problems of Modernisation in Islam', *The Muslim World*, 65, 3.

Al-Sayyid, M. (1997) 'Theoretical Issues in the Arab Human Rights Movement', *Arab Studies Quarterly*, 12, Winter.

Alston, P. (1992) 'The Committee on Economic, Social and Cultural Rights', in P. Alston (ed.) *The United Nations and Human Rights: A Critical Appraisal*, Oxford: Clarendon Press.

Al-Suwaidi, J. (1995) 'Arab and Western Conceptions of Democracy', in D. Garnham and M. Tessler (eds) *Democracy, War, and Peace in the Middle East*, Bloomington: Indiana University Press.

Altug, Y. (1968) 'Legal Rules Concerning Land Tenure in the Ottoman Empire', *Annales de la Faculté De Droit Istanbul*, 18.

Amawi, A. (1996) 'Women and Property Rights in Islam', in S. Sabbagh (ed.) *Arab Women, Between Defiance and Restraint*, New York: Olive Branch Press.

Amnesty International (2004) *Re-drafting the Arab Charter on Human Rights: Building for a Better Future*, London: Amnesty International.

Anderson, J. N. D. (1967) 'The Eclipse of the Patriarchal Family in Contemporary Islamic Law', in J. N. D. Anderson (ed.) *Family Law in Asia and Africa*, London: George Allen and Unwin.

Anderson, M. (1996) *Islamic Law and the Colonial Encounter in British India*, Occasional Paper 7, Women Living under Muslim Laws (WLUML) 2.

An-Naim, A. (1990) *Toward an Islamic Reformation: Civil Liberties, Human Rights, and International Law*, Syracuse, NY: Syracuse University Press.

—— (1994) 'Cultural Transformation and Normative Consensus on the Best Interests of the

Child', in P. Alston (ed.) *The Best Interests Principle: Towards a Reconciliation of Culture and Human Rights*, Oxford: Clarendon.

—— (ed.) (2002) *Islamic Family Law in a Changing World*, London and New York: Zed Books.

—— (2004) '"The Best of Times" and "the Worst of Times": Human Agency and Human Rights in Islamic Societies', *Muslim World Journal of Human Rights*, 1, 1.

Annan, K. (2005) *In Larger Freedom: Towards Development, Security and Human Rights for All*, New York: UN Report.

Antoun, R. (1990) 'Litigant Strategies in an Islamic Court in Jordan', in D. H. Dwyer (ed.) *Law and Islam in the Middle East*, New York: Bergin and Garvey.

Anwar, M. (2003) 'Islamicity of Banking and Modes of Islamic Banking', *Arab Law Quarterly*, 18, 1.

Arjomand, S. A (1998) 'Philanthropy, the Law, and Public Policy in the Islamic World before the Modern Era', in W. F. Ilchman, S. Katz, and E. L. Queen II (eds) *Philanthropy in the World's Traditions*, Bloomington: Indiana University Press.

Arkoun, Mohamed (1998) 'Rethinking Islam Today', in C. Kurzman (ed.) *Liberal Islam: A Source Book*, New York: Oxford University Press.

Asian Development Bank (2004) *Technical Assistance for the Development of International Prudential Standards for Islamic Financial Services*: Asian Development Bank, July.

Awde, N. (2000) *Women in Islam: An Anthology From the Qur'an and Hadiths*, New York: St Martin's Press.

Ayubi, N. N. (1991) *Political Islam: Religion and Politics in the Arab World*, London: Routledge.

—— (1995) *Over-Stating the Arab State: Politics and Society in the Middle East*, London: I. B. Tauris.

Baderin, M. (2001) 'Macroscopic Analysis of the Practice of Muslim State Parties to International Human Rights Treaties: Conflict or Congruence?', *Human Rights Law Review*, 1, 2.

—— (2003) *International Human Rights and Islamic Law*, Oxford: Oxford University Press.

Badran, M. (1985) 'Islam, Patriarchy and Feminism in the Middle East', *Trends in History*, 4, 1, Fall.

—— (1999) 'Toward Islamic Feminisms: A Look at the Middle East', in A. Afsaruddin (ed.) *Hermeneutics and Honour: Negotiating Female "Public" Space In Islamic/ate Societies*, Cambridge, MA: Harvard University Press.

Baer, G. (1962) *A History of Landownership in Modern Egypt, 1800–1950*, New Haven: Oxford University Press.

—— (1969) *Studies in the Social Histories of Modern Egypt*, Chicago: University of Chicago Press.

—— (1983) 'Women and *Waqf*: An Analysis of the Istanbul Tahrir of 1546', *Asian and African Studies*, 17, 1.1.

—— (1997) '*Waqf* as Prop for the Social System (Sixteenth–Seventeenth Centuries)', *Islamic Law and Society*, 4, 3.

Bahaa-Eldin, Z. (1999) 'Formal and Informal Finance in Egypt', in B. Dupret, M. Berger and L. al-Zwaini (eds) *Legal Pluralism in the Arab World*, The Hague and London: Kluwer.

Barakat, H. (1993) *The Arab World: Society, Culture, and State*, Berkeley: University of California Press.

Barkan, O. L. and Ayverdi, E. H. (1970) *Istanbul Vakiflari Tahrir Defteri*, Istanbul: Fetih Cemiyeti.

Barlas, A. (2002) *Unreading Patriarchal Interpretations of the Qur'an*, Austin: University of Texas Press.

Basar, H. (1987) *Management and Development of Awqaf Properties*, Jeddah: Islamic Research and Training Institute, Islamic Development Bank.

Baskan, B. (2002) '*Waqf* System as a Redistribution Mechanism in the Ottoman Empire', paper presented at *17th Middle East History and Theory Conference*, 10–11 May, Center for Middle Eastern Studies, University of Chicago.

Basu, A. (1999) *The Challenge of Local Feminisms: Women's Movements in Global Perspective*, Delhi: Kali for Women.

BBC (British Broadcasting Corporation) (2005) 'Islamic Banking "Goes Mainstream"',

Tuesday, 15 February, <http://news.bbc.co.uk/1/hi/business/4264939.stm>.

Becker, L. (1980) 'The Moral Basis of Property Rights', in J. R. Pennock and J. W. Chapman (eds) *Nomos XXII: Property*, New York: New York University Press.

Behdad, S. (1989), 'Property Rights in Contemporary Islamic Economic Thought: A Critical Survey', *Review of Social Economy*, 47, 2.

—— (1992) 'Property Rights and Islamic Economic Approaches', in K. S. Jomo (ed.) *Islamic Economic Alternatives*, London: Macmillan.

Bell, D. A. (1996) 'The East Asian Challenge to Human Rights: Reflections on an East West Dialogue, *Human Rights Quarterly*, 18, 3.

Benthall, J. (2002) 'Organized Charity in the Arab-Islamic World: A View from the NGOs', in H. Donnan (ed.) *Interpreting Islam*, London: Sage.

—— (2003) 'Humanitarianism and Islam after 11 September', in J. Macrae and A. Harmer (eds), *Humanitarian Action and the 'Global War on Terror': A Review of Trends and Issues*, HPG Report 14, London: Humanitarian Protection Group.

Bentham, J. (1931 [1802]) *The Theory of Legislation*, London: C. K. Ogden.

Berween, M. (2000) 'The Fundamental Human Rights: An Islamic Perspective', *International Journal of Human Rights*, 6, 1.

Bethell, T. (1994) 'The Mother of All Rights: Without Secure Property, the Islamic World Can't Escape Tyranny and Stagnation', *Reason*, 25, April.

Bhabha, H. (1994) *The Location of Culture*, London: Routledge.

Bhatnagar, J. P. (1992) *Commentary on the Muslim Women: Containing the Muslim Women (Protection of Rights on Divorce) Act, 1986*, Allahabad: Ashoka Law House.

Bhatty, M. A. (2001) *Takaful Industry: Global Profile and Trends*, <www.islamic-banking.com/insurance/takaful_aom/ma_bhatti.php> 29 April 2005.

Bielefeldt, H. (1995) 'Muslim Voices in the Human Rights Debate', *Human Rights Quarterly*, 17, 4.

Biezeveld, R. (2004) 'Discourse Shopping in a Dispute over Land in Rural Indonesia', *Ethnology*, 43, 2.

Billah, M. M. and S. Patel (2005) *An Opportunity for ICMIF Members to Provide Islamic Insurance (Takaful) Products*, Altrincham, ICMIF, <www.icmif.org/takaful> 29 April 2005.

Biyik, C. and L. T. Yomralio (1994) *Land Information Systems in the 1500s*, Figure XX, International Congress, Commission 1, Melbourne, Australia.

Bjorkelo, A. (1998) 'Islamic Contracts in Economic Transactions in the Sudan', paper presented at *The Fourth Nordic Conference on Middle Eastern Studies: The Middle East in a Globalizing World*, Oslo, August.

Bobbio, N. (1996) *The Age of Rights*, Cambridge: Polity Press.

Bonine, M. E. (1979) 'The Morphogenesis of Iranian Cities', *Annals of the Association of American Geographers*, 69, 2.

—— (1987) 'Islam and Commerce: *Waqf* and the Bazaar of Yazd Iran', *Erdkunde*, 41, 3.

—— (1997) *Population, Poverty and Politics in Middle East Cities*, Gainesville, FL: University Press of Florida.

Bonne, A. (1960), *State and Economics in the Middle East: A Society in Transition*, London: Routledge and Kegal Paul.

Bowen, J. (2003) *Islam, Law and Equality in Indonesia*, Cambridge: Cambridge University Press.

Bowman, K. and J. Green (1997) 'Urbanization and Political Instability in the Middle East', in Michael Bonine (ed.) *Population, Poverty, and Politics in Middle East Cities*, Gainesville: University Press of Florida.

Brandsma, J. and D. Burjorjee (2004) *Microfinance in the Arab States: Building Inclusive Financial Sectors*, New York: UNCDP.

Brandsma, J. and R. Chaouali (1998) *Making Microfinance Work in the Middle East and North Africa*, New York: Human Development Group, World Bank.

Brandsma, J. and L. Hart (2004) *Making Microfinance Work Better in the Middle East and North Africa*, Washington DC: World Bank.

Bremer, J. (2004) '*Islamic Philanthrophy: Reviving Traditional Forms for Building Social Justice*', paper submitted at the 5th Annual Conference, Center for the Study of Islam and Democracy Annual Conference on Defining and Establishing Justice in Muslim Societies, Washington: CSID.

Brown, N. J. (1997) *The Rule of Law in the Arab World*, Cambridge: Cambridge University Press.

—— (2001) *Arab Judicial Structures: A Study Prepared for the United Nations Development Program*, Program on Governance in the Arab Region, Geneva: United Nations.

Brumberg, D. (2002) 'Democratization in the Arab World? The Trap of Liberalized Autocracy', *Journal of Democracy*, 13, 4.

Bukhari, Saleem M. (1982) 'Squatting and the Use of Islamic Law', *Habitat International*, 6, 5/6.

Bunton, M. (2000) 'Demarcating the British Colonial State: Land Settlement in the Palestinian *Jiftlik* villages of Sajad and Qazaza', in R. Owen (ed.) *New Perspectives on Property and Middle East*, Cambridge MA: Harvard University Press.

Bush, R. (2004) *Civil Society and the Uncivil State*, Paper Number 9, Civil Society and Social Movements Programme, United Nations Research Institute for Social Development (UNRISD).

Cammack, M. (2000) *Inching Toward Equality: Recent Developments in Indonesian Inheritance Law*, London: Women Living under Muslim Laws (WLUML), Dossier 22.

Caponerea, D. (1973) *Water Laws in Muslim Countries*, Rome: Food and Agriculture Organization (FAO).

Carroll, L. (2001) 'Life Interests and Inter-Generational Transfer of Property: Avoiding the Law of Succession', *Islamic Law and Society*, 8, 2.

Cattan, H. (1955) 'The Law of *Waqf*', in M. Khadduri and H. J. Liebsney (eds) *Law in the Middle East – Vol. 1*, Washington: Middle East Institute.

Chapra, M. U. (1970) 'The Economic System of Islam: A Discussion of its Goals and Nature', *The Islamic Quarterly*, 14.

—— (1992) *Islam and the Economic Challenge*, Leicester: Islamic Foundation.

—— (2003) 'The Nature of *Riba* in Islam', *Hamdard Islamicus*, 7, 1.

Charlesworth, H., C. Chinkin and S. Wright (1991) 'Feminist Approaches to International Law', *American Journal of International Law*, 85.

Charrad, M. (2001) *States and Women's Rights: The Making of Postcolonial Tunisia, Algeria, and Morocco*, Berkeley: University of California Press.

Chaudhry, Z. (1997), 'The Myth of Misogyny: A Reanalysis of Women's Inheritance in Islamic Law', *Albany Law Review* 61, Winter.

CHF International (2005) *Practical Guide for Housing Microfinance in Morocco*, CHF International.

Choudhury, M. A. and Malik. U. A. (1992) *The Foundations of Islamic Political Economy*, London: Macmillan.

CIHRS (Cairo Institute for Human Rights Studies) (1996) 'Lift the Reservations on CEDAW', *Sawasiah*, 12, September.

Çizakça, M. (2000) *A History of Philanthropic Foundations: The Islamic World From the Seventh Century to the Present*, Istanbul: Bogazici University.

—— (2004) *Ottoman Cash* Waqfs *Revisited: The Case of Bursa 1555–1823*, Manchester: Foundation for Science, Technology and Civilization.

Coban, A. R. (2004) *Protection of Property Rights within the European Convention*, London: Ashgate Publishing.

Collier, J. F. (1996) 'Intertwined Histories: Islamic Law and Western Imperialism' *SEHR*, 5, 1.

Consultative Group to Assist the Poor (2001) 'Microfinance, Grants and Non-Financial Responses to Poverty Reduction: Where Does Microfinance Fit?', *Focus Note No. 20*, May 2001.

Cook, R. (1993) 'Women's International Human Rights Law: The Way Forward', *Human Rights Quarterly*, 15, 1.

Cosgel, M. (2004) 'The Economics of Ottoman Taxation', Department of Economics Working Paper Series, University of Connecticut.

Cotula, L. (2002) *Gender and Law – Women's Rights in Agriculture*, Rome: Food and Agriculture Organization (FAO) Legislative Study.

Coulson, N. J. (1969) *Conflicts and Tensions in Islamic Jurisprudence*, Chicago and London: University of Chicago Press.

Craven, M. (1995) 'Economic and Social Rights: The Dynamics of Implementation', *Interights Bulletin*, 9, 3.

Crecelius, D. (1995) 'Introduction', *Journal of the Economic and Social History of the Orient*, 38, 3.

Cummings, J. T., H. Askari and A. Mustafa, (1980) 'Islam and Modern Economic Change', in J. Esposito (ed.) *Islam and Development: Religion and Sociopolitical Change*, Syracuse, NY: Syracuse University Press.

Cuno, K. M. (1980) 'The Origins of Private Ownership of Land in Egypt: A Reappraisal', *International Journal of Middle East Studies*, 12, 3.

d'Hellencourt, N. Y., S. Rajabov, N. Stanikzai and A. Salam (2003) *Preliminary Study of Land Tenure Related Issues in Urban Afghanistan with Special Reference to Kabul City*, Kabul: UN-Habitat.

Daily Star (2005), 17 February.

Dale, S. F. and A. Payind (1999) 'The Ahrari *Waqf* in Kabul in the Year 1546 and the Mughul *Naqshbandiyyah*', *Journal of the American Oriental Society*, 119, 2.

de Soto, Hernando (2000) *The Mystery of Capital: Why Capitalism Triumphs in the West and Fails Everywhere Else*, London: Black Swan.

Deguilhem, R. (1994) 'Le *Waqf* en Syrie Independante', in F. Bilici (ed.) *Le Waqf dans le monde musulman contemporain (XIXe–Xxe siecles)*, Istanbul: Institut Francais d'Études Anatoliennes.

DfID (2002) *Better Livelihoods for Poor People: The Role of Land Policy*, consultation document, London: Department for International Development.

Dhumale, R. and A. Sapcanin (1998) *An Application of Islamic Banking Principles to Microfinance: A Technical Note*, Regional Bureau for Arab States, UNDP and Middle East and North Africa Region, World Bank.

Doi, A. R. (1997) *Shariah: The Islamic Law*, London: Ta Ha Publishers.

Donnelly, J. (1998) 'Human Rights: A New Standard of Civilization?' *International Affairs*, 74, 1.

—— *Universal Human Rights in Theory and Practice*, Ithaca: Cornell University Press.

Donohue, J. J. (2000) 'A Note on the Theory and Practice of Islamic Banking', *Yearbook of Islamic and Middle Eastern Law*, London: Kluwer Law International.

Doumani, B. (1998) 'Writing Family: *Waqf*, Property and Gender in Tripoli and Nablus, 1800–1860', *Comparative Studies in Society and History*, 40, 1.

—— (2003) *Family History in the Middle East: Household, Property, and Gender*, Albany: SUNY Press.

Ehlers, E. (1992) 'The City of the Islamic Middle East', in E. Ehlers (ed.) *Modelling the City: Cross-Cultural Perspectives*, Bonn: Ferd Dumlers.

Eide, A. (1989) 'Realization of Social and Economic Rights and the Minimum Threshold Approach', *Human Rights Law Journal*, 10, 2.

Eisenman, R. H. (1997) *Islamic Law in Palestine and Israel: A History of the Survival of Tanzimat and Shari'a in the British Mandate and the Jewish State*, New York: Brill.

El Ayachi, M., S. El Hassane, M. Ettarid, D. Tahiri and P. Robert (2003), *New Strategy towards a Multipurpose Cadastral System to Support Land Management in Morocco*, Second FIG Regional Conference, Marrakech, Morocco, 2–5 December.

El Ghonemy, M. R. (2005) *Land Reform Development Challenges of 1963–2003 Continue into the Twenty-First Century*, Food and Agriculture Organization (FAO) <http://www.fao.org/DOCREP/006/ J0415T/j0/ j0415t05.htm 29/06/2005>.

El Saadawi, N. (2001) Interview Reported on Monday 9 July as 'Egypt Apostasy Trial Adjourned', BBC Online.

El-Alimi, S. and D. Hinchcliffe (1996) *Islamic Marriage and Divorce Laws of the Arab World*, London and Boston: Kluwer Law International.

El-Diwany, T. (2003) *The Great Islamic Mortgage Caper?* <http://www.islamic-finance.com/item122_f.htm>.

El-Gamal, M. A. (2001) 'An Economic Explication of the Prohibition of *Riba* in Classical Islamic Jurisprudence', Occasional Paper, Houston: Rice University.

El-Hawary, D., W. Grais and Z. Iqbal (2004) *Regulating Islamic Financial Institutions: The Nature of the Regulated*, World Bank Policy Research Working Paper 3227, Washington, DC: World Bank.

Engelmann, K. E. (2001) *Rural Development in Eurasia and the Middle East: Land Reform, Demographic Change, and Environmental Constraints*, Seattle: University of Washington Press.

Esposito, J. L. (1982) *Women in Muslim Family Law*, Syracuse, NY: Syracuse University Press.

—— (1983) *Voices of Resurgent Islam*, Oxford and New York: Oxford University Press.

—— (1987) *Islam and Politics*, Syracuse, NY: Syracuse University Press.

—— (1999) *The Oxford History of Islam*, Oxford and New York: Oxford University Press.

Esposito, J. L. with N. J. DeLong-Bas (2001) *Women in Muslim Family Law*, Syracuse, NY: Syracuse University Press.

Evans, M. and R. Murray (2002) *The African Charter on Human and Peoples' Rights: The System in Practice, 1986–2000*, New York: Cambridge University Press.

Fadel, M. H. (2004) *Islamic Finance*, American Association of Law Schools (AALS), American Society of Comparative Law and Law and Society.

Faruqui, N, I., A. K. Biswas and M. J. Bino (2001) *Water Management in Islam*, Tokyo: International Development Research Centre (IDRC)/United Nations University (UNU) Press.

Fay, M. A. (1998) 'From Concubines to Capitalists: Women, Property and Power in Eighteenth-Century Cairo', *Journal of Women's History*, 10, 3.

Feillard, A. (1997) 'Indonesia's Emerging Muslim Feminism: Women Leaders on Equality, Inheritance and Other Gender Issues', *Studia Islamika*, 4, 1.

Ferchiou, S. (1985) *Les Femmes dans l'Agriculture Tunisienne*, Aix on Provence: Edisud.

Fernandes, E. and A. Varley (1998), *Illegal Cities: Law and Urban Change in Developing Countries*, London: Zed Books.

Ferro, N. (2005) *Value Through Diversity: Microfinance and Islamic Finance and Global Banking*, Milan: Fondazione Eni Enrioco Mattei.

Forni, N. (2005) *Land Tenure Policies in the Middle East*, <http://www.fao.org//docrep/005/Y8999T/y8999t0f.htm>.

Freeman, M. D. A (1998), *Legal Theory at the End of the Millennium*, Oxford: Oxford University Press.

Freeman, M. (2002), 'Equality and Rights': background paper for the proposed general comment on the International Covenant on Economic, Social and Cultural Rights (ICESCR) Article 3, 13 May.

Fuccaro, N. (2001), 'Visions of the City – Urban Studies on the Gulf', *Middle East Studies Association Bulletin*, 35, 2.

Fyzee, A. A. A. (1974) *Outlines of Muhammedan Law*, New Delhi: Oxford University Press.

Gallagher, A. (1997) 'Ending the Marginalization: Strategies for Incorporating Women into the United Nations Human Rights System', *Human Rights Quarterly*, 19, 2.

Gerber, H. (1988) *Economy and Society in an Ottoman City Bursa 1600–1700*, Jerusalem: The Hebrew University.

—— (1999) 'Muslims and Zimmis in Ottoman Economy and Society: Encounters, Culture and Knowledge', in R. Motika, C. Herzog and M. Ursinus (eds) *Studies in Ottoman Social and Economic Life*, Heidelberg: Heidelberger Orientverlag.

—— (2002) 'The Public Sphere and Civil Society', in M. Hoexter, S. N. Eisenstadt and N. Levtzion (eds) *The Public Sphere in Muslim Societies*, Albany: State University of New York Press.

Gerrard, P. and B. J. Cunningham (1997) 'Islamic Banking: A Study in Singapore', *International Journal of Bank Marketing*, 15, 6.

Ghai, Y. (1998) 'Appendix I: Our Common Humanity — Asian Human Rights Charter', *Netherlands Quarterly of Human Rights*, 16, 4.

Ghazzal, Z. (2005) *The Grammars of Adjudication: The Economics of Judicial Decision Making in fin-de-siècle Ottoman Beirut and Damascus*, Cambridge: Cambridge University Press.

Ghozzi, K. (2002) 'The Study of Resilience and Decay in Ulama Groups: Tunisia and Iran as an Example', *Sociology of Religion*, 63, 3.

Goldstone, J. A. (2003) 'Islam, Development, and the Middle East: A Comment on Timur Kuran's Analysis' in the series *Institutional Barriers to Economic Change: Cases Considered*, Washington DC: USAID.

Goodwin-Gill, G. (1996) *The Refugee in International Law*, Oxford: Clarendon Press.

Grace, L. and A. Al-ZamZami (2002) *Islamic Banking Principles Applied to Microfinance Case Study: Hodeidah Microfinance Program, Yemen*, Geneva: UNCDF.

Gran, P. (1998) *Islamic Roots of Capitalism*, Syracuse, NY: Syracuse University Press.

Grant, A. and Tessler, M. (2002), 'Palestinian Attitudes toward Democracy and its Compatibility with Islam: Evidence from Public Opinion Research in the West Bank and Gaza' *Arab Studies Quarterly*, 24, 4.

Guiso, L., P. Sapienza and L. Zingales (2002) *People's Opium? Religion and Economic Activities*, NBER Working Paper 9237, Cambridge, MA: National Bureau of Economic Research.

Guity, N. and J. E. Tucker (1999) *Women in the Middle East and North Africa: Restoring Women to History*, Bloomington: Indiana University Press.

Guner, O. (2005) 'Poverty in Traditional Islamic Thought: Is it Virtue or Captivity?', *Studies in Islam and the Middle East*, 2, 1.

Haeri, S. (1989) *Law of Desire: Temporary Marriage in Shi'i Iran*, Syracuse: Syracuse University Press.

Haji Buang, H. S. (1989) *Malyasian Torrens System*, Kuala Lumpur: Percetekan Dewan Bahasa dan Pustaka.

Halim, A. (1994) 'Challenges to Women's International Human Rights in the Sudan', in R. Cook (ed.) *Human Rights of Women: National and International Perspectives*, Philadelphia: University of Pennsylvania Press.

Hallaq, W. (1984) 'Was the Gate of Ijtihad Closed?', *International Journal of Middle East Studies*, 16, 1.

—— (1997) *Islamic Legal Theories*, Cambridge: Cambridge University Press.

Hamidullah, M. (1977) *The Muslim Conduct of State*, Lahore, Pakistan: Sheikh Muhammad Ashraf.

Hamza, Manaf (2002) 'Land Registration in Bahrain: Its Past, Present and Future within an Integrated GIS Environment', unpublished PhD thesis, University of East London.

Haneef, S. S. S. (2002) 'Principles of Environmental Law in Islam', *Arab Law Quarterly*, 17, 3.

Hanna, M. M. (1985) 'Real Estate Rights in Urban Egypt: The Changing Sociopolitical Winds' in A. E. Mayer (ed.) *Property, Social Structure and Law in the Modern Middle East*, Albany, NY: State University of New York Press.

Harper, M. (1994) '"*Musharaka*" Partnership Financing – An Approach to Venture Micro-Enterprise', *Small Enterprise Development*, 5, 4.

Harris, J. W. (1996) *Property and Justice*, Clarendon Press: Oxford.

Hartmann, B. and J. K. Boyce (1983) *A Quiet Violence: View from a Bangladeshi Village*, Dhaka: University Press Ltd.

Harvard Research Group (2000) *Housing Microfinance Initiatives, Synthesis and Regional Summary: Asia, Latin America and Sub-Saharan Africa with Selected Case Studies*, Boston: Center for Urban Development Studies, Harvard University Graduate School of Design.

Hasan, A. (1984) *The Doctrine of Ijma' in Islam. A Study of the Juridical Principle of Consensus*, Islamabad: Saqi.

Hashemi, S. M. and S. R. Schuler (2002) *Sustainable Banking with the Poor: A Case Study of Grameen*, Dhaka: Programme for Research on Poverty Alleviation (PRPA), Grameen Trust.

Hassan, R. (1982) 'On Human Rights and the Qur'anic Perspective', in L. Swindler (ed.) *Human Rights in Religious Traditions*, New York: Pilgrim Press.

Hassan, S. Z. S. and S. Cedrroth (1997) *Managing Marital Disputes in Malaysia: Islamic Mediators and Conflict Resolution in the Syariah Courts*, Nordic Institute of Asian Studies Monograph Series, 75, Surrey: Curzon Press.

Hatem, M. (1998) 'Secularism and Islamist Discourses on Modernity in Egypt and the Evolution of the Postcolonial Nation-State', in Y. Haddad and J. Esposito (eds) *Islam, Gender and Social Change*, Oxford: Oxford University Press.

Hawting, G. R. (1989) 'The Role of *Qur'an* and Hadith in the Legal Controversy about the Rights of a Divorced Woman during her Waiting Period (*'Idda*)', *Bulletin of the School of Oriental and African Studies*, 52, 3.

Haykal, M. (1976) *Life of Muhammad*, Indianapolis: American Trust.

Hennigan, P. C. (2004) *The Birth of a Legal Institution: The Formation of the* Waqf *in Third-Century A.H. Hanafi Legal Discourse*, London: Brill.

Higgins, R. (1994) *Problems and Process: International Law and How We Use It*, Oxford: Clarendon.

Hirsch, S. F. (1998) *Pronouncing and Persevering: Gender and the Discourses of Disputing in an African Islamic Court*, Chicago: University of Chicago Press.

Hodgson, M. G. S. (1974) *The Venture of Islam: Conscience and History in a World Civilization, Vol. 2*, Chicago: University of Chicago Press.

Hoexter, M., S. N. Eusenstadt and N. Leutzion (2002) *The Public Sphere in Muslim Societies*, New York: State University of New York Press.

Home, R. and H. Lim (2004) 'Conclusions' in R. Home and H. Lim (eds) *Demystifying the Mystery of Capital*, London: Cavendish Publishing.

Hoodfar, H. (1998) 'Muslim Women on the Threshold of the Twenty-First Century' in *Dossier 12: Women Living Under Muslim Laws*, London: WLUML.

Huda, S. (1996) '"Born to be Wed": Bangladeshi Women and the Muslim Marriage Contract', unpublished PhD thesis, University of East London.

Huff, T. E. (1993) *The Rise of Early Modern Science: Islam, China and the West*, Cambridge: Cambridge University Press.

Human Rights First (2004), *Revised Arab Charter on Human Rights Must Guarantee Full Protection for Basic Rights*, New York: Human Rights First, 24 March.

Human Rights Watch (2004) *Divorced from Justice*, Human Rights Watch, 16, 8E, December.

Humphrey, J. P. (1984) *Human Rights and the United Nations: A Great Adventure*, Dobbs Ferry, New York: Transnational Publishers.

Humphreys, R. S. (1995) *Islamic History, a Framework for Inquiry*, London, New York: I. B. Tauris, revised edition.

Hussain, M. (1997) 'Islamic Law and the Modern Age', *Hamdard Islamicus*, 22, 1.

Hussain, J. (1999) *Islamic Law and Society*, Annandale, New South Wales: Federation Press.

Husseini, K. and A. Baidoun (2001) *The Multi-Sector Review of East Jerusalem: Review of Land*, Jerusalem: Multi-Sector Team.

ICWC, UNCDF and Ford Foundation (2001) *Innovating from Experience – Gender Initiatives in Microfinance: Roundtable Proceedings*, New York: International Coalition on Women and Credit, United Nations Capital Development Fund and Ford Foundation.

Ignatieff, M. (1999) 'Human Rights: The Midlife Crisis', *The New York Review*, 20 May.

—— (2001) 'The Attack on Human Rights', *Foreign Affairs*, November/ December.

Ihsanoglu, E. (2004) *Science, Technology and Learning in the Ottoman Empire; Western Influence, Local Institutions and the Transfer of Knowledge*, Aldershot: Variorum, [reprinted articles].

Imber, C. (1997) *Ebu's-su'ud: The Islamic Legal Tradition,* Stanford: Stanford University Press.

Inalclk, H. (1969) 'Capital Formation in the Ottoman Empire', *The Journal of Economic History*, 23, 1.

Indian Express News Service (1999) Thursday, 13 May.

Institute of International Studies (1998) *The Moral Economy of Islam*, Institute of International Studies, University of California, Berkeley<http://globetrotter.berkeley.edu/ Islam/>

Interights (1996) 'Status of Selected International Human Rights Instruments in Relation to States Members of the Organisation of Islamic Conference', *Interights Bulletin*, 10, 1.

International Commission of Jurists (2003) 'The Process of "Modernizing" the Arab Charter on Human Rights: A Disquieting Regression', Geneva: Position Paper, 20 December.

Iqbal, M. (2002) *Islam and Science*, Burlington: Ashgate.

Iqbal, Z. (1997) *Islamic Financial Systems*, Washington, DC: World Bank.

Irani, G. and N. Funk (1998) 'Rituals of Reconciliation: Arab-Islamic Perspectives', *Arab Studies Quarterly*, 20, 4.

Ishaque, K. M. (1983) 'The Islamic Approach to Economic Development', in J. Esposito (ed.) *Voices of Resurgent Islam*, New York and Oxford: Oxford University Press.

Islamic Conference of Foreign Ministers (2001), *Resolution Adopted at the Twenty-eighth Session of the Islamic Conference of Foreign Ministers Held in Bamako*, Republic of Mali, 25–27 June.

Islamic Development Bank Group (2003), *Report of the 28th Annual Meeting*, Almaty, Republic of Kazakhstan: Islamic Development Bank Group, 2-3 September.

Islamoglu-Inan, H. (1987). 'Oriental Despotism in World System Perspective', in H. Islamoglu-Inan (ed.) *The Ottoman Empire and the World Economy*, Cambridge and Paris: Cambridge University Press and Maison des Sciences.

—— (2000) 'Property as a Contested Domain: A Reevaluation of the Ottoman Land Code of 1858', in R. Owen (ed.) *New Perspectives on Property and Land in the Middle East*, Cambridge, MA: Harvard University Press.

Issawi, C. (1966) *The Economic History of the Middle East, 1800–1914*, Chicago: University of Chicago Press.

—— (1984) 'The Adaptation of Islam to Contemporary Economic Realities' in Y. Haddad, B. Haines and E. Findly (eds) *The Islamic Impact*, Syracuse, NY: Syracuse University Press.

Jefferey, P. (1999) 'Agency, Activism and Agendas', in P. Jefferey and A. Basu (eds) *Resisting the Sacred and the Secular: Women's Activism and Politicised Religion in South Asia*, New Delhi: Kali for Women.

Jennings, R. C. (1975) 'Women in Early Seventeenth-Century Ottoman Judicial Records – the Shari'a Court of Anatolian Kayseri', *Journal of the Economic and Social History of the Orient*, 18, 2/3.

Johansen, B. (1988) *The Islamic Law on Land Tax and Rent: the Peasants' Loss of Property Rights as Interpreted in the Hanafite Legal Literature of the Mamluk and Ottoman Periods*, London and New York: Croom Helm and Methuen.

Johnson, D. (1992) 'Cultural and Regional Pluralism in the Drafting of the UN Convention on the Rights of the Child', in M. Freeman and P. Veerman (eds) *The Ideologies of Children's Rights*, Dordrecht, Boston and London: Martinus Nijhoff.

Johnson, N. and E. Balla (2004) 'The Islamic Origins of Institutional Stagnation: France and the Ottoman Empire During the Early-Modern Period', paper presented at the Eighth Annual Conference of the International Society for New Institutional Economics, Tucson, USA, 1 October.

Johnson, P. (2004) 'Agents for Reform: the Women's Movement, Social Politics and Family Law Reform', in L. Welchman (ed.) *Women's Rights and Islamic Family Law*, London: Zed Books.

Jorgens, D. (2000) 'A Comparative Examination of the Provisions of the Ottoman Land Code and Khedive Said's Law of 1858' in R. Owen (ed.) *New Perspectives on Property and Land in the Middle East*, Cambridge, MA: Harvard University Press.

Joseph, S. (1990) 'Working the Law: A Lebanese Working-Class Case', in D. H. Dwyer (ed.) *Law and Islam in the Middle East*, New York: Bergin and Garvey.

Kabeer, N. (1985) 'Do Women Gain from High Fertility', in H. Afshar (ed.) *Women, Work and Ideology in the Third World*, London: Tavistock.

Kadivar, M. (2003), 'An Introduction to the Public and Private Debate in Islam – Part I: Public/Private: the Distinction', *Social Research*.

Kahf, M. (1998), 'Financing the Development of *Awqaf* Property', seminar paper, Islamic Research and Training Institute (IRTI), Kuala Lumpur, Malaysia, March 2-4.

—— (1999), 'Towards the Revival of *Awqaf*: A Few *Fiqhi* Issues to Reconsider', paper presented at the Harvard Forum on Islamic Finance and Economics, 1 October.

Kamal, N., A. Jamal and K. Al-Khatib (1999) 'Islamic Banking: A Study of Customer Satisfaction and Preferences in Jordan', *International Journal of Bank Marketing*, 17, 3.

Kamali, M. (1998) *Revolutionary Iran: Civil Society and State in the Modernization Process*, Aldershot: Ashgate.

Karsten, I. (1982) *Efforts to Develop Islamic Financial Systems: Focus on the Abolition of Fixed Interest Rate*, IMF Survey

Katulis, B. (2004) *Women's Freedom in Focus: Morocco*, Freedom House Survey, Washington DC: Freedom House.

Kedar, A. (2001) 'The Legal Transformation of Ethnic Geography: Israeli Law and the Palestinian Landholder 1948–1967', *International Law and Politics*, 33, 4.

Keddie, N. (1964) 'The Roots of the Ulama's Power in Modern Iran', *Studia Islamica*, 10.

Kedourie, E. (1994) *Democracy and Arab Political Culture*, London and Portland, OR: Frank Cass.

Kelsay, J. (1988) 'Saudi Arabia, Pakistan, and the Universal Declaration of Human Rights', in *Human Rights and the Conflict of Cultures: Western and Islamic Perspectives on Religious Liberty*, Columbia, SC: University of South Carolina Press.

Kemicha, F. (1996) *The Approach to Mediation in the Arab World*, paper presented at the Conference on Mediation, Geneva, Switzerland, 29 March.

Kennedy, D. (1994) 'Neither the Market nor the State: Housing Privatization Issues', in G. Alexander and G. Skapska (eds) *A Fourth Way? Privatization, Property, and the Emergence of New Market Economies*, New York: Routledge.

Khadduri, M. (2002) trans. *The Islamic Law of Nations: Shaybani's Siyar*, Baltimore, MD: Johns Hopkins University Press.

Khadduri, M. and Liebesny, H. (1955) *Law in the Middle East. Volume: 1*, Washington, DC: Middle East Institute.

Khalid, F. M. (2002), 'Islam and the Environment', *Social and Economic Dimensions of Global Environmental Change*, in P. Timmerman (ed.) *Encyclopedia of Global Environmental Change*, Chichester: John Wiley.

Khaliq, U. (1995) 'Beyond the Veil? An Analysis of the Provisions of the Women's Convention in the Law as Stipulated in the Shari'a', *Buffalo Journal of International Law*, 2, 2.

Khan, M. A. (1994), *An Introduction to Islamic Economics*, Islamabad: International Institute of Islamic Thought and Institute of Policy Studies, Pakistan.

Khan, M. M. (1989) *Islamic Law of Inheritance*, New Delhi: Nusrat Ali Nasri for Kitab Bhavan.

Khan, M. S. and A. Mirakhor (2003) *Islamic Banking: Experience in The Islamic Republic of Iran and in Pakistan*, Joman Al-Khaleej Centre for Islamic Finance Consultancy.

Khan, M. Z. (1989) *Islam and Human Rights*, Islamabad: Islam.

Kogelmann, F. (2002) 'Ahbas', in H. Weiss (ed.) *Social Welfare in Muslim Societies in Africa*, Stockholm: Nordic Africa Institute.

Koraytem, T. (2001) 'Arab Islamic Developments on Human Rights', *Arab Law Quarterly*, 16, 3.

Kozlowski, G. (1985) *Muslim Endowments and Society in British India*, Cambridge: Cambridge University Press.

Kuran, T. (1977) 'Islamic Economics and the "Clash of Civilisations"', in *Middle Eastern Lectures, Volume 2*, Tel Aviv: Tel Aviv University.

—— (1995) 'Islamic Economics and the Islamic Subeconomy', *Journal of Economic Perspectives*, 9, 4.

—— (2001) 'The Provision of Public Goods under Islamic Law: Origins, Impact, and Limitations of the *Waqf* System', *Law and Society Review*, 35, 4.

—— (2002) *The Islamic Commercial Crisis: Institutional Roots of Economic Underdevelopment in the Middle East*, Research Paper No. C01-12, Los Angeles: USC Center for Law, Economics, and Organization.

—— (2003) 'Why the Middle East Is Economically Underdeveloped: Historical Mechanisms of Institutional Stagnation', <http://www.international.ucla.edu/cms/files/ kuran.0130.pdf>, 30 November.

—— (2004) 'Why the Middle East is Economically Underdeveloped: Historical Mechanisms of Institutional Stagnation', *Journal of Economic Perspectives*, 18, 3.

Lambton, A. K. S. (1953) *Landlord and Peasant in Persia: A Study of Land Tenure and Land Revenue Administration*, London: Oxford University Press.

Lampe, G. E. (ed.) (1997) *Justice and Human Rights in Islamic Law*, Washington DC: International Law Institute.

Lapidus, I. (1973) 'The Evolution of Muslim Urban Society', *Comparative Studies in Society and History*, 15, 1.

Larsson, G. (1991) *Land Registration and Cadastral Systems*, London: Longman.
Layish, A. (1994) 'The Muslim *Waqf* in Jerusalem after 1967: Beneficiaries and Management' in F. Bilici (ed.) *Waqf dans le monde musulman contemporain (XIXe–Xxe siecles)*, Istanbul: Institut Francais d'Études Anatoliennes.
—— (1997) 'The Family *Waqf* and the *Shar'i* Law of Succession in Modern Times', *Islamic Law and Society*, 4, 3.
LeBlanc, L. (1995) *The Convention on the Rights of the Child: United Nations Lawmaking on Human Rights*, Lincoln and London: University of Nebraska Press.
Leckie, S. (2000) 'Housing and Property Restitution Issues for Refugees and Internally Displaced Persons in the Context of Return: Key Considerations for UNHCR Policy and Practice', *Refugee Survey Quarterly*, 19, 3.
Ledgerwood, J. (1998) *Microfinance Handbook: Sustainable Banking with the Poor Project*, Washington, DC: World Bank.
Leilani, F. (2002) 'Re/Conceiving the Human Right to Housing', background paper for the proposed general comment on Article 3 of the International Covenant on Economic, Social and Cultural Rights (ICESCR) Covenant on the equal right of men and women to the enjoyment of economic, social and cultural rights, Monday, 13 May.
Lewis, B. (1979) 'Ottoman Land Tenure and Taxation in Syria', *Studia Islamica*, 50.
Lim, H. (2000) 'The *Waqf* in Trust', in S. Scott-Hunt and H. Lim (eds) *Feminist Perspectives on Equity and Trusts*, London: Cavendish.
—— (2003) 'AIDS Pandemic Denies Secure Tenure for Women, Children', *Habitat Debate*, 9, 4.
Loqman, M. (1999) 'A Brief Note on the Islamic Financial System', *Managerial Finance*, 25, 5.
MacIntyre, A. (1988) *Whose Justice? Which Rationality?* Notre Dame: University of Notre Dame Press.
McChesney, R. D. (1991) *Waqf in Central Asia: Four Hundred Years in the History of a Muslim Shrine, 1480–1889*, Princeton, NJ: Princeton University Press.
Maher, E. (1974) 'Divorce and Property in the Middle East and Morocco', *Journal of the Royal Anthropological Institute*, 9.
Mahmood, T. (1988) 'Islamic Family *Waqf* in Twentieth Century Legislation: A Comparative Perspective', *Islamic and Comparative Law Quarterly*, 8, 1.
Majid, A. (2000) *Unveiling Traditions: Postcolonial Islam in a Polycentric World*, Durham, NC: Duke University Press.
Makdisi, J. (1985) 'Legal Logic and Equity in Islamic Law', *American Journal of Comparative Law*, 33.
—— (2004) *Islamic Property Law: Cases and Materials for Comparative Analysis with the Common Law*, Durham: Carolina University Press.
Makhoul, J. and L. Harrison (2004) 'Intercessory *Wasta* and Village Development in Lebanon', *Arab Studies Quarterly*, 16, 3.
Mallat, C. (1988) 'The Debate on *Riba* and Interest in Twentieth-Century Jurisprudence', in C. Mallat (ed.) *Islamic Law and Finance*, London: Graham and Trotman.
Mamdani, M. (1996) *Citizens and Subjects: Contemporary Africa and the Legacy of Late Colonialism*, Princeton: Princeton University Press.
Mandaville, J. E. (1973) 'Give to the *Waqf* of Your Choice', *Saudi Aramco World*, 24, 6, November/December.
—— (1979) 'Usurious Piety: The Cash *Waqf* Controversy in the Ottoman Empire', *International Journal of Middle East Studies*, 10, 3.
Mannan, M. A. (1970) *Islamic Economics: Theory and Practice*, Lahore: Muhammed Ashraf.
—— (1984) *The Frontiers of Islamic Economics*, New Delhi: Idarahi Adabiyati Delli.
Marcus, A. (1989) 'Men, Women and Property', *Journal of the Economic and Social History of the Orient*, 26, 2.
Mardin, S. (1983) 'Religion and Politics in Modern Turkey', in J. Piscatori (ed.) *Islam in the Political Process*, Cambridge: Cambridge University Press.
Marsot, A. L. al-S. (1996) 'Entrepreneurial Women', in Yamani, M. (ed.) Feminism in Islam,

Legal and Literary Perspectives, Reading: Ithaca.

Mastura, M. (2001) 'The Making of Civil Society through the *Waqf* Institution in Midnao', in N. Mitsuo, S. Siddique and O. F. Bajunid (eds) *Islam and Civil Society in Southeast Asia*, Singapore: Institute of Southeast Asian Studies.

Masud, K., B. Messick and D. Powers (1996) *Islamic Legal Interpretation: Muftis and their Fatwas*, Cambridge, MA: Harvard University Press.

Mawdudi, A. A. (1980) *Human Rights in Islam*, Leicester: Islamic Foundation, second edition.

Mayer, E. A. (1994), 'Universal Versus Islamic Human Rights: A Clash of Cultures or a Clash with a Construct', *Michigan Journal of International Law*, 15, 2.

—— (1999a) *Islam and Human Rights: Tradition and Politics*, Boulder, CO: Westview Press.

—— (1999b) 'Islamic Law and Human Rights: Conundrums and Equivocations' in C. Gustafon and P. Juvilier (eds) *Religion and Human Rights: Competing Claims?* Armonk, NY: M. E. Sharpe.

—— (1999c) 'Religious Reservations to the Convention on the Elimination of All Forms of Discrimination against Women: What Do They Really Mean?' in C. W. Howland (ed.) *Religious Fundamentalism and the Human Rights of Women*, New York: St Martin's Press.

Medina, C. (1993) 'Do International Human Rights Laws Protect Women?', in J. Kerr (ed.) *Ours by Right: Women's Rights as Human Rights*, London: Zed Books.

Meier, A. (2002) 'Urban Institutions between Centralization and Autonomy', in J. Hanssen, T. Philipp, and S. Weber (eds) *The Empire in the City: Arab Provincial Capitals in the Late Ottoman Empire*, Beiruter Texte und Studien, Würzburg: Ergon in Kommission.

Mengers, R. (2002) *Islamic Banking in Europe – the Reintegration of Faith and Economy*, Fifth SLIM Annual Lecture, Southwark Cathedral, London.

Messick, B. (1993) *The Calligraphic State: Textual Domination and History in a Muslim Society*, Berkeley: University of California Press.

—— (2003) 'Property and the Private in a Shari'a System', *Social Research*, 70, 2.

Metawa, S. A. and M. Almossawi (1998) 'Banking Behaviour of Islamic Bank Customers: Perspectives and Implications', *International Journal of Bank Marketing*, 16, 7.

Mills, P. and J. Presley (1999) *Islamic Finance: Theory and Practice*, London: Macmillan.

Minault, G. (1997) 'Women, Legal Reform, and Muslim Identity', *Comparative Studies of South Asia, the Middle East, and Africa*, 17, 2.

Mirakhor, A. (2002) 'Hopes for the Future of Islamic Finance', Lecture at the Institute of Islamic Banking, London.

Mir-Hosseini, Z. (1993) *Marriage on Trial: A Study of Islamic Family Law, Iran and Morocco Compared*, London and New York: I. B. Tauris.

Mitchell, R. (1997) 'Family Law in Algeria before and after the 1404/1984 Family Code', in R. Gleave and E. Kermeli (eds) *Islamic Law Theory and Practice*, London and New York: I. B. Tauris.

Mitchell, T. (1991) *Colonizing Egypt*, New York: Cambridge University Press.

Moaddel, M. (2002) 'Discursive Pluralism and Islamic Modernism in Egypt', *Arab Studies Quarterly*, 24, 1.

Modaressi, H. (1983) *Kharaj in Islamic Law*, London: Anchor.

Moghul, U. (1999) 'Approximating Certainty in Ratiocination: How to Ascertain the *'Illah* (Effective Cause) in the Islamic Legal System and How to Determine the *Ratio Decidendi* in the Anglo-American Common Law', *The Journal Of Islamic Law*, 4, Fall/Winter.

Mohanty, C. (1991) 'Under Western Eyes: Feminist Scholarship and Colonial Discourses', in C. Mohanty, A. Russo and L. Torres (eds) *Third World Women and the Politics of Feminism*, Bloomington: Indiana Press.

Molla, R. I., R. A. Moten, S. A. Gusau and A. A. Gwandu (1988), *Frontiers and Mechanics of Islamic Economics*, University of Sokoto, Nigeria.

Momen, M. A. (1996) 'Land Reform and Landlessness in Bangladesh', unpublished PhD thesis, University of East London.

Moors, A. (1995) *Women, Property and Islam: Palestinian Experience, 1920–1990*, New York: Cambridge University Press.

—— (1999) 'Debating Islamic Family Law: Legal Texts and Social Practices', in Margaret L. Meriwether and Judith E. Tucker (eds) *Social History of Women and Gender in the Modern Middle East*, Boulder, CO: Westview Press.

Mulla, M. (1990) *Principles of Muhammedan Law*, Bombay: N. M. Tripathi Private Ltd, nineteenth edition.

Mundy, M. (1979) 'Women's Inheritance of Land in Highland Yemen', *Arabian Studies*, 5.

Munzer, S. R. (1990) *A Theory of Property*, Cambridge: Cambridge University Press.

Murad, A. H. (1995) *Understanding the Four Madhhabs*, London: Ta Ha.

Nagata, J. (2002) *The Changing Perceptions of* Waqf, *as Social, Cultural and Symbolic Capital in Penang*, Penang: Penang Story Project.

Najjar, F. M. (1996) 'The Debate on Islam and Secularism in Egypt', *Arab Studies Quarterly*, 18, 2.

Nasir, J. J. (2002) *The Islamic Law of Personal Status*, The Hague, London and New York: Kluwer Law International.

Nesiah, V. (1994) 'Towards a Feminist Internationality: A Critique of US Feminist Legal Scholarship', *Harvard Women's Law Journal*, 16, Spring.

New York Times (2004) Editorial, 21 March.

Nicholson, F. and P. Twomey (1999), *Refugee Rights and Realities: Evolving International Concepts and Regimes*, Cambridge: Cambridge University Press.

Nickel, J. W. (1987) *Making Sense of Human Rights: Philosophical Reflections on the Universal Declaration of Human Rights*, Berkeley: University of California Press.

Noland, M. (2003) 'Religion, Culture, and Economic Performance', Working Paper No. 03-8, Washington, DC: Institute for International Economics <http://www.iie.com/ publications/wp/2003/03-8.pdf>

Normani, F. and A. Rahnema (1995) *Islamic Economic Systems*, Kuala Lumpur: S. Abdul Majeed and Co.

Nyazee, I. K. (1994) *Theories of Islamic Law: The Methodology of Ijtihad*, Kuala Lumpur: A. S. Noordeen.

OHCHR (2004), *Status of Ratifications of the Principal International Human Rights Treaties*, Geneva: Office of the United Nations High Commissioner for Human Rights, 9 June.

Omar, M. A-K. (1997) 'Reasoning in Islamic Law: Part One', *Arab Law Quarterly*, 12, 2.

OIC (Organization of Islamic Conference) (1998), 'On Coordination among Member States in the Field of Human Rights', Twenty-fifth Session of the Islamic Conference of Foreign Ministers Doha, State of Qatar, 15–17 March 1998, Resolution No. 51/25-P.

—— (2000), 'Promoting *Waqfs* and Their Role in the Development of Islamic Societies', Report of the Secretary General to the Twenty-seventh Session of the Organisation of Islamic Conference, Kuala Lumpur, Malaysia, 27–30 June.

—— (2005), *Enhancing Refugee Protection in the Muslim World,* Draft, 18 March, Working Document 1.

Osman, B. B. (1999) 'The Experience of the Sudanese Islamic Bank in Partnership (*Musharakah*) Financing as a Tool for Rural Development among Small Farmers in Sudan', *Arab Law Quarterly*, 14, 3.

Owen, Roger (2000a) *State, Power and Politics in the Making of the Modern Middle East*, London: Routledge.

Owen, R. (2000b) 'Introduction' in R. Owen (ed.) *New Perspectives on Property and Land in the Middle East*, Cambridge, MA: Harvard University Press.

Parker, M. (2004) 'Private Liquidity in MENA Crosses $2 Trillion Mark', *Arab News*, London: 2 August.

Patel, S. (2005) 'Takaful and Povery Alleviation', Altrincham: International Cooperative and Mutual Insurance Federation (ICMIF) <www.icmif.org/ takaful29/04/05>.

Payne, G. (2001) 'Innovative Approaches to Tenure', *Habitat Debate*, 7, 1.

—— (ed.) (2002) *Land, Rights and Innovation: Improving Tenure for the Urban Poor*, London: ITDG.

Pearl, D. and M. Werner (1998) *Muslim Family Law*, London: Sweet and Maxwell.

Peirce, L. P. (1993) *The Imperial Harem: Women and Sovereignty in the Ottoman Empire*, New York and Oxford: Oxford University Press.

Pennell, C. R. (2005) 'Muhammad Ali's Tax Inspectors', Historical Texts Archives, <http://historicaltextarchive.com/sections.php?op=viewarticle&artid=14>.

Peters, R. (2001), *The Reintroduction of Islamic Criminal Law in Northern Nigeria*, Lagos: European Commission.

Pollis, A. (1996) 'Cultural Relativism: Through a State Prism', *Human Rights Quarterly*, 18, 2.

Pollis, A. and P. Schwab (1979) *Human Rights: Cultural and Ideological Perspectives,* New York: Praeger.

Posner, R. (1992) *Economic Analysis of Law*, Boston: Little Brown and Company.

Powers, D. S. (1992), 'On Judicial Review in Islamic Law', *Law and Society Review*, 26, 2.

—— (1993) 'The Islamic Inheritance System: A Socio-Historical Approach', in C. Mallat, and J. Connors (eds) *Islamic Family Law*, London: Graham and Trotman.

—— (1999) 'The Islamic Family Endowment (*Waqf*)' , *Vanderbilt Journal of Transnational Law*, 32, 4.

—— (2002) *Law, Society, and Culture in the Maghrib, 1300–1500*, Cambridge, Cambridge University Press.

Pryor, F. L. (1985), 'The Islamic Economic System', *Journal of Comparative Economics*, 9, 2.

Rahim, H. Z. (1991) 'Ecology in Islam: Protection of the Web of Life a Duty for Muslims', *Washington Report on Middle Eastern Affairs.*

Rahman, F. (1983) 'Law and Ethics in Islam', in R. Hovannisian (ed.) *Ethics in Islam*, Atlanta: Scholars Press.

Rahman bin Kamsani, F. (2005) 'Islamic Real Estate Finance and Middle East Opportunities', Powerpoint presentation at Real Estate Developers' Association of Singapore (REDAS) seminar on 'Construction and Property Prospects', Singapore.

Raissouni, A. (2005), 'Islamic Waqf Endowment – Scope and Implications', translated by Abderrafi Benhallam, revised by Ahmed Alaoui, Islamic Educational, Scientific and Cultural Organization (ISESCO) <http://www.isesco.org.ma/pub/Eng/WAQF/ waqf. htm>.

Ray, N. D. (1995) *Arab Islamic Banking and the Renewal of Islamic Law*, London: Graham and Trotman.

Rayner, S. E. (1991) *The Theory of Contracts in Islamic Law*, London: Graham and Trotman.

Razzaz, O. M. (1998) 'Land Disputes in the Absence of Ownership Rights: Insights from Jordan', in E. Fernandes and A. Varley (eds) *Illegal Cities*, London and New York: Zed Books.

Reiter, Y. (1994) 'The Administration and Supervision of *Waqf* Properties in Twentieth-Century Jerusalem', in F. Bilici (ed.) *Le Waqf dans le monde musulman contemporain (XIXe–Xxe siecles)*, Istanbul: Institut Francais d'Études Anatoliennes.

Rishmawi, M. (1996) 'The Arab Charter on Human Rights: A Comment', *Interights Bulletin*, 10, 1.

Rivlin, P. (2001) *Economic Policy and Performance in the Arab World*, Boulder, CO: Lynne Rienner Publishers.

Roded, R. (1999) *Women in Islam and the Middle East*, London and New York: I. B. Tauris.

Rodinson, M. (1973), *Islam and Capitalism*, translated from the French by Brian Pearce, Pantheon.

Rosen, L. (1989) *The Anthropology of Justice: Law as a Culture in Islamic Society*, Cambridge: Cambridge University Press.

—— (1999) 'Legal Pluralism and Cultural Unity in Morocco', in B. Dupret, M. Berger and L. al-Zwaini (eds) *Legal Pluralism in the Arab World*, The Hague: Kluwer Law International.

—— (2000) *The Justice of Islam: Comparative Perspectives on Islamic Law and Society*, Oxford: Oxford University Press.

Rosser, B. and M. Rosser (1999) 'The New Traditional Economy: A New Perspective for Comparative Economics?', *International Journal of Social Economics*, 26, 6.

Saad, R. (2002) 'Egyptian Politics and the Tenancy Law', in R. Bush (ed.) *Counter Revolution in the Egyptian Countryside: Land and Farmers in the Era of Economic Reform*, London: Zed Books.

Sahibzada, M. H. (1997) *Conceptualizing an Islamic Approach to Poverty Alleviation*, Islamabad: Institute of Policy Studies, Pakistan.
Sahliyeh, E. (2000) 'The Limits of State Power in the Middle East', *Arab Studies Quarterly*, 22, 4.
Said, E. W. (1993) *Culture and Imperialism*, New York: Alfred A. Knopf.
Sait, S. (2000) 'Islamic Perspectives on Rights of the Child', in D. Fottrell (ed.) *Revisiting Children's Rights: Ten Years of the UN Convention on the Rights of the Child*, London: Kluwer.
—— (2002) 'International Refugee Law: Excluding the Palestinians' in J. Strawson (ed.) *Law after Ground Zero*, Sydney, London and Portland, OR: Cavendish.
—— (2003) 'Child Participatory Rights in the Arab World', *Interights Bulletin*, 14, 2.
—— (2004) 'Have Palestinian Children Forfeited Their Rights?', *Journal of Comparative Family Studies*, 35, 2.
Sajoo, A. B. (2001) 'The Ethics of the Public Square - A Preliminary Muslim Critique', *Polylog: Forum for Intercultural Philosophy*, 3.
—— (2002) *Civil Society in the Muslim World: Contemporary Perspectives*, London: I. B. Tauris in association with the Institute of Ismaili Studies.
Salih, N. A. (1992) *Unlawful Gain and Legitimate Profit in Islamic Law*, London: Graham and Trotman.
Salih, S. A. (1999) *The Challenges of Poverty Alleviation in IDB Member Countries*, Jeddah: Islamic Development Bank.
Santos, B. de S. (1995) *Toward a New Legal Common Sense: Law, Globalization and Emancipation*, London, New York: Routledge.
Sayne, P. (1993) 'Ideology as Law: Is There Room for Difference in the Right to Housing?', in H. Dandekar (ed.) *Shelter, Women and Development: First and Third World Perspectives*, Ann Arbor, MI: White Raven.
Schabas, W.(1997) 'Reservations to the Convention on the Elimination of All Forms of Discrimination against Women and the Convention on the Rights of the Child', *William and Mary Journal of Women and the Law*, 3, 1.
Schacht, J. (1986 [1964]) *An Introduction to Islamic Law*, Oxford, Clarendon Press.
Schaebler, B. (2000) 'Practising *Musha*: Common Lands and the Common Good in Southern Syria under the Ottomans and the French', in R. Owen (ed.) *New Perspectives on Property and Land in the Middle East*, Cambridge, MA: Harvard University Press.
Schoenblum, J. A. (1999) 'The Role of Legal Doctrine in the Decline of the Islamic *Waqf*: A Comparison with the Trust', *Vanderbilt Journal of Transnational Law*, 32, October.
Schramm, M. and M. Taube (2003) 'Evolution and Institutional Foundation of the *Hawala* Financial System', *International Review of Financial Analysis*, 12, 4.
Scott-Hunt, S. and H. Lim (2001), *Feminist Perspectives on Equity and Trusts*, London: Cavendish.
Shatzmiller, M. (1995) 'Women and Property Rights in Al-Andalus and the Maghrib: Social Patterns and Legal Discourse', *Islamic Law and Society*, 2, 3.
—— (2001) 'Islamic Institutions and Property Rights: the Case of the Public Good *Waqf*', *Journal of Economic and Social History of the Orient*, 43, 1.
Sherif, A. O. and N. Brown (2002) *Judicial Independence in the Arab World*, New York: UNDP Arab Governance Programme.
Siddiqui, M. Z. (1993) *Hadith Literature: Its Origin, Development and Special Features*, London: Islamic Texts Society.
Siddiqui, M. (1995) 'Mahr: Legal Obligation or Rightful Demand', *Oxford Journal of Islamic Studies*, 6, 1.
Singer, A. (2000) 'A Note on Land and Identity: from *Zeamet* to *Waqf*', in R. Owen (ed.) *New Perspectives on Property and Land in the Middle East*, Cambridge MA: Harvard University Press.
Sloane, R. D. (2001) 'Outrelativizing Relativism: A Liberal Defense of the Universality of International Human Rights', *Vanderbilt Journal of Transnational Law*, 34.
Sonbol, A. El-A. (ed.) (1996) *Women, the Family, and Divorce Laws in Islamic History*, Syracuse, NY: Syracuse University Press.
—— (2003) *Women of Jordan*, Syracuse, NY: Syracuse University Press.
Spies, O. (1972) 'Arabische Quellenbeitschrift zum Rechtsinstitut der Delegation' *Zeit fur ver-*

gleichende Rechtswissenschaften einschlieflich der ethnologischen Rechtsforschung, 73.
Starr, J. (1992) *Law as Metaphor: From Islamic Courts to the Palace of Justice*, Albany, NY: State University of New York Press.
Stauth, G. (1990) 'Women, Properties, and Migration: Access to Land and Local Conflicts in Rural Egypt', *Zeitschrift Der Deutschen Morgenlandischen Gesellschaft*, 140, 1.
Strawson, J. (1997) 'A Western Question to the Middle East: Is There a Human Rights Discourse in Islam?', *Arab Studies Quarterly*, 19, 1.
Sundararajan, V. and L. Errico (2002) *Islamic Financial Institutions and Products in the Global Financial System: Key Issues in Risk Management and Challenges Ahead*, IMF Working Papers 02/192, International Monetary Fund.
Swain, A. (1998) 'A New Challenge: Water Scarcity in the Arab World', *Arab Studies Quarterly*, 20, 1.
Tabandeh, S. (1970) *A Muslim Commentary on the Universal Declaration of Human Rights*, London: F. T. Goulding and Company, English edition.
Takkenberg, L. (1998) *The Status of Palestinian Refugees in International Law*, Oxford: Clarendon Press.
Talal, H. (2004) 'The Arab Human Development Report 2002: review and reform' *Arab Studies Quarterly*, 26, 2.
Thier, A. and J. Chopra (2002) 'Considerations for Political and Institutional Reconstruction in Afghanistan', *Peace Initiatives*, 8, 1–3.
Thornberry, P. (1993) *International Law and the Rights of Minorities*, Oxford: Oxford University Press.
Tilley, J. J. (2000) 'Cultural Relativism', *Human Rights Quarterly*, 22, 2.
Timberg, T. A. (2003) *Risk Management: Islamic Financial Policies – Islamic Banking and Its Potential Impact*, case study funded in part by US Agency for International Development, Virginia: Nathan Associates, Inc.
Timmer, P. and D. McClelland (2004), *Economic Growth in the Muslim World: How Can USAID Help?* US Agency for International Development.
Tomasevki, K. (1994) 'Human Rights: Fundamental Freedoms for All', in E. Childers (ed.) *Challenges to the United Nations*, London: St Martin's Press.
Tripp, C. (1997) '"The Enemy Within": Islamic Responses to Capitalism in the Middle East', in *Middle Eastern Lectures, Volume 2*, Tel Aviv: Tel Aviv University.
Tucker, J. E. (1979) 'Decline of the Family Economy in Mid-Nineteenth-Century Egypt', *Arab Studies Quarterly*, 1, 1.
—— (1985) *Women in Nineteenth Century* Egypt, Cambridge: Cambridge University Press.
—— (1993) 'Gender and Islamic History, Problems in the Study of Gender', in M. Adas (ed.) *Islamic and European Expansion: The Forging of a Global Order*, Philadelphia: Temple University Press.
—— (1994) 'Muftis and Matrimony: Islamic Law and Gender in Ottoman Syria and Palestine', *Islamic Law and Society*, 1, 3.
—— (1998) *In the House of the Law: Gender and Islamic Law in Ottoman Syria and Palestine*, Berkeley: University of California Press.
Udovitch, A. L. (1974) 'Technology, Land Tenure, and Rural Society: Aspects of Continuity in the Agricultural History of the Pre-Modern Middle East', in A. L. Udovitch (ed) *The Islamic Middle East 700–1900: Studies in Economic and Social History*, Princeton NJ: Princeton University Press.
UNDP (1999) *Essentials of Microfinance: A Synthesis of Lessons Learned*, Evaluation Office, No. 3, Washington: UNDP, December.
UNDP (2004) *Arab Human Development Report 2004: Towards Freedom in the Arab World*, Washington: UNDP.
UN-HABITAT (2003), *The Challenge of Slums: Global Report on Human Settlements*, London: Earthscan Publishers.
Usmani, M. T. (2000), *The Text of the Historic Judgement on* Riba *(23 December 1999) Given by the Supreme Court of Pakistan*, Islamabad: Islamic Book Trust.

Van Bueren, G. (1995) 'Children's Rights: Balancing Traditional Values and Cultural Plurality', in G. Douglas and L. Sebba (eds) *Children's Rights and Traditional Values*, Aldershot: Ashgate.
van der Molen, P. (2004), 'The Future Cadastres – Cadastres after 2014', *FIG Working Week 2003*, Paris, 13–17 April.
Vandevelde, K. (1981) 'The New Property of the Nineteenth Century: the Development of the Modern Concept of Property', *Buffalo Law Review*, 29.
Vasile, E. (1997) 'Devotion as Distinction, Piety as Power: Religious Revival and the Transformation of Space in the Illegal Settlements of Tunis', in M. Bonine (ed.) *Population, Poverty and Politics in Middle East Cities*, Gainesville, FL: University Press of Florida.
Vikor, K. S. (1998) 'The Shari'a and the Nation State: Who Can Codify the Divine Law?', in U. Utvik and K. S. Vikor (eds) *The Middle East in a Globalized World*, London: Hurst and Co.
Visser, W. A. M. and A. Macintosh (1998) 'A Short Review of the Historical Critique of Usury', *Accounting, Business and Financial History*, 8, 2.
Vogel, F. (2000) *Islamic Law and Legal System: Studies of Saudi Arabia*, Leiden: Brill.
Voll, J. O. (1994) *Islam, Continuity and Change in the Modern World*, Syracuse, NY: Syracuse University Press.
Von Grunebaum, G. (1955) 'The Structure of the Muslim Town', in G. von Grunebaum, *Islam: Essays in the Nature and Growth of a Cultural Tradition*, London: Routledge and Kegan Paul.
Wadud, A. (1999) *Qur'an and Woman: Rereading the Sacred Text from a Woman's Perspective*, New York: Oxford University Press.
Wahlin, L. (1994) 'Inheritance of Land in the Jordanian Hill Country', *British Journal of Middle Eastern Studies*, 21, 1.
Warriner, D. (1948) *Land and Poverty in the Middle East*, London: Royal Institute of International Affairs.
Watson, A. M. (1983) *Agricultural Innovation in the Early Islamic World: the Diffusion of Crops and Farming Techniques, 700–1100*, Cambridge: Cambridge University Press.
Webb, G. (2000) (ed.), *Windows of Faith: Muslim Women Scholar-Activists in North America*, Syracuse, NY: Syracuse University Press.
Weeramantry, C. G. (1988) 'Islam and Human Rights', in *Islamic Jurisprudence*, London: Macmillan.
Weiss, B. (1978) 'Interpretation in Islamic Law: The Theory of *Ijtihad*', *American Journal of Comparative Law*, 26.
—— (1998) *The Spirit of Islam*, Athens, GA: University of Georgia Press.
Welch, C. and R. Meltzer (1984) *Human Rights and Development in Africa*, Albany, NY: State University of New York Press.
Welchman, L. (2000) *Beyond the Code: Muslim Family Law and the Shari'a Judiciary in the Palestinian West Bank*, The Hague: Kluwer.
Wilkinson, J. C. (1990) 'Muslim Land and Water Law', *Journal of Islamic Studies*, 1, 1.
Williamson, I. and D. Grant (2002), 'United Nations – FIG Bathurst Declaration on Land Administration for Sustainable Development: Development and Impact', *FIG XXII International Congress*, Washington DC, 19–26 April.
Wilson, R. (1987) 'Islamic Banking: the Jordanian Experience', *Arab Law Quarterly*, 3, 2.
Wily, L. A. (2005) 'Resolution of Property Rights Disputes in Urban Areas: Rethinking the Orthodoxies', World Bank, unpublished MS.
Witte, J. (1996) 'Law, Religion and Human Rights', *Columbia Human Rights Law Review*, 28, 1.
Woodman, G. R. (1999) 'The Idea of Legal Pluralism', in B. Dupret, M. Berger and L. al-Zwaini (eds) *Legal Pluralism in the Arab World*, The Hague: Kluwer Law International.
World Bank (2002) 'MNA Governance Workshop in Beirut: Summary of Discussions', Beirut, 21-23 October.
Yanagihashi, H. (2004), 'A History of the Early Islamic Law of Property', *Reconstructing the Legal Development, 7th–9th Centuries*, Leiden: Brill.
Yediyildiz, B. (1982) 'Maessese-Toplum Minisebetleri Cercevesinde XVIII. Asir Turk Toplumu ve Vakif Mu essesesi,' *Vaka, flar Dergisi*, 15.
Younis, M. (2005) 'Grameen Bank at a Glance', <http://www.grameen-info.org/bank/

GBGlance.htm 31/03/2005>.

Yousef, T. M. (1996) 'Islamic Banking, Financial Development and Growth', *Newsletter of the Economic Research Forum for the Arab Countries, Iran and Turkey*, September.

Yusof, Dato' M. F. (2005) *An Overview of the Takaful Industry*, London: Institute of Islamic Banking and Finance, <http://www.islamic-banking.com/aom/takaful/ mf_yusof. php 29/04/05>.

Zaid, A. M. (1986) *The Islamic Law of Bequest*, London: Scorpion Publishing.

Zakaria, F. (1997) 'The Rise of Illiberal Democracy', *Foreign Affairs*, 76, 6.

Za'za, B. (2005) *Gulf News*, 4 June.

Ziadeh, F. J. (1960) '*Urf* and Law in Islam', in J. Kritzeck and R. B. Winder (eds) *The World of Islam*, London: Macmillan.

—— (1979) *Property Law in the Arab World*, London: Graham and Trotman.

—— (1985) 'Land Law and Economic Development in Arab Countries', *The American Journal of Comparative Law*, 33.

—— (1993) 'Property Rights in the Middle East', *Arab Law Quarterly*, 8, 1.

Ziai, F. (1997) 'Personal Status Codes and Women's Rights in the Maghrib', in M. Afkahmi and E. Friedl (eds) *Muslim Women and the Politics of Participation*, Syracuse, NY: Syracuse University Press.

Zubaida, S. (1993) *Islam, the People and the State: Political Ideas and Movements in the Middle East*, London: I. B. Tauris.

—— (2003) *Law and Power in the Islamic World*, London and New York: I. B. Tauris.

Documents

American Convention on Human Rights, OAS Treaty Series No. 36, 1144 UNTS 123 entered into force 18 July 1978, reprinted in Basic Documents Pertaining to Human Rights in the Inter-American System, OEA/Ser.L.V/II.82 doc.6 rev.1 at 25 (1992).

Arab Charter on Human Rights, Council of the League of Arab States, adopted on 15 September 1994.

Cairo Declaration on Human Rights in Islam**,** adopted by member states of the Organization of the Islamic Conference, 5 August 1990, and presented before the 1993 Vienna Conference. See UN Doc.A/CONF.157/PC/62/Add.18 (9 June 1993).

Casablanca Declaration of the Arab Human Rights Movement (1999) , 23–25 April 1999, 17 *Netherlands Quarterly of Human Rights* 363.

Convention Relating to the Status of Refugees, 1951 189 UNTS 150 entered into force 22 April 1954.

Convention concerning Basic Aims and Standards of Social Policy (ILO Convention 117), Geneva, 46th ILO Conference, 22 June 1962.

Convention on the Rights of the Child, adopted 20 November 1989, GA Res 44/25, UNGAOR, 44th Sess., Supp. No. 49 at 165, UN Dc. A/44/79 (1989).

Convention Against Torture and Other Cruel, Inhuman, Degrading Treatment or Punishment, adopted 10 December 1984, GA Res 39/4, UNGAOR, 39th Sess., Supp. No. 51 at 197, UN Doc A/3/51 (1984).

Convention on the Elimination of All Forms of Discrimination Against Women, adopted 18 December 1979, GA Res 34/180, UNGAOR, 34th Sess., Supp. No. 36 at 193, UN Doc A/34/36 (1979).

Convention Concerning Indigenous and Tribal Peoples in Independent Countries (ILO No. 169), 72 ILO Official Bull. 59, entered into force 5 September 1991.

Committee for Economic, Social and Cultural Rights, General Comment 4: The Right to Adequate Housing (Art. 11(1) of the Covenant, UN ESCOR, 6th Sess., UN Doc. E/C.12/1991/4 (1991).

Committee for Economic, Social and Cultural Rights, General Comment 7: The Right to

Adequate Housing (art. 11(1)): Forced Evictions, UN ESCOR, 16th Sess., UN Doc. E/C.12/1997/4 (20 May 1997).

European Convention for the Protection of Human Rights and Fundamental Freedoms (as amended by Protocol No. 11) Rome, 4. XI. 1950.

International Covenant on Civil and Political Rights, adopted 16 December 1966, 999 UNTS 171, GA Resolution 2200A (XXI), Supp. No.16, at 49, UN Doc A/6316 (1966), entered into force 23 March 1976.

International Covenant on Economic, Social and Cultural Rights, adopted 16 December 1966, GA Resolution 2200 (XXI), UNGAOR Supp. (No 16) at 49, UN Doc A/6316 (1966), entered into force 3 January 1976.

International Covenant on the Elimination of All Forms of Racial Discrimination, adopted 21 December 1965, 660 UNTS 195.

International Convention on the Suppression and Punishment of the Crime of Apartheid, General Assembly Resolution 3068 (XXVIII) of 30 November 1973.

International Convention on the Protection of the Rights of All Workers and Members of Their Families, UN General Assembly resolution 45/158 of 18 December 1990.

'Limburg Principles on the Implementation of the International Covenant on Economic, Social and Cultural Rights' (1987), E/CN.4/1987/17, Annex, reproduced in 9 *Human Rights Quarterly,* 122–35.

'Maastricht Guidelines on Violations of Economic, Social and Cultural Rights' (1998) 20 *Human Rights Quarterly*, 691–701.

Tunis Declaration of 16th Arab Summit, adopted by member states of the League of Arab States, meeting in Tunis, Tunisia on 22–23 May 2004.

United Nations Conference on Human Settlements (Habitat II), Istanbul, 3–14 June 1996 (United Nations publication, Sales No. E.97.IV.6), chap. I, resolution 1, annex II.2 Resolution S-25/2, annex.

United Nations Fact Sheet (1996), Fact Sheet No. 21, 'The Human Right to Adequate Housing', UN Centre for Human Rights.

United Nations Fact Sheet (1996), Fact Sheet No 16, 'The Committee on Economic, Social and Cultural Rights', UN Centre for Human Rights.

Universal Declaration of Human Rights, adopted 10 December 1948, GA Res. 217A (III), 3 UN GAOR (Resolutions, part 1), UN Document A/810 (1948).

Universal Islamic Declaration of Human Rights, 19 September 1981 (UNESCO document, Paris) (adopted by the Islamic Council of Europe).

Vienna Declaration and Programme of Action of 25 June 1993, reprinted in 14 *Human Rights Law Journal* 353 (1993).

World Summit on Sustainable Development, Johannesburg, South Africa, 26 August–4 September 2002 (United Nations publication, Sales No. E.03.II.A.1 and corrigendum), chapter I, resolution 1, annex.

Glossary of Arabic, Ottoman and Islamic Terms

Background Note

Though the language of the *Qur'an* and most traditional/classical literature is Arabic, Muslims speak dozens of languages where Arabic terms are often absorbed into native languages with variations in spellings and pronunciation. In turn, the local languages and customs generate newer expressions approximating to the original Islamic terminology. Arabic terms have also been supplemented by Persian modifications (particularly in Shi'a literature, for example *vaqf* for *waqf*) and Turkish words (through the Ottoman period, for example *siyaset* for *siyasa*). There are also terms, as in other parts of the Muslim world, which are customary in origin or have no relation to Arabic but are nevertheless now part of local or regional Muslim lingo.

Transliterating Arabic concepts into English poses particular problems as Islamic terms have been freely changed to make them more easily pronounceable for English speakers. For example Qur'an becomes Koran, *Uthmani* Empire is called Ottoman, and in British India *waqf* written as wakf. Where possible, the English spelling closest to the original Arabic, Turkish or Persian word has been chosen but some well-entrenched colonial terms such as Ottoman have been retained for easy reference.

There are elaborate guidelines for transliteration in the field of Arabic and Islamic studies. For example, it is important to distinguish between *hamza* and *'ayn* (or apostrophe) but the model followed here is simply to make the glossary more accessible for a non-Muslim, non-specialist audience. No effort is made to trace the linguistic origins of a term or its current geographical usage (unless relevant), for this is again a matter of enquiry. The reader must keep in mind that there would be an additional extensive glossary specific to a particular country owing to its Islamic school, linguistic and historical context.

Where there are two equally popular spellings, for example mawat and mewat, either both or one of them is used. A superfluous 'h' ending, for example in Sunnah or Shariah has been dropped. Similarly 'al' (or the) prefixed to Arabic terms has been dropped. Where possible, the Arabic plurals have been used for example *awqaf* (Islamic endowments) instead of waqfs, unless such authenticity creates complications. Rather, this glossary operates as a ready referencer for the particular vocabulary used in the main eight position papers, bearing in mind that these terms are often complex, have varied meanings and are often subject to much debate.

adl — justice, one of the fundamental concepts in the *Qur'an*

adl wal ihsan — equilibrium, the endeavour to balance competing interests, for example, striking an appropriate balance between the needs of present and future generations

Abbasids — Muslim dynasty which ruled between 750 and 1258

adab al-qadi	field of study or rules concerning the model behaviour of the judge and the courtroom
Ahmadi	name of a Muslim religious movement, which is not a part of mainstream Sunni Islam and founded by Hazrat Mirza Ghulam Ahmad (d. 1908)
akhira	the eternal life after death with God
amana	*Qur'anic* principle of trust: land and resources are owned by God and human beings exercise control over them in trust
Al-Medina	the City, commonly referring to Medina, the sister city to Makkah in Saudi Arabia inhabited by the Prophet's generation and an important Muslim holy city
aql	intellect, the protection of intellect is one of the five *daruriyyat* (essentials) of Islamic law and is to be protected by *maslaha* (public interest)
ard-i mahdar	individual or official petitions filed by members of the public before the Ottoman rulers, for example with regard to abuse of power by officials
aradi mudawana	used in Syria to describe villages where land had been registered personally in the name of Sultan Abd' al-Hamid but was 'turned over' to the Ottoman Treasury in 1908, although the occupants regarded themselves as having full ownership. See also *jiftlik*
arkan	essential components
ar-raqid	honour killings
asaba	deceased's closest surviving male agnate, the deceased's father, brothers, uncles, cousins or more distant male relative
ayn	tangible property right
Ayyubids	Muslim dynasty which ruled between 1171 and 1250
bai 'urbun	credit transaction with a down payment, rejected by the majority of Islamic jurists
bai' salam	a sale with advance payment for future delivery
bai'mua'jjal	credit sale or deferred payment sale: allows products to be purchased on instalment payments or for a lump sum paid at a later date
bashari	human (for example human endeavour or interpretation), as well as state preferences that determine how contemporary society actualises the Shari'a
bay	sale
bayt-al-mal	the state treasury for welfare, also the means for managing *zakat* funds
birr	benevolent
darura	necessity and need, supplementary principle in the methodology of Islamic law (*usul al fiqh*)
daruriyyat	essential, one of the three categories of public interest (*maslaha*) which includes protection of property (*mal*)
defter-i khaqani	central register in the Ottoman sphere, concerned primarily with accountancy and taxation, also commonly known as the *tahrir defterleri*
dhimmi	'protected' or 'covenanted' people, non-Muslim subjects, specifically Christians and Jews. A *dhimmi* has extensive rights in an Islamic state, although his land is subject to higher taxes (see *kharaj* and *jizya*) in lieu of his exemption from military duty and *zakat* tax.
din	religion: protection of religion is one of the five *daruriyyat* (essentials) of Islamic law which is to be protected by *maslaha* (public interest)
dirlik	fief, or right to control the land productively in a local area. Also the official, appointed by an Ottoman Sultan, who held this right
duniya	worldly life in the here and now on earth
Emir land	Sultanic land, often used synonymously with state land (*miri*)
fard	(plural *faraid*) an act considered to be obligatory under Islamic law, also the duty to act
fatwa	(plural *fatawa*) formal advice from a competent authority (mufti) on a point

	of Islamic law or dogma. It is given in response to a question.
feddan	a measurement of land, 1.038 acres and 0.42 of a hectare
fiqh	Islamic jurisprudence, practical rules of Shari'a derived from the detailed evidence in the textual sources. *Fiqh* is thus the end product of *usul al-fiqh*.
firman/ferman	orders of the Sultan (for example, declarations of taxes); the orders were disseminated or read out to the people directly
fuqaha	jurists or those well versed in *fiqh*
Futawa Alumgeeree	legal compilation during the reign of Mughal Indian emperor Aurangzeb by eminent lawyers of the time (about 1670), translated in 1850 by Neil Baillie
ghah	a declaration
gharar	uncertainty, risk or speculation
hadith	plural *ahadith*, the sacred tradition: studies of the recorded actions and sayings of the Prophet
hajiyyat	category of complementary rights, protected by public interest, in contrast to the more *daruriyyat* (essentials) or the less significant *tahsiniyyat* (embellishment)
hajj	annual Muslim pilgrimage to Makkah and Medina, one of the five pillars of Islam, incumbent once in a lifetime on every Muslim who can make it
halal	permitted, lawful
hammam	public bath, a common feature of urban space
Hanafi	name of a Sunni school of law, associated with the early religious leader (Imam) Abu Hanifa (d. 767)
Hanbali	name of a Sunni school of law, associated with the early religious leader (Imam) Ahmad ibn Hanbal (d. 855)
haqq	truth or rights, used in the *Qur'an* 227 times, sometimes referred to as rights of God, thereby creating obligations for human beings
haram	forbidden, unlawful under Islamic law or religion
has	large fief (*dirlik*) during the Ottoman period
hadood/hadd	fixed punishment for designated serious crimes
hawala	informal system of banking and debt transfer
Hedaya	literally the guide, it is a compendium of Hanafi law. An orientalist influential translation is that by Charles Hamilton in 1870.
hiba	lifetime transfer or gift, in Islamic law a contract without consideration
hijab	Muslim veil worn by women
hikma	wisdom; sound rational judgment based on cause and effect, to be exercised in the spirit of Islamic law
hikrs	long leases with advance lump sums
hima	special reserves, for example, those established by the state for use as conservation zones
hisbah	an Islamic institution or ombudsman for enforcement of public interests or vigilance powers. An independent officer appointed since the days of the Prophet to ensure compliance with Islamic regulations. Often had broad powers, functioning like a chief inspector of weights and measures and chief public health officer rolled into one, as well as environmental protection 'czar'.
hujja	document recording the contract of sale and the deed of ownership
hujjat al-ikhbariyya	a Shari'a court document recording the inheritance of land
hujjat al-tabayu	sale document issued by a Shari'a court
hokum	assessment or final product through Islamic legal reasoning
ibadat	matters of worship and practice of religion
Icmal	summaries of the details from *mufassal* books kept during the Ottoman period

ihya' al-Mawat reclamation or the revival of dead *(mewat/mawat)* land, creates a right of ownership with the claimant being given a *tapu* (grant or document)

ijara lease in commercial or financing context, land may also be leased for its usufruct by the state to achieve its reclamation and development

Ijaza authorisation or licence, used in a variety of contexts including commercial transactions

ijitarayn lease with 'two rents'

ijma consensus of opinion, one of the four main sources of Islamic law (*Shari'a*) but supplementary to the *Qur'an* and *Sunna*

ijtihad personal reasoning or interpretation, a tool of Islamic jurisprudence

ikhlaf 'variant' in Islamic legal reasoning

ikhtiy'ar free will: individual freedom to interpret Islamic path

Illah determination of effective cause or rationale in Islamic legal reasoning

ilmiye religious sector in Turkey, corresponds to *ulema*

iltizam (plural *iltimazat*), (*multazim*) tax farm/s, created by Ottomans in favour of a wealthy notable for collecting land revenues for the state, initially for a year although later it came to be seen as a lifetime enjoyment. There were charges of exploitation of peasants and the system was abolished in 1813.

Imaan faith in God

Imam religious leader

Imama/imamate Islamic ideal theory of the caliphate or leadership, particularly Shi'a, where the Imam has extensive powers and the final word on religion

imaret soup kitchen

infaq spending in the way of God

iqta/iqta tamlik grants of land by the state, historically land given to Ottoman soldiers in lieu of regular wage, which by itself did not create juridical or hereditary rights. Could also be a grant for other purposes, for example land reclamation or development

irsadat endowments formed out of state land for the benefit of those who are entitled to such benefits from the state treasury for welfare and the needy (*bayt al mal*)

islah reform or atonement, a *Qur'anic* concept whereby a wrongdoer is able to make amends

Islam from Arabic word *s-l-m*, which refers to peace and submission, the religion of 1.2 billion Muslims worldwide

istinbat inferences during the process of Islamic legal reasoning

istishab presumption of continuity or permanence, a subsidiary legal tool associated with the Shafii school of law

istihsan juristic preference to achieve equity and avoid a harsh result, a legal method particularly associated with the Hanafi school of law

istislah public interest or social welfare as a supplementary tool of juristic interpretation, associated with the Maliki school of law

jiftlik term used to describe villages in Palestine where land had been registered personally in the name of Sultan Abd' al-Hamid but was 'turned over' to the Ottoman Treasury in 1908, although the occupants regarded themselves as having full ownership, see also *aradi mudawana*

jizya a poll tax paid by non-Muslims in classical times: originates from the Arabic word 'compensate' in the context of higher taxes being paid by non-Muslims in lieu of their exemption from other obligations, used synonomously with *kharaj*

kadi/khadi *qadi* or judge in an Islamic court

kaffara a penitential charitable contribution for the breaking of an oath

Kanunname-i	an Ottoman land registration
Kitabet-I Vilayet	guide, available in the Ottoman archives
Khalifa	successor, vice-regent; caliph stewardship, an Islamic political concept indicating leadership on behalf of the Muslim community (*Umma*)
Khalil	source of Maliki law, based on the writings of Mukhtasar of Sîdî Khalîl; the widely used translation is that of F. H. Ruxton (1916)
kharaj	land under state control upon which a tax is paid by those in possession; it describes both the land itself and the tax
khoms	general obligation for a charitable payment on all gains from trade or other economic activities for Shi'a Muslims
khula	a judicial divorce, granted through a decree
Khutbatul Wada'	Prophet's Farewell Sermon (632 AD), an important Islamic document
Kitab al-Kharaj	(The Book of Land Tax), Abu Yusuf's wide ranging treatise on the Islamic theory of taxation (Cairo, 1382)
Kuyud-u	Ottoman period land information
Hakani	records (particularly between 1534–1634) containing all land-related information
'ma	water; water rights are widely discussed in the *Qur'an* and the documented sayings of the Prophet
mabi'	the good (property) being sold or purchased
madhab	(plural *madhahib*), a school of legal thought with distinctive elements to its methodology, associated with a particular religious leader (Imam) of the classical period
madrassa	a religious school
mafsada	harm *maslaha* (public interest) includes the duty to prevent harm
maisir	gambling
Majalla	the Ottoman Civil Code based on Islamic law (Shari'a), enacted in 1876. Based on the perspective of the Hanafi School of Muslim jurisprudence, but following a Napoleonic form. Its full title is *Majallat-I Ahkami Adliye*, the Book of Rules of Justice.
Makkah	Mecca, the holiest Muslim city, which houses the *Kaaba* or the 'black stone'; destination for the Muslim pilgrimage (*Hajj*)
makruh	an act considered repugnant under Islamic law or faith
mal	property, the protection of property is one of the five *daruriyaat* (essentials) of Islamic law which is to be protected by *maslaha* (public interest)
Maliki	name of a Sunni school of law, associated with the early religious leader Malki ibn Anas (d. 796)
Mamluks	Muslim dynasty which ruled between 1250–1517
manat	anchor point in Islamic legal reasoning
Mandub	an act recommended under Islamic law or faith
maqasid e sharia	hierarchy of legal aims or objectives of Islamic law also the title of an influential book by Al-Ghazzali (1058–1111)
maruf	good or acceptable behaviour that is to be encouraged by other Muslims
Maslaha/maslaha	Islamic public interest principle;
marsala	literally means benefit or interest in Islamic jurisprudence and is often perceived as overriding public interest; used synonymously with *istislah*
matruk/metruke	public land for general use, such as pastures for the use of particular towns and villages, markets, parks and places to pray
matruk mahmiyya	property for general public use such as roads
matruk murfaqa	property for use by a specific community such as market places and cemeteries
mawat	see *mewat*
mawquf	specific property settled in an endowment (*waqf*)

mawquf 'alayh	beneficiaries of an endowment (*waqf*)
mehlul/mahlul	land left uncultivated, state land (*miri*) under the Ottoman Land Code 1858, if left uncultivated for three years could be taken back by the state, depriving the owner of possession
mehr/mahr	the payment of money from the husband to the wife at the time of marriage, known as dower
memuru marifetiyle	Ottoman state agents
mewat	dead or empty land, which can be reclaimed or revived (*ihya'al mawat*)
microtakaful	Islamic micro-insurance, based on mutual responsibility and mutual guarantee
Minhaj	source of Shafi law, written by Mahiudin Abu Zakaria Yahya ibn Sharif en Nawawi, translated by E. C. Howard (1914)
mirath	the Islamic law of succession
mu'amalat	sphere of Islamic law governing human or social relationships such as most property rights, as distinct from *ibadat*, matters relating to worship
mubah	an act considered permissible under Islamic law of faith
mudaraba	limited partnership, trust financing
mudarib	the client in a trust financing (*mudaraba*) transaction who provides know-how, labour or management expertise
mufti	theologian who is competent to issue an advisory Islamic legal opinion (*fatwa*) in response to a specific question
muhtasib	one who is appointed to implement *hisbah*; must be experienced, honest, knowledgeable in his profession, pious in his dealings, and of good standing in the community
mujadad	the first registration of land, also a land registration document created by the Jordanians in the West Bank as part of its land reform, which was abandoned in 1967
mujtahid, plural *mujtahidun*	a person who practises independent reasoning (*ijtihad*)
mujtahidat	woman practising Islamic reasoning (*ijtihad*)
mukhabara	sharecropping where the owner provides only the land
mulk	land in full ownership
multazim	tax farmer: wealthy notable given charge of collecting land revenues for the state (tax farm or *iltizam*) during Ottoman period
munkar	unacceptable behaviour or wrongful, that which other Muslims have a duty to stop, in contrast to *maruf*, good conduct to be encouraged
Muqaddimah	'Prolegomena' – an influential treatise by Muslim writer Ibn Khaldun (1332–95)
murabaha	purchase and resale agreement, mark-up/cost plus sale
musha'	communal land, also a term deployed by colonial officials during Mandate rule in the Middle East to describe a system by which most of a village's arable land was held in common and in shares which were periodically redistributed
musharaka	partnership, joint venture
Muslim	follower of Islam, one who makes the declaration of faith (*shahada*) or submission to Islam
mustahab	desirable practices/acts for a Muslim
mut'a	temporary marriage
mutat	compensation from a husband to a divorced wife
mutawalli	the administrator, manager or superintendent of endowment (*waqf*) property, equivalent to *nazir* in South Asia
muzara'a	agricultural contract, a form of sharecropping in which the landowner

provides both land and seed for the crop, the worker provides the labour

nafs life; the protection of life is one of five *daruriyyat* (essentials) of Islamic law and is to be protected by *maslaha* (public interest)

naskh necessity; or the repeal of inoperative or contradictory *Qur'anic* verses in favour of those considered more fundamental

nasl progeny, the protection of progeny is one of the five *daruriyyati* (essentials) of Islamic law and is to be protected by *maslaha* (public interest)

nazir administrator, manager or superintendent of an endowment (*waqf*) in South Asia, equivalent to *mutawalli* in the Arab world

ni'mah God's gift or bounty: the *Qur'anic* view holds that everything on the earth was created for humankind. Human beings can enjoy these gifts, particularly in relation to the environment, land and water, but the rights have to be exercised with care as a trusteeship (*amana*)

nushuq disobedience in marriage

Ottoman Empire Uthmani, most recent and significant Muslim dynasty, which ruled between 1281 and 1918, with its seat of power in Istanbul. It had an extensive land administration system and the Ottoman Land Code (1858) is still influential as a codification of Islamic law, though it also absorbed other legal sources. Ottoman archives are an important source of the application of Islamic law in context

qadi religious judge

qanun decree to supplement Islamic law (Shari'a)

qard hasana an interest free loan

qat'i clear and unambiguous as in the main features of the Islamic inheritance rules, explicit *Qur'anic* injunctions are not open to reinterpretation

qiwama the concept of male guardianship, prerogative of the male guardian (*wali*)

qiyas reasoning, deduction by analogy, a source of Islamic law (Shari'a)

Qur'an the Holy *Qu'ran*, the revelation of God, the sourcebook of Islamic values and the primary source of Islamic law (Shari'a)

qurbah pious purpose, as in relation to the creation of an endowment (*waqf*)

rabal-maal the financier in a trust financing (*mudaraba*) transaction, for instance a bank

raqaba full property ownership, often in the context of private individual land (*milk/mulk*)

Ramadhan the Islamic holy month of fasting

riba usury, the Islamic prohibition of interest

riba al-fadl prohibited transactions that give one party more than 'fair exchange' value and produce an interest-like payment

riba al-nasi'a a prohibited transaction whereby a lender receives an additional excess payment to the principal amount of a loan, whether by fixed or variable interest, set out in advance

sadaqa religiously inspired voluntary almsgiving or discretionary charitable donation, not necessarily monetary in nature

sadaqa jaaria continous charity, as in a endowment (*waqf*)

Safavids Muslim dynasty which ruled between 1501 and 1722

sahm-e-Imam 'share of the Imam', a practice by which every Muslim should pay 10 per cent of his annual income to the religious élite (*ulama*) for religious institutions

sahms the term used to describe shares in a village where land is held communally (*musha'*)

salat/salah prayer or worship performed five times a day by Muslims

sanjak provinces or large administrative units under Ottoman territories

Shafi name of a Sunni school of law, associated with the early religious leader Muhammed al-Shafii (d. 820)

shahada	declaration of faith in Islam, in the oneness of God (Allah or the God, in Arabic) and acceptance of the Prophet as the last messenger of God
Shari'a	Islamic law
Shi'a	minority branch of the Muslim community which claims that the Prophet named Ali, his nephew and son-in law, as his successor
shura	concept of consultation discussed in the *Qur'an*, relevant in the context of democracy in Islam
shuf'a	pre-emption, a barrier upon the free disposal of land and the means by which a co-inheritor, or in some cases a neighbour, may use a privileged option to purchase land when it is for sale
silsila	scholarly genealogy stretching back, in some cases, to the Prophet and companions, which often creates authority for a scholar
sipahi	an individual cavalryman
Sinirname	an approved Ottoman demarcation certificate given to landholders; the boundaries demarcated on land by stones, based on the written boundary descriptions
siyar	international law or law of nations, derived from the same sources as Islamic law (Shari'a)
siyasa	policy, governance, administration
sulah	conciliation, an Islamic dispute resolution technique which requires compromise between two parties
sultan	ruler, literally power or authority, sometimes referred to as emir
Sunni	the largest group within the Muslim community, who believe that the Prophet died in 632 AD without choosing any successor
Sunna	tradition, deeds, utterances and tacit approvals of the Prophet, the second source of Islamic law (Shari'a)
ta'a	obedience in marriage
tabu/tapu/tabo	an Ottoman land title registration office or document, still referred to as such for example in Palestinian territories and Israel. Also a title deed granting usufruct rights in state land (*miri*)
tahkim	arbitration, an Islamic dispute resolution technique which involves a mutually acceptable arbitrator
tahrir defterleri	Ottoman imperial registers or *defter-i khan*
Tahsiniyyat	embellishment, the least important of the three categories of rights protected by public interest (*maslaha*). The other two are *daruriyyat* (essentials) and *hajiyyat* (complements)
takaful	mutual responsibility, mutual guarantee, Islamic insurance
takhayyur	Islamic legal method of selection amongst competing legal principles
talaq	husband's unlimited right to divorce his wife
talfiq	the legal method of 'patchwork', combining approaches or principles from different Islamic schools of law
tanazul	a customary practice by which a person, typically a woman, renounces her inheritance rights
taqlid	adherence to a tradition, relying upon the opinion of other jurists, not practising *ijtihad*
tassaruf	possession of land vested in an individual cultivator
tawhid	Islamic doctrine of unity in God
Temessuk Belgeleri	Title Deed Records, the name for the *Kuyud-u Hakani* registration books from 1634 to 1847
thimmah	a separate and independent financial personality
timar	small fief (*dirlik*) during Ottoman rule; a right to revenue in relation to land
ulama/ulema	clerical leadership, religious scholars
umma	universal Muslim community, which defies national boundaries

Ummayads	Muslim dynasty after the 'rightly guided Caliphs' which ruled between 661–750
*'urf*or *'urf wa adah*	custom and usage, a general or local model of behaviour, social understanding, or mode of expression, that is generally accepted by the population and does not contract a definitive rule of Islamic law (Shari'a)
ushr	land on which a tithe is paid, belonging to a Muslim at the time of his conversion or distributed to a Muslim soldier as his share of the spoils of war; *ushr* is describes both the land itself and the tithe. It is an obligatory charge on farm produce ranging from one-tenth to one-twentieth of the produce – a lower rate than *kharaj* paid by non-Muslims.
usul al-Fiqh	methodology applied to the *Qur'an* and *Sunna* to deduce the rules of *fiqh*, or substantive law
vaqf, Persian, plural *auqaf*	charitable endowment in Shi'a practice
wajib	a highly recommended act for a Muslim under Islamic law or religion
wali	guardian, also a local governor in Ottoman times
waqf, plural *awqaf*	general term for charitable endowment
waqf ahli	a family endowment where the usufruct or income is held for the family of the founder/creator (*waqif*) or other specific individuals, until the extinction of his or her descendants, whereupon it is diverted to a charitable purpose
waqf al aulad	a family endowment in South Asia, equivalent of *waqf ahli* in the Arab world
waqf dhurri	an alternative name to *waqf ahli* for the family endowment in Arab countries
waqf fi-sabilillah	endowment in the way of Allah, to set up a pious endowment
waqf gayri sahih	State endowment, created either because it was established from the State treasury (*bait al-mal*) or because the endowment (*waqf*) was taken into state control
waqf khairi/ khayri	a charitable endowment, which involves the 'permanent' dedication of the property for charitable purposes
waqf mushtarak	a quasi-public endowment (*waqf*), which primarily provides for particular individuals or a class of individuals including the founder's family, but also serves certain outside public interests, such as a mosque which is convenient for, but not exclusive to, family members
waqif	the founder of an endowment (*waqf*)
wasata	mediation, an Islamic dispute resolution technique whereby one or more persons intervene in a dispute either on their own initiative or at the request of one of the parties
wasaya	an Islamic will
wudu	obligatory ablution which precedes the five-times-daily prayer (*salat*)
Yoklama	land title inspection or record books used by Ottomans after 1847
zakat	general charitable payment, levied on property such as gold, silver, merchandise and income-producing animals, as well as land, required of all Muslims to purify both themselves and their wealth
zam zam	water from the *Makkan* aquifer having a religious significance
zeamat	middle-size fief (*dirlik*) during Ottoman rule

Index

Index

www.ingramcontent.com/pod-product-compliance
Lightning Source LLC
Chambersburg PA
CBHW022307280326
41932CB00010B/1011

* 9 7 8 1 8 4 2 7 7 8 1 3 5 *